MERLEAU-PONTY'S PHILOSOPHY

MERLEAU-PONTY'S PHILOSOPHY

Lawrence Hass

INDIANA
UNIVERSITY
PRESS
*Bloomington
and Indianapolis*

This book is a publication of

Indiana University Press
601 North Morton Street
Bloomington, IN 47404-3797 USA

http://iupress.indiana.edu

Telephone orders   800-842-6796
Fax orders   812-855-7931
Orders by e-mail   iuporder@indiana.edu

The paper used in this publication meets the minimum requirements of
American National Standard for Information Sciences—Permanence of
Paper for Printed Library Materials, ANSI Z39.48-1984.

Manufactured in the United States of America

Library of Congress Cataloging-in-Publication Data

Hass, Lawrence.
    Merleau-Ponty's philosophy / Lawrence Hass.
        p.   cm. — (Studies in Continental thought)
    Includes bibliographical references and index.
    ISBN-13: 978-0-253-35119-7 (cloth : alk. paper)
    ISBN-13: 978-0-253-21973-2 (pbk. : alk. paper)
    1. Merleau-Ponty, Maurice, 1908–1961. I. Title.
    B2430.M3764H38 2008
    194—dc22

                                                          2007038417

1 2 3 4 5   13 12 11 10 09 08

Dedicated to the memory of

Martin Dillon

Mentor, Friend, Provocateur

Contents

Acknowledgments

It is no exaggeration to say that this book is the result of a process that has been unfolding for nearly twenty years. As one might imagine, my thinking and writing about Merleau-Ponty has been touched by many people during this long time, and it is my deep pleasure to acknowledge them here.

A first thank-you goes to Arthur Melnick at the University of Illinois at Urbana-Champaign for all the "metaphysics" I learned through his hands. My thanks also go to Richard Schacht, Fred Schmitt, and Stephen Watson for all their work on my behalf and support. I am also especially indebted to two other teachers: William Schroeder for his excellent course on Merleau-Ponty, taken in my second year of graduate school, and Seale Doss who inspired my phenomenological leanings as an undergraduate.

After completing my Ph.D. in 1991, during my early years at Muhlenberg College, I spent much of my research time writing, presenting, and then publishing essays on Merleau-Ponty in journals and anthologies. For their enthusiasm about my essays and their sage advice, I want to thank Fred Evans, Leonard Lawlor, James Morley, Dorothea Olkowski, and Gail Weiss, and the editors at *Continental Philosophy Review* (formerly *Man and World*).

I began to work on this book in earnest during a sabbatical leave from Muhlenberg in the spring semester of 1999. In 2000–2001, I was able to work intensely on it by receiving course relief as the Muhlenberg College "Class of 1932 Research Professor." Further, I have received several Faculty Research Grants from the College. Thus, I am grateful to Muhlenberg for the important ways it has supported my work on this book. I also want to thank a number of my Muhlenberg faculty colleagues for support of this project and friendship, in particular: Ludwig Schlecht, Alec Marsh, Linda Miller, Jack Gambino, Rich Niesenbaum, Jim Peck, Francesca Coppa, Susan Schwartz, Scott Sherk, Laura Edelman, David Tafler, Curtis Dretsch, and Nelvin Vos.

I am also profoundly appreciative of the many Muhlenberg students who have studied Merleau-Ponty with me in seminars and courses during the years that this book was being written. It is not possible to recognize them all here, but special mention must go to Abram Anderson, Michael Bernstein, Heather Blakeslee, Lydia Brubaker, Frank Christmann, Eve DeVaro, Lee Dury, Jamie Ebersole, Susan Frederick, Ardalan Keramati, Kara Gebhart, Doug Herreshaft, Linda Hertzberg, Jon Katz, Rich Meagher, Samir Pandya, Thomas Kay

Peri, Andrew Smith, Meredith Sossman, Danielle Spang, Victor van Buchem, Aaron Wolf, and Kristin Wustholz.

As the book was being written, chapter by chapter, I received comments and good advice from my friends and colleagues Alec Marsh, Ludwig Schlecht, and Andrew Smith. This book has directly benefited from the hours they put in on its behalf. There is no sufficient way to thank them, but I remain deeply grateful for their support of the project. I am also appreciative to Jim Adams for editing suggestions for one of the chapters, and to David Dusenbury for excellent work as copy editor of the manuscript. Special thanks too go to Leonard Lawlor and Dorothea Olkowski who reviewed the book for Indiana University Press and made many important suggestions that have been incorporated into it. Finally, I want to thank Dee Mortensen and her assistant Laura MacLeod at Indiana University Press for their many efforts on behalf of the book. Amidst all these close readers and their excellent advice, it goes without saying that I am responsible for any remaining deficiencies.

I also want to acknowledge the flourishing intellectual community of the International Merleau-Ponty Circle. I have been attending and presenting papers at its annual conferences since 1987. For those readers who may be unaware of this organization, the community of these conferences is truly remarkable: it is characterized by the unique combination of supportive collegiality and rigorous critical scholarship on Merleau-Ponty's thought. I have developed many friendships and professional relationships in this community and they have nurtured my career-long fascination with Merleau-Ponty. There is no way to acknowledge all of the people whose ideas, presentations, and feedback over the years have informed my thinking, but I would be remiss if I did not mention Galen Johnson, Dorothea Olkowski, Stephen Watson, Alphonso Lingis, Hugh Silverman, Robert Bernasconi, Michael B. Smith, Forrest Williams, Pat Burke, Fred Evans, Leonard Lawlor, James Morley, Duane Davis, Susan O'Shaughnessy, Gail Weiss, Helen Fielding, Joanne Dillon, David Abram, Carolyn Woolson, Glen Mazis, Ted Toadvine, Debbie Mullen, Susan Cataldi, and Isaac Ruedin. Among these friends and colleagues, I want to thank Dorothea Olkowski, James Morley, and Susan O'Shaughnessy for encouraging my work in profound ways.

Also from this community, I want to especially recognize Martin "Mike" Dillon—author of the groundbreaking book *Merleau-Ponty's Ontology*, longtime General Secretary of the International Merleau-Ponty Circle, and a senior mentor and friend. I never had Mike as a classroom teacher, but throughout my career he provided incisive commentary on my writings and much wise professional advice. Mike read virtually every word of an earlier draft of this book, wrote a glowing review of it, and encouraged me every step of the way—

despite his disagreements, sometimes on substantial issues. Mike Dillon was the kind of person who liked you because you were willing to disagree with him; he was not one much for sycophancy. I am very sad to say that Mike did not live to see the publication of this book. He died unexpectedly in the spring of 2005 at the early age of 66. This book is dedicated to his memory: may it serve in some small way to commemorate him and his important contributions to the study of Merleau-Ponty.

Outside of the profession, I have been inspired, encouraged, and supported in my philosophical pursuits by family members and loving friends. I especially want to recognize and thank Eugene Burger, Tom Cardinal, Marc DeSouza, Jeffrey Frank and Kristin Illick, Michael and Sally Hoit, Jeff McBride, Steve Montgomery, Robert E. Neale, Cary Oshins and Beth Hyde, Larry Reichlin, Ruth Setton, Sally Tramel, and my parents, Robert and Mary Hass.

Finally, my deepest thanks go to my wonderful family: Marjorie, Cameron, and Jessica. Our lives and loving experiences together have been written between the lines of these pages. We have all lived a long time with this project in our midst. There is no way I could have gotten started, much less finished without your love, support, and constant encouragement. Thank you, my dearest ones.

Abbreviations of Texts by Merleau-Ponty

CD   "Cézanne's Doubt," in *The Merleau-Ponty Aesthetics Reader*

EM   "Eye and Mind," in *The Merleau-Ponty Aesthetics Reader*

IS   "Introduction" to *Signs*

N   *Nature*

PP   *Phenomenology of Perception*

PP-F *Phénoménologie de la perception*

PS   "The Philosopher and His Shadow," in *Signs*

PW   *The Prose of the World*

PW-F *La Prose du monde*

SB   *The Structure of Behavior*

UT   "The Unpublished Text," in *The Primacy of Perception and Other Essays*

VI   *The Visible and the Invisible*

VI-F *Le Visible et l'invisible*

WP   *The World of Perception*

MERLEAU-PONTY'S PHILOSOPHY

Introduction to Merleau-Ponty's Philosophy: "Singing the World"

My Overarching Project

Most philosophies—once vibrant and fresh—pass quietly into the history of philosophy. There they become the province of a handful of specialists and episodes in a grand narrative that has since moved on. However, nearly fifty years after his death (in 1961), this has not happened to the philosophy of Maurice Merleau-Ponty. At the time of this writing, major new books and essays about his thought continue to be published around the world.[1] Further, previously unpublished lectures, essays, interviews, and radio talks by Merleau-Ponty are starting to emerge and they reveal surprising new dimensions of his thought.[2] There are flourishing scholarly organizations and international conferences in North America, France, Italy, and Japan. Dissertations on his work continue to be written and published world-wide. Even Anglo-American philosophers, who frequently eschew all things "Continental," have realized there is something vital going on here, particularly for philosophy of mind and aesthetics.[3] In short, despite its mid-twentieth-century vintage, Merleau-Ponty's philosophy continues to live and breathe. It continues to offer resources that solve traditional philosophical problems. It continues to offer promising insights for our most contemporary concerns.

Yet, for all that, I believe Merleau-Ponty's thought is not well-understood in the wider philosophical community. After nearly twenty years of studying, writing, and lecturing intensively on Merleau-Ponty, I remain surprised by how many excellent philosophers say that they "still haven't read him." I remain surprised by the number of very smart people who essentially ignore his writings even though they are working on closely related topics or thinkers. I remain surprised by established professionals who confess that they really don't understand what he is saying. Consider, for instance, Daniel Dennett's *Philosophical Lexicon* where the word "merleau-ponty" is offered as an adjective for confusion.[4] If that is the state of some professional philosophers, then imagine the plight of educated laypersons: they may have heard of Merleau-Ponty and seen his books, but they have little sense of his philosophical project and its importance.

While I find it surprising, I also have a pretty good understanding of how this situation has come to be. For one thing, Merleau-Ponty never published a short, accessible text that introduces his philosophy as a whole. Indeed, it is notoriously difficult to know where to begin reading him: the two main options—*Phenomenology of Perception* and *The Visible and the Invisible*—would seem to fall somewhere in the range between formidable and impossible. Further, it must be said that despite his exceptional talents as a prose stylist, Merleau-Ponty writes in an idiom that is dense, complicated, and at times elusive. And his writings are often wrestling with ideas, views, and programs that animated the French academy in the 1940s and 1950s but which really didn't catch fire across the English Channel or the Atlantic: Hegelianism, neo-Kantianism, and structuralism. Even his philosophical method—phenomenology—remains badly understood by many contemporary philosophers.

Be all that as it may, this book is written to ameliorate the situation. It is designed to be a readable, carefully argued, and critical appreciation of Merleau-Ponty's philosophy as a whole. It aims to help readers—professional and lay philosophers alike—understand why Merleau-Ponty's thought continues to remain vital and productive for so many contemporary philosophers around the world. Indeed, I believe that his philosophy has a peculiar power to alleviate traditional, malingering philosophical problems and open new vistas for thinking and living. By the time you are done with this book, I hope to have persuaded you that this strong claim is plausible, if not true.

Having clarified these overarching values, I can be more specific about the two-fold orientation of the arguments in this book. On one hand, as just indicated, they seek to offer an accessible, yet systematic presentation of what I take to be the major elements in Merleau-Ponty's philosophy. That is, (1) his commitment to phenomenology as a philosophical method, (2) his phenomenology of perceptual experience, (3) his philosophy of embodiment, (4) his groundbreaking work on intersubjectivity, (5) his later ontology of the flesh, (6) his philosophy of expression, and (7) his philosophy of language. My goal in this arc of the book is to present—clearly and with a minimum of jargon—these central elements and their philosophical justification. In this way, my book offers an entrée, an invitation into Merleau-Ponty's philosophy. Along the line of this arc I will measure, test, and adjudicate the strengths and weaknesses of his views in relation to a number of contemporary philosophers and movements. In many cases this testing and weighing will be done in relation to Merleau-Ponty's French successors: Levinas, Derrida, Foucault, Deleuze, and Irigaray. Since the work of these important thinkers pervades much contemporary philosophical discourse, this first arc of argumentation will participate in, and hopefully advance, some of the current scholarship being done on their complex relationship to Merleau-Ponty's thought.

The second orientation of this book, and an extension of the first, is to offer an accessible, yet systematic presentation of an important dimension of Merleau-Ponty's philosophy that has so far eluded most commentators (including his direct, French successors): his account of thinking, knowing, and language as processes of *expression*.[5] Given the extraordinary importance of this account to Merleau-Ponty's philosophy as a whole, a few preliminary words about it seem in order. First of all, it must be said that in contemporary English we use this word "expression" frequently and casually; it has a very wide-ranging use. However, in Merleau-Ponty's philosophy, "expression" is a complex, yet precise technical term: for him it refers to a specific, observable process that happens in our cognitive life and which, he argues, has been systematically overlooked by thinkers since the dawn of western philosophy. Indeed, Merleau-Ponty's account of expressive cognition is explicitly offered as an alternative to the ancient picture of thinking, language, and knowing as *representation*. The view (or paradigm) that thought and language fundamentally *represent* reality is classical in origin; it is installed in western philosophy by Plato and Aristotle. It then flourishes during the so-called "modern" period of philosophy (the Enlightenment) and has persisted throughout the nineteenth and twentieth centuries. To be sure, a considerable amount of work in contemporary epistemology, metaphysics, philosophy of mind, and philosophy of language starts from assuming the representational character of mind, thinking, speaking, and knowing. Again, it is this representational view that Merleau-Ponty's philosophy of expressive cognition will show is mistaken.

As these comments perhaps begin to convey, the implications of the second arc of this book are substantial: Merleau-Ponty's philosophy of expression offers dramatic possibilities for re-conceiving human cognition. It is not possible to rehearse specific arguments here in the introduction, but in general terms Merleau-Ponty shows that the representational view of thought and language is predicated upon a long, developing tradition of essentially mistaken notions of the mind's relationship to nature. On Merleau-Ponty's account, acknowledging and embracing the mind's rootedness in nature permits us to see that human thought and language are not merely representational (mimetic); they do not merely imitate, mirror, and copy some outside reality. Instead, he argues, those processes are essentially, fundamentally *creative*. That is, they involve processes of transformation—acts of expression—in which the overflowing meaning of perceptions or language are reorganized to yield new, especially powerful ways of thinking and speaking. I hasten to add that this is not, for Merleau-Ponty, to hold that thought and language cannot or do not represent; he clearly believes that they can and sometimes do. His view is rather that the representational, mimetic, reflective power of thought and language is essentially, inescapably based upon creative cognition. This means that the representational definition of thought and language, so constitutive of western philosophy, mistakes a second-order possibility for the primary process of expressive transformation.

What more fully are these creative processes, these acts of expression? How do they work? For Merleau-Ponty, understanding cognition as expressive allows us to understand the creative, productive life of the mind within a thoroughly naturalistic framework, one that is compatible with Darwinian evolution. How precisely will this relationship between mind and nature go? Again, the second arc of this book will elucidate Merleau-Ponty's answers to these important questions. By the time you are done with the book you should have a clear grasp of his answers and their philosophical implications. However, it must be stressed that these specific answers cannot be given prematurely—they do not just stand on their own. In particular, Merleau-Ponty's account of expressive cognition is an extension of his perceptual ontology, and so I must carefully lay out the elements of his philosophy that will allow sufficient understanding of his philosophy of expression.

The fact that it is an extension of his ontology also helps us understand why Merleau-Ponty's account of expressive cognition has been largely overlooked. Indeed, it is already an enormous occupation for commentators to elucidate his exceptionally fecund ontology, a fact that is reflected in the large number of essays and books on the subject. It must also be said that Merleau-Ponty himself contributes to the problem: in virtually every case he begins his books and major essays by developing ontological claims and then, toward the end, if at all, works his way into the phenomena of expression. Be all that as it may, this book seeks to rectify the imbalance. By the end I hope to show that Merleau-Ponty gives us a very promising account of the mind's subtle relationship with the body that finally leaves behind the exhausted binary of dualism and reductive materialism. And it does so in a way that embraces our natural life and natural history rather ignores or denies them.

Nonetheless, there is still the question of "phenomenology." What really is this thing, this method, called *phenomenology*? I believe it has been the persistent failure of many philosophers to understand phenomenology that makes my elucidation of Merleau-Ponty's philosophy still necessary. In the rest of this introduction I hope to say enough to put some of these confusions to rest, or at least at bay, so that we can later understand and test Merleau-Ponty's phenomenological approach on it own, best terms.

A "Discourse on Method"

In the wider philosophical community there have been a great many confusions about phenomenology, as well as "straw man" denunciations of it, that have contributed to a widespread failure to understand this way of doing philosophy. I believe that phenomenology is both less and more than many philosophers seem to realize. It is less vacuous, less metaphysically loaded, and more promising, more interesting. For the purpose of getting started, I would say in general terms that phenomenology is correctly understood in a two-fold way: both as a specific form of argumentation and as a philosophical movement. Let's start with the first of these understandings.

One of the deepest misconceptions about phenomenology is the lingering notion that it is essentially "irrational," that its proponents "offer no arguments." At this late date it is clear that the contrary is true: phenomenology is a way of arguing, reasoning, and persuading; it is a way of establishing a conclusion. It does, however, function differently than deduction and induction. Further, it is different than Peirce's "abduction," what is now typically called "inference to the best explanation." And it does not reason to the "necessary conditions of possibility" (transcendental argumentation), nor elucidate hidden tensions (aporias) in a text or a concept (deconstruction). Rather, to borrow a phrase from Heidegger, a phenomenological argument "says to show."[6] That is, such an argument uses language to direct our attention to something in our worldly experience, to show us something, to help us notice and see it. Phenomenological argument then is not mere description (a listing of properties), but rather a use of evocative language (for example, descriptive, metaphorical, analogical, gestural language) toward the end of seeing, noticing, or understanding something specific in or about our direct, living experiences.

We can grasp this more fully by way of an analogy with how one teaches chess. To be sure, I could try to teach my son how to move the rook with a defining proposition: "The rook is the piece that moves vertically or horizontally on the board for any number of squares." Or instead, I can do what teachers of chess have been doing for centuries: pick up the rook, hold it above the board, and *show* him how it moves. In doing so, I need not say a word: I move the rook relative to the board, and my son *gets* it; he passes from non-understanding to understanding through this act of showing.

This "passage" from non-understanding to understanding, from non-seeing to seeing, qualifies phenomenology as a form of inference, a way of "reasoning." Through showing gestures ("the premises"), we move others toward a desired recognition or understanding ("the conclusion"). Indeed, when phenomenological arguments are effective they involve something like a light bulb going on: "Oh, I get it! I see it now!" Of course we can use our bodies to show other people things—as in the chess example. But when we aren't in physical proximity with them then we can (and must) use words and language-gestures to evoke their awareness of what we wish them to see or understand. I should also mention that there is nothing automatic about phenomenological reasoning. As with any form of inference, this kind of argument can be flawed, for example, when my showing gestures or words do not reveal or uncover the desired phenomenon. Imagine the unsatisfactory results if I waved the rook up in the air with no visible relation to the chessboard. Thus, there are better and worse phenomenological arguments—"successful" and "unsuccessful" ones—determined by their success in having us see or grasp what they aim to show. To be sure, just as there are potential errors specific to deductive and inductive reasoning, so too are there unique pitfalls for phenomenological showing.

It has been the persistent failure of many philosophers to appreciate the specific character of phenomenological reasoning that has led some of them to make the false objection that "phenomenology can't be criticized." Of course it can, but doing so effectively requires that we understand its method of inference (as a "saying to show") and criticize such reasoning on its own terms. I might add that what I have just claimed about phenomenological reasoning—that it must be understood and criticized on it own terms—holds equally true for any mode of inference, for example, deduction, induction, transcendental reasoning, or deconstruction. To criticize and dismiss a mode of inference by demanding it meet the specific standards of another mode is what we might call "a category mistake"—a fallacy committed, for example, by Hume when he criticizes inductive reasoning for (in effect) not meeting the standards of deduction.

With these insights in place, we are now in a position to reject a final criticism of phenomenology, a criticism so widespread in philosophy, the human sciences, and literary theory that it has become a platitude: the criticism that "phenomenology is essentially subjectivistic." On the contrary, there is nothing at all in phenomenological method that is essentially subjectivistic or a "mere intuitionistic report of subjective states." For one thing, this mistaken notion is predicated upon failing to understand the character of phenomenological method as a method of *reasoning*. But it also takes hold because people tacitly accept Husserl's famous explorations as the very essence of phenomenology. There is no question that Husserl is a pivotal figure in the use of phenomenological method. And there is no question that he, at times, practiced phenomenological reasoning in the service of a subjectivistic ontology. However, it does not follow that phenomenological method is equivalent to subjectivism. To slide from a method of reasoning to a particular ontological outlook is—once again—a kind of category mistake.

But also this equation, this slide, simply ignores Heidegger's and Merleau-Ponty's rigorous arguments that disentangle phenomenological method from Husserl's inclinations to transcendental subjectivism. The equation ignores their constant efforts to show that being in the world, with other people, amid language, in history and culture, are the necessary conditions for articulating a subjectivistic ontology in the first place. Therefore, the proper thing to say after Heidegger and Merleau-Ponty is that phenomenological method is essentially *intersubjective:* such reasoning takes shape in the real world, with and toward others, using language that is sedimented by culture. The method "says to show" features of this shared, lived world, just as, for example, I might try to help my friend see the red cardinal hiding in a tree. Far from "subjective intuitions, take them or leave them," phenomenological arguments succeed or fail in relation to the real world we share. Sometimes the person "gets" it: "Yes! I see the cardinal!" Sometimes, perhaps if I can't say it right or my friend isn't really listening, he misses what I am trying to show. And sometimes we discover something new altogether, for example, that it was only a leftover red leaf stuck up in the branches. In the early chapters of this book, as I elaborate Merleau-Ponty's perceptual ontology, what is properly called "perceptual realism" or "experiential realism," we will see his arguments against the subjectivistic tradition founded by Descartes—a tradition from which Husserl simply could not disentangle himself.[7] With these arguments in place, I hope to rather decisively expose the errors and dualistic sediments that attend the widespread notion that phenomenology is subjectivistic—a notion that unfortunately continues to persist in a good deal of contemporary Anglo-American philosophy of mind.[8]

We see then, on one hand, that phenomenology is a particular way of reasoning, a method that aims to direct and amplify our "knowledge by acquaintance." If it is true, as it clearly seems, that acquaintance with something through experience is a necessary condition for what is called "knowledge by description" about that thing (or propositional knowledge), then this method of reasoning is far from peripheral or irrelevant, but rather indispensable in our efforts for knowledge.

Phenomenology is thus a method of reasoning and one fundamental way of knowing the world—knowing by acquaintance. At the same time, the word "phenomenology" refers to a twentieth-century philosophical movement that grows out of the insight that certain modes of thinking get in the way of seeing important features of our living experiences. These modes of thinking get in the way of *realizing* our living experiences—"realizing" them in the sense of understanding them, but also in the sense of living in consonance with them. For this reason, thinkers in the phenomenological movement carry out a substantial critical project: the ongoing effort to remove certain conceptual veils, to expose those modes of thinking and the models based upon them as *abstract*. What this vigilance about "abstraction" means precisely for a phenomenologist is that the mode of thinking in question presupposes living experience for its formulation and therefore neither this mode nor its formulation is itself metaphysically basic. I have already hinted at one example of this criticism: Merleau-Ponty's and Heidegger's arguments that Husserl's transcendental subjectivism, adopted from Descartes and Kant, presupposes one's already being in an intersubjective world. However, that is just one example, for the error of asserting some derivative view as fundamental can be found far and wide throughout the history of philosophy, the empirical sciences, and even in our everyday thinking and common notions. I want to underscore this last phrase, "even in our everyday thinking and common notions." Indeed, it is important to understand—because some critics have missed this—that phenomenology is no appeal to "common sense."

Therefore, as a movement phenomenology enacts a kind of vigilance about views, models, practices, and pedagogies; it seeks to uncover abstraction in them so that we don't become problematically invested in ontologically derivative notions. On one level, as Merleau-Ponty argues time and time again, these abstractions lead to bad metaphysics, to mistakenly reifying some second-order concept as primary fact. On another level, if we embrace abstractions we become blind to the actual character of worldly experience. That is, we can find ourselves in the bizarre, contradictory position of believing that reality is one way while we live and experience it in quite another. These abstract views must be revealed, then, not only in pursuit of sound thinking, but also as a way to promote coherence between thought and life. I want to stress that in practice the critical mode of phenomenology typically works in tandem with the affirmative mode of "saying to show" what has been obscured by these abstractions. That is, with a kind of to-and-fro movement between critique and showing, phenomenology seeks to illuminate our living experiences in the natural world with other people and other living creatures.

With all this in mind, we can discern that the phenomenological practice of philosophy is actually ancient in its origins. We find its kind of double intention—the critique of abstraction and the practice of "saying to show" experience—throughout early Buddhist texts and in the classic works of Taoism. (This fact provides a clue about the extraordinary interest that western phenomenology has generated in parts of Asia.) And we can find examples of phenomenological arguments throughout the western tradition as well—in Plato, Aristotle, Descartes, and Nietzsche, to name a few. But there is no question that Husserl (following Brentano) gives voice, name, and legitimacy to this approach in an unprecedented way; he is the "father" of phenomenology as a twentieth-century movement. Equally certain is the fact that Heidegger and Merleau-Ponty find the Cartesian assumptions in Husserl to be thoroughly "abstract," and that they reconfigure the practice of phenomenology in ways that continue to inspire many contemporary philosophers.

We see then the sense in which Merleau-Ponty is a formative practitioner of phenomenology. After Husserl, yet deeply critical of Husserl, he radicalizes the double gesture of phenomenology—the critique of intellectual abstraction and the affirmative revelation of important features of living experience: perception, embodiment, intersubjective life, thinking, and language. However, as this book unfolds I will be able to eventually show that he radicalizes phenomenological method as well, for he gradually comes to understand his own philosophical practice as *expression*. In this last set of arguments, we will see a final cost of overlooking Merleau-Ponty's account of expressive cognition. For in this neglect, we have failed to understand the full extent of his philosophical method and, with it, his revitalized vision for philosophy itself. This vision is not conceived as "the end of philosophy" (Heidegger), a ladder or raft to be thrown away (Wittgenstein, Buddha), "a revaluation of all values" (Nietzsche), "edifying philosophy" (Rorty), or "writing with two hands" (Derrida). As Merleau-Ponty puts it otherwise: "Expressing what *exists* is an endless task" (CD 66). Philosophy, re-conceived by Merleau-Ponty as expressing the world, as "singing the world," *chanter le monde* (PP 187, PP-F 218), is an endless task, but not a futile one. It is the ongoing work of renewing our connections to the world, of embracing our very being as flesh and nature, of remaining alive to our being with each other. At the same time, it is also about celebrating the creative, transformative powers of thought, language, and philosophy itself.

In this introduction, I have issued a number of promissory notes. To make good on them, the first five chapters of this book will elucidate central elements of Merleau-Ponty's perceptual ontology: his justification of phenomenological method, his still-unsurpassed phenomenology of perceptual experience, his breakthrough work on embodied subjectivity and intersubjectivity, and his later, deep revisions to this ontology in *The Visible and the Invisible*. My purpose in these chapters is not to exhaust all the topics or issues that are germane to these subjects, but rather to articulate these elements and their philosophical justification in a way that invites the reader into the richness of Merleau-Ponty's philosophy. Along the way, as previously indicated, I will test his views in light of contemporary ideas or objections, and adjudicate those debates as truth demands. Nonetheless, these early chapters serve a dual purpose, for they also provide the groundwork that will allow me to elucidate Merleau-Ponty's account of expressive thinking, language, and knowing in chapter 6 and beyond.

Before we proceed with this plan however, I believe it is important to offer a prelude that highlights the philosophy to which Merleau-Ponty's thought stands in sharpest contrast: Descartes's philosophy. It should be said that Merleau-Ponty is not a vigorously polemical thinker—as is Nietzsche, for example. But there is no question that Descartes is Merleau-Ponty's nemesis.[9] Few thinkers have taken Descartes more seriously than Merleau-Ponty; few have studied him more closely or criticized him more exhaustively. This is because, for him, Descartes's epoch-shaping philosophy is responsible for the dualistic and mechanistic categories that continue to haunt western ways of thinking. Further, Merleau-Ponty recognizes that Descartes renews the representationalism of Plato and Aristotle, driving it deep into the heart of modern conceptions of perception, cognition, language, and knowledge. I believe that briefly seeing how these categories emerge in Descartes's philosophy will be illuminating as we approach Merleau-Ponty's philosophy. It will also be helpful as we seek to acknowledge Merleau-Ponty's achievement: his remarkable reconfiguration of being and knowing beyond the ancient paradigm of representation.

In closing, I should say a few words about my own method in this book. My overarching aim is to treat Merleau-Ponty's philosophy in a way that resonates with his texts—that reveals and amplifies what is already there in them. I want to illuminate his views and arguments in those texts rather than violate them; I want to "get them right." Having said that, I also insist there could be quite different, powerful ways of organizing and elaborating the same material. In my commitment to this complex conjunction—of "getting it right" and a genuine plurality of interpretation—I will not be *representing* Merleau-Ponty's texts. On the contrary, my project in this book is to *express* Merleau-Ponty's philosophy, to "let it sing" along some particularly powerful lines of possibility. I suspect that this complex conjunction doesn't make much sense yet, nor does my talk of "expressing powerful lines of possibility." But I hope that it will by the time you finish this book, and that you will find Merleau-Ponty's account of expressive cognition as provocative and promising as I do.

Prelude: Scenes from the Cartesian Theater

1. Descartes's Revolution

The philosophy of René Descartes (1596–1650) was revolutionary to the core. There is little question that he intended it to be. As he wrote to his close friend, Father Mersenne: "I may tell you, between ourselves, that these six Meditations contain all the foundations of my physics. . . . I hope that readers will gradually get used to my principles, and recognize their truth, before they notice that they destroy the principles of Aristotle."[1]

When we recall the nearly exclusive extent to which the Scholastic education of his day was Aristotelian, and that, at one point, Descartes planned to write a volume that would replace the standard textbooks,[2] we can see that Descartes was seeking to create a radical paradigm shift. The extraordinary thing is that he succeeded: his philosophy laid down the terms, categories, and problems that shaped—and continue to shape—much western thinking about mind, reality, and knowledge. Indeed, to a significant extent, we remain *Cartesians*.

I realize that this claim may seem flawed or provocative. After all, much late-twentieth-century philosophy of mind, cognitive science, and psychology begin by criticizing or ridiculing Descartes's thought. We have heard that the "Cartesian Theater" should be shut down as a model of mind.[3] And his quest for secure, certain foundations has been pronounced dead, about as viable as his biological notion of "animal spirits." All that is true: we are "recovering" Cartesians, to be sure. But I also believe that we have not clearly, decisively rejected a central innovation in Descartes's thought. I further believe that this innovation, this metaphysical artifact at the heart of his revolution, continues to shape our language, fundamental concepts, and sensibilities. I am speaking here, not of Descartes's radical skepticism, nor his metaphysical dualism, but rather of his *representation theory of perception*. This theory of perception is really, finally, Descartes's legacy. For decades after him, then centuries, and in our own time, the latent ontology and language of his theory of perception has been accepted in the west as axiomatic, or "scientific," or "just plain fact." But more vigorously than any other philosopher, Merleau-Ponty argues that the representation theory of perception introduces a schism at the heart of life—

a radical separation of consciousness from the world, of self from others—and rends nature as matter-machine. If post-Cartesian philosophy finds itself wrestling with idealism, relativism, subjectivism, mechanism, and reductive materialism, Merleau-Ponty teaches us that it is because they so naturally follow from Descartes's representation theory of perception. In any event, Merleau-Ponty's ontology lies on the other side of this theory. It lies on the other side as an alternative through its sustained critique of the theory. In order to appreciate the character and promise of Merleau-Ponty's ontology, and then later his account of expressive cognition, I want to elucidate Descartes's radical innovation of perceptual representation—its context, its bizarre logic, and its curious half-life. Perhaps then, as Merleau-Ponty says, we can better reject "the age-old assumptions that put . . . the world and the body in the seer as in a box."[4]

2. The Context and Arguments for Perceptual Representation

The emergence of Descartes's philosophy is best understood at the nexus of two primary influences at work in his life and times, the "natural-philosophic" and the Scholastic.[5] On one hand, there was a burgeoning micro-mechanical movement in natural philosophy—a movement into which Descartes was initiated by his formative meeting with Isaac Beeckman in 1618.[6] Since the Renaissance, of course, European culture had been gradually adopting quantificational techniques and mechanistic models for practical affairs.[7] But at the dawn of the seventeenth century natural philosophers were applying such models and techniques to the workings of the cosmos with remarkable results. Beeckman was an early innovator in this movement. Inspired by his many discussions with Beeckman, Descartes went on to make several breakthroughs in mathematics, optics, and theoretical physics; he wrote the *Rules* (1619–1620, 1626–1628) and *The World* (1633) as early attempts to legitimize this "natural-philosophic" enterprise.

At the same time, Descartes was deeply infused with the Aristotelian scholasticism of his Jesuit education at La Flèche. In this profoundly theological milieu, the world was not depicted as an aggregation of "corpuscles" or "atoms" in motion which could be captured numerically. Rather it was extolled, following Aristotle and Aquinas, as a hierarchical kingdom of substances differentiated by their qualities: God, human, animal, plant, living or dead. In the great schools of the era knowledge proceeded not by mathematical analysis, but through the syllogism and sheer authority. And metaphysics was the bread and butter course of study. There is no question that Descartes railed against many aspects of this education.[8] But it would be a mistake to conclude from this fact that Descartes's metaphysics and theology are mere artifice designed to appease the church and protect his real scientific interests. On the contrary, Descartes abandoned the *Rules* because his project there had not sufficiently secured its metaphysical foundations.[9] And while he extols natural philosophy as the path to all progress, he also insists upon "first philosophy" as the essential propaedeutic. Without it, Descartes insists, one is prey not only to the Aristotelian-Thomistic prejudices of worldly forms and final causality, but also to the vicissitudes of the skeptical and probabilistic movements that were flourishing at the time. As a result, Descartes says that "the whole of philosophy is like a tree. The roots are metaphysics, the trunk is physics."[10]

It is amid the larger cultural conflict between metaphysics, theology, and natural philosophy—a conflict played out in the trial and submission of Galileo—that Descartes writes his extraordinary text, *Meditations on First Philosophy* (published in 1641). On one level, the book seeks to resolve this cultural conflict by reconciling theological metaphysics with the new science—marking out the domain proper to each. Descartes begins his great book in dramatic terms:

> Some years ago I was struck by the large number of falsehoods that I had accepted as true in my childhood, and by the highly doubtful nature of the whole edifice that I had subsequently based on them. I realized that it was necessary, once in the course of my life, to demolish everything completely and start again right from the foundations if I wanted to establish anything . . . that was stable and likely to last.[11]

We see here Descartes's basic commitment to distinguishing "opinions" from truths that are "completely certain and indubitable"; we see his desire to identify a secure, permanent foundation for human knowledge. We also see his paradoxical plan to find those certainties by "destroying all his former opinions." Indeed, Descartes reasons that without this destructive prelude, any forthcoming foundation might be infected by some unwitting falsehood, just as any new apple would be if rotten apples were left in the basket.[12]

Thus, as is well known, Descartes continues his First Meditation by wielding a "method of doubt": if a belief is open to the slightest doubt it will be abandoned on his quest for certainty. To raise these doubts, Descartes offers three skeptical arguments of escalating force. The first is an argument by the senses: his recognition that all one's beliefs are based on the senses and that one's senses are sometimes deceptive. The second argument is his famous claim that "there are never any sure signs by means of which being awake can be distinguished from being asleep," hence any belief one holds might be based on a dream.[13] However, Descartes rejects the full effectiveness of these arguments and goes on to offer a third argument he accepts as utterly decisive. He famously argues that all his former beliefs are open to doubt because "it is *possible* that an evil demon is deceiving me right now, not only about all sensible things, but also about the basic truths of math and geometry." And since, he says, laziness might draw him back into the slumbers of everyday opinion, Descartes tells us he will persist in a radical hypothesis:

"I shall think that the sky, the air, the earth, colours, shapes, sounds and all external things are merely the delusions of dreams which [the evil demon] has devised. . . . I shall consider myself as not having hands or eyes, or flesh, or blood or senses."[14] We see then that in offering this "evil demon" argument, Descartes believes he has "destroyed" all his former opinions, but he has also simultaneously defined the standard of his desired certainty: from here on, "knowledge" will be truth that isn't vulnerable to the evil demon hypothesis.

With the Cartesian stage thus set, Descartes purports to find knowledge in the Second Meditation. He begins to answer the radical doubt with the so-called *cogito* argument, an argument that is in fact composed of two phases. The first phase is Descartes's most famous reasoning of all: his recognition that precisely insofar as he doubts, using the evil demon hypothesis, he necessarily, certainly must exist. "I think therefore I am." The second phase of the argument is Descartes's further claim that this "I" which necessarily, certainly exists, even while it doubts the existence of the world and all flesh, is a thinking thing, a *mind.* As Descartes says:

> But what shall I now say that I am, when I am supposing that there is some supremely powerful and . . . malicious deceiver, who is deliberately trying to trick me in every way he can? Can I now assert that I possess even the most insignificant of all the attributes which I have just said belong to the nature of a body? . . . [N]othing suggests itself. . . . Thinking? At last I have discovered it—thought; this alone is inseparable from me. . . . I am, then, in the strict sense only a thing that thinks.[15]

"I exist as a thinking being"—in this tacitly theological conclusion, Descartes believes he has found an indubitable point of purchase against the radical doubt, an undeniable truth about which even an evil spirit could not possibly deceive us.

It is at this juncture in the text that we find the essential arguments on which I want to focus. For with the *cogito* in place, Descartes goes on to establish his theory that perception as we know it is an internal mental representation of an external world. Before we see the details of his argument, it is worth emphasizing the novelty of this representation theory of perception. For Descartes, the theory is a huge innovation beyond the alternative accounts alive in his day. One such account was the extramission theory of Galen (and Plato to some extent), according to which perception proceeds from the eye to the object; the eye "sends out" rays that, in effect, caress the object. The other leading option was Aristotle's causal account: perception involves the organ "being affected" by the object, just as "wax takes on the impress of a signet-ring."[16] For Descartes, neither theory is acceptable: they cannot address the facts of perceptual error and illusion (a notorious problem for Aristotle), but even more, they are part and parcel of the old Scholastic ontology of substantial forms. For Descartes then, establishing that perception is a mental representation of external, homogeneous matter is a breakthrough of the first order. Not only does it overthrow these ancient views still dominant in the Schools, but it permits "the great synthesis" between the micro-mechanical and theological domains, between what he and legions of philosophers after him call the "external" world of matter and the "internal" world of consciousness.

Descartes begins to establish his theory of perception in the Second Meditation by acknowledging a "strangeness" that has resulted from his earlier reasoning. Indeed, in making the *cogito* argument he suggested that perception is a form of thinking and not a bodily operation, but he sees that this view needs to be more fully earned. To this end, he offers what is known as the "wax argument." Descartes begins by observing that even though all the sensible qualities of a piece of wax are altered when passed through a flame, it is nonetheless indubitable that the puddle before him is the same entity: "no one denies it, no one thinks otherwise."[17] Observing the total transformation of sensory qualities between wax$_1$ (the honeycomb) and wax$_2$ (the puddle), Descartes reasons that he doesn't *sense* or *see* that wax$_1$ and wax$_2$ are the same entity. Nor could he *imagine* those "immeasurable changes." He concludes, rather that he must *perceive* wax$_1$ and wax$_2$ are the same, where "perceive" explicitly means "conceived with his mind." Precisely put, Descartes concludes that perceptions are *judgments* made by the mind's faculty of understanding.[18] And given the radical doubt, the still-telling possibility "that what I see is not really the wax, . . . that I do not even have eyes," an implicit corollary follows—a corollary Descartes explicitly asserts in the Third Meditation: that the wax *as perceived* is a conceptual object or "impression," an *idea*. As Descartes puts it: "But what was it about [the earth, sky, stars, and everything else I apprehended with the senses] that I perceived clearly? *Just that the ideas, or thoughts, of such things appeared before my mind.*"[19]

In the wax argument then, Descartes has offered his revolutionary premise, his key innovation: perception is strictly a mental or cognitive operation, and perceived objects—the sky, the stars, tables, chairs, one's own body, etc.—are *ideas*. It is an initially counter-intuitive view, but Descartes insists upon it: perceptions are ideas "appearing before my mind," mental objects playing as though on a screen (the Cartesian Theater). As Descartes puts it in the *Optics:* "it is the soul which sees, and not the eyes."[20] What a strange conclusion this is! How contrary it is to everything we experience! What could be more self-evident to us than the fact that we perceive worldly things with our eyes, ears, hands, and tongues—with our bodies? What seems more self-evident to us than the fact we perceive worldly things themselves? But in reply, Descartes would remind us to follow his chain of reasoning: (1) we can doubt the existence of all corporeal objects by the possibility of the evil demon, (2) at the exact same time, we know our existence as a thinking being and we know that we have all these perceptions of worldly things, such as wax and my own body, therefore (3) those perceptions must be *thoughts,* a tissue of ideas. For Descartes, our commonsense notion that we perceive and know worldly things with our bodies is one of those vague, confused (Aristotelian) *opinions* that the method of doubt is designed to eradicate. As Descartes puts it at the very end of the Second Meditation: "I now know that even bodies are not strictly perceived by the senses . . . but by the intellect alone, and that this perception derives not from their being touched or seen but from their being understood; and in view of this I know plainly that I can achieve an easier . . . perception of my own mind [and its ideas] than of anything else."[21]

To be sure, Descartes adds more to this theory of perception: in the Sixth Meditation he adds a mechanistic world of matter to underlie and inform the mental-perceptual appearances. I will elucidate this addition in section 4, below, and it will help us understand the extraordinary prestige enjoyed by Descartes's theory of perceptual representation. But first it is important to establish how deeply fallacious the above web-work of argument has been.

3. The Problems of Perceptual Representation

You will recall that when "push comes to shove," when commonsense objections are raised, Descartes always has recourse to his apparently simple chain of reasoning: (1) one can doubt that material objects and one's own body exist, and yet (2) one still perceives such things, therefore (3) those perceptions are ideas in one's mind. To be fair, Descartes does not explicitly offer this argument to the reader, even though it is strongly implied. Perhaps he doesn't explicitly make this argument because he senses that it is fallacious. It commits what Bernard Williams calls "the masked man fallacy."[22] To see the problem for Descartes, consider the following analogous reasoning: (1) I do not know who this masked man is, (2) I do know my father, therefore (3) this masked man is not my father. Clearly this kind of reasoning is unsound. It slides from my *ignorance* about whether X is Y to a claim that X *is not* Y, and this is illegitimate. Even though—on the evil demon hypothesis—I don't know for sure that I have a body while I perceive, it doesn't at all follow that perception is not performed by my body. It doesn't at all follow that "it is the soul which sees and not the eyes."

Recognizing the masked man fallacy is devastating to Descartes's first, implicit argument for perceptual representation. Further, it means that the plausibility of the representation theory of perception rests entirely upon the wax argument. Does this argument fare any better? We will see that it does not. Indeed, if the *cogito* is one of the most famous arguments in the history of philosophy, the wax argument is one of the most vexed. It contains a number of deep, but subtle internal problems that decisively undermine its plausibility.

The first of these internal problems is that the wax argument depends upon Descartes's illicitly shifting his standard of certainty. We might recall that at the end of the First Meditation the standard of certainty was some fact or belief known to be true despite the possibility of an evil demon. As we saw, he appears to meet that standard with the first phase of the *cogito* argument: "I must exist while I am thinking. Not even an evil deceiver could fool me about that." But the founding premise for the wax argument—that wax_1 (the honeycomb) and wax_2 (the puddle) are the same entity—is only secured by Descartes through an appeal to the crowd: as he puts it, "no one denies it."[23] This is a major problem for Descartes. First of all, it must be stressed that the evil demon hypothesis prevents him from appealing to other people at this point. According to his chain of reasoning they may not even exist. Still more problematic is the fact that this new standard of "certainty" is far weaker than the one Descartes had earlier insisted on. Indeed, if all that was needed for certainty was this kind of appeal to the crowd, then certainty might well be claimed against Descartes's skeptical arguments in the First Meditation. For instance: "Who would ever think they can't tell the difference between waking life and a dream? No one! Thus I am certain I am awake." No, until the evil demon hypothesis is eliminated, as he purports to do in the Third Meditation, Descartes must meet the higher standard of certainty, and it is clear that this founding premise of the wax argument does not. After all, if a hypothetical demon could deceive me about my mathematical beliefs (for example, that $2 + 3 = 5$), why couldn't it deceive me into thinking wax_1 and wax_2 are the same entity? In short, the wax argument is unsound because Descartes has equivocated over certainty.

But the wax argument involves a subtler and deeper equivocation. For in the course of it Descartes shifts the meaning of perceptual experience itself in a way that undoes his chain of reasoning in the first two Meditations. To show this will take a bit of close, textual work. Directly prior to offering the wax argument, Descartes reflects on what his mind is and does. He says "it *thinks*," that is, it doubts, understands, affirms and denies, wills, imagines, and perceives.[24] Offering a few words on each of these mental operations, Descartes asserts that perception is incorrigible; *that* I perceive wax is not open to doubt. As he puts it: "For example, I am now seeing light, hearing a noise, feeling heat. But [perhaps] I am asleep, so all this is false. Yet I certainly *seem* to see, to hear, and to be warmed. This cannot be false."[25] From this point forward in the text, Descartes will treat all perceptions as themselves indubitable in this way: *that* I perceive, say, a tree, light, or heat cannot be false. From here on the possibility of perceptual error is solely about whether or not my internal perceptual idea *corresponds* to some real external entity, that is, whether there really is a tree "out there" corresponding to my internal, mental idea of a tree.

Seeing this new sense of perceptual incorrigibility—a sense Descartes uses throughout the wax argument—allows us to grasp his second, deeply problematic equivocation. For this new incorrigibility contradicts the way Descartes treated perception in the First Meditation to achieve his skeptical ends. Indeed, it was only by treating perceptions (referred to there as "the senses") as themselves internally corrigible that Descartes was able to empty the basket of all his former beliefs so he could go on to establish the certainty of his thinking ego. Thus his chain of reasoning is torn by a dilemma. On one hand, he can stick with his First Meditation view that perceptual experience is open to doubt, that "his senses deceive him." But this decision, consistently applied, blocks his later claim that perceptions themselves are "internal mental states that cannot be false," and thus the wax argument cannot get off the ground. Conversely, Descartes can appear to save the wax argument by insisting that his reduction to the thinking mind has revealed perception to be an internal, incorrigible "seeming to see." But this claim ripples back and undoes the skepticism about "the senses," in the First Meditation, that was necessary for his reduction to the ego. To be sure, if Descartes's perceptions are incorrigible *now*, they were in fact *then*, and his chain of reasoning through skepticism and the reduction to the mind, to the theory that perceptions are internal ideas, dissolves like a snake swallowing its own tail.

The truth of the matter is that Descartes's reasoning requires both of these incompatible things: he requires perceptual experience to be worldly and doubtful in the First Meditation, so he can establish the ego as the indubitable foundation for knowledge. However, once the ego is established, he then needs perceptions to be internal, incorrigible *ideas* so he can use them to try and escape his egocentric predicament. I am convinced that this is a fatal flaw in the

Meditations. It is this kind of flaw Merleau-Ponty has in mind when he says: "Once one is settled in it, [the philosophy of] reflection is an inexpugnable philosophical position. . . . But are we to enter into reflection? In its inaugural act is concealed a decision to play a double game which, once unmasked, divests it of its apparent evidence" (VI 44).

The "philosophy of reflection" is Merleau-Ponty's name for those philosophical programs that perform a reduction of living experience to ideas before the mind, the philosophies of Descartes, Kant, and Husserl, among others. Throughout his main writings, Merleau-Ponty offers extensive, compelling analyses of the fallacious "double games" required by this type of philosophy to launch itself.[26] Nonetheless, we have seen enough for the purposes of this prelude. We have seen, specifically, that Descartes does not legitimately establish the first half of his representation theory of perception—his theory that perceived things are ideas in the subjective confines of the Cartesian Theater. He does not legitimately establish the dichotomy between "internal" perception and "external" objects. This means that, contrary to traditional assumptions, Descartes's project utterly breaks down in the Second Meditation, and not merely in the theological arguments of the Third and the Fourth Meditations. In short, philosophy cannot legitimately begin from a radical subjectivism: be skeptical if you must, recognize perceptual illusion by all means, but it does not legitimately follow that perception is an internal mental screen of appearances or "veil of ideas."

4. Descartes's "Physical World"

We have just seen that Descartes's wax argument is unsound, and that his arguments to establish perceptions as internal mental ideas fail decisively. One might then expect that our intellectual tradition moved on to essentially different theories of perception, theories that respect perceptual error and illusion without making perception into "a veil of ideas," an "internal representation of an external world." But historically—in philosophy, psychology, and the physical sciences, with leakage into everyday discourse—quite the contrary has occurred: our intellectual culture has gotten mired in the language and ontology of Descartes's representation theory of perception. We have remained stuck in its conceptual matrix, with its intractable subjectivism and its threat of solipsism. How and why did this happen? I think this is a fascinating question about the history of ideas in the western world. While answering it fully is a task for a historian of such ideas, I will soon lay out some strands of this intellectual morass. But first, I need to show how Descartes seeks to complete his theory of perception in the Sixth Meditation. For it is in its finished form that the representation theory of perception came to feel so compelling, lost its metaphysical aura, and started to be taken as "just plain fact."

Descartes opens the Sixth Meditation by stating his one remaining task: to examine "whether material things exist."[27] His premises are all in place: in the Third Meditation he has argued that God exists as a perfect being and hence that no evil demon can possibly exist. In the Fourth he has further argued that all error is caused, not by God, but rather by one's mind affirming or denying things that one doesn't clearly and distinctly understand. These two claims have allowed Descartes to establish a new standard for knowledge, the so-called "divine guarantee": if one affirms only what one understands clearly and distinctly one can never be mistaken.[28] So armed, in the Sixth Meditation, Descartes offers his argument that material objects must certainly exist beyond one's veil of perceptual ideas: "[God] has given me a great propensity to believe that my [perceptual ideas] are produced by corporeal things, so I do not see how God could be understood to be anything but a deceiver if the ideas were transmitted from a source other than corporeal things. It follows that corporeal things exist."[29]

This argument is not particularly remarkable: once a philosopher installs a perfect being into his/her ontology, just about anything follows. What *is* remarkable are some of its corollaries. For one thing, Descartes confirms what I have shown above, something that many people who have held the representation theory of perception tend to ignore: on this theory a person, a mind, has no direct, conscious access to bodies, flesh, things, the natural world, or other people. One's only relation to such things is *mental:* an intellectual *judgment* that such things exist—a judgment, Descartes maintains, that is only guaranteed as true by the certainty that God exists. Thus, for Descartes, the thorny problem of radical subjectivism is solved by quintessential theology: all knowledge of other people, all knowledge of the world, all knowledge of my own flesh flows through God; it is guaranteed by the strength of my epistemological relationship with God. Without Him, all is darkness.

A second corollary to this "proof" is the specific character of the material world beyond "the veil of ideas." That world is not an Aristotelian multiplicity of substantial forms and qualities (such as color or hardness): all such forms and qualities now belong merely to subjective perceptual appearances. Descartes argues instead that external material reality is a homogeneous tableau of pure extension, *res extensa,* "the subject-matter of pure mathematics."[30] While perception cannot access this reality in any way, Descartes holds that geometrical physics allows us to formulate clear and distinct judgments about its workings that are thus (divinely) guaranteed as true. As for differentiation and change in this external material reality, Descartes accounts for them in terms of *motion*. Not motion as Aristotelian potentiality, but rather motion cast in terms of a new micro-mechanical concept: motion is "the transference of one part of matter or of one body . . . into the neighborhood of others."[31] There are, to be sure, problems in both of these claims about external reality. On one hand, Descartes's reduction of corporeality to extension is unsound; his arguments only establish that extension belongs to material objects, not that extension is their sole defining essence.[32] Scholars also agree that it is highly doubtful that his theory of motion can explain basic concepts such as rest, direction, and speed.[33] Historical influence, however, is often not rational: what emerges in the Sixth Meditation is an account of physical reality in terms of purely extended objects in a system of strict, point-by-point, mechanistic causality. In other words, he installs and legitimates, if not gives birth to, our modern concept of *matter*—the so-called "physical world," the world Newton was to explore and extend with such proficiency.

Be that as it may, with the world of extended physical objects existing "out there," Descartes is able to complete his representation theory of perception in the closing pages of the Sixth Meditation. For now he is able to add that his perceptual ideas are subtended by a whole layer of independent material processes, processes that are, not surprisingly, mechanistic in function. To begin, Descartes says, just as a clock "constructed of wheels and weights observes all the laws of its nature," so too we might "consider the body of a man as a kind of machine . . . made up . . . in such a way that, even if there were no mind in it, it would still perform all the same movements."[34] In this "body-machine," Descartes adds, there is a specific process called *sensation*: "When the nerves are pulled in the foot, they in turn pull on inner parts of the brain to which they are attached, and produce a certain motion in them; and nature has laid it down that this motion should produce in the mind a sensation of pain."[35] Indeed, "out there" and "below" my perceptual ideas is the point-by-point causality of sensory functioning: nerve points ABCD are a "cord" from foot to brain; stimulation to one of those physical points passes through each succeeding point until a sensation arrives in the immaterial mind through the pineal gland. These discrete material sensations form the basis of my perceptual ideas and judgments about them. And so, in the Sixth Meditation Descartes's theory finally, fully earns its name: perception is a mental representation, a *re-presentation* of those extended bodies that are in mechanistic, point-by-point causal relations. It is a *copy* of that original presentation, a *mimēsis*, with color, depth, texture, size, and shape added by the mind.[36] Thus, the famous distinction between so-called "primary" and "secondary" qualities—the qualities that belong to matter and those that are added by the mind—is legitimized for an age.[37]

At this point, I believe we have seen enough of Descartes's representation theory of perception. We have seen it from the opening wax argument in the Second Meditation to its completion in the Sixth. By now, setting aside the notion of nerves being "pulled," this theory ought to sound familiar. It is, in essence, a dominant modern theory. It has gone by several names since Descartes—the idea theory, the judgment theory, the propositional theory, the causal representation theory, and recently the computational theory—but the core elements remain the same. It is the view that perception is "built up" out of discrete sensations causally activated from "outside," that perception is an internal mental representation or subjective appearance of an external, essentially mechanistic physical reality. Many philosophers, psychologists, and scientists hold this view as just stated. Others try to revise this or that aspect of the theory to overcome specialized problems. Nonetheless, Descartes's theory is the base matrix that underlies many discussions in contemporary philosophy, philosophy of mind, and cognitive studies. It is the basic view that operates alongside many interpretations of physical and quantum data. Its categories and language have found their way into popular science and literature, into our everyday expressions. Indeed, its dualistic language of subjective/objective, internal/external, mind/matter is no less entrenched in modern consciousness than Aristotle's substance-talk was in the Renaissance.

However, if we can set aside our blinding familiarity with this account, I have tried to say enough here to earn a number of claims that should give us pause. First, we have seen that the notion of perception as an internal, mental representation did not fall from the sky; it is not just a "given." It is a *theory*, and it is Descartes's theory through and through: his key innovation, the breakthrough that achieves his desired synthesis between theology and natural philosophy. Insofar as we accept the notion that perception is an "internal, subjective representation of an external world" we remain trapped in the Cartesian Theater. Further, we have seen that its premises are not scientific, but *metaphysical*: it is based on the mere possibility of an evil demon (the ghost of a doubt) and a metaphysical reduction of living experience to pure thought. And finally, we have seen some of the implausible, even disastrous consequences of Descartes's reductive theory. Its ontological dualism literally cuts one's mind off from the world of things and flesh. It severs mind from body, me from you. One has no direct experience of one's body, or other people, or nature: all one ever has are intellectual judgments that are more or less clear and distinct. And since so many philosophers after Descartes have been willing to tolerate, if not embrace, this framework, it is imperative to remember that Descartes does not legitimately establish that perceptual experience is a subjective, private, veil of ideas. Again, be skeptical if you must, rehearse the *cogito* argument if you will, it just doesn't follow that perception is an internal representation.

In this prelude I have also sought to reveal the inextricable connection between the representation theory of perception and the "physical world," the so-called *objective* world of the sciences. As we have seen, the representation theory of perception is an essential premise in Descartes's Sixth Meditation argument for the existence and specific character of this "physical reality." But it is also the case that without the reduction of perceptual experience to "subjective appearances before the mind," the sparse, colorless world of "physical objects" in mechanistic motion and causality would stand revealed as a total *abstraction*. That is to say, this world of pure, mechanistic objects would stand revealed as a second-order, manifestly incomplete *model* derived from corporeal, natural, and worldly experience, rather than accepted as its fundamental reality. In short, perceptual subjectivism *founds* "the physical world" in fact and in principle, a relationship no one understood more clearly than Descartes. This is precisely why he insists that metaphysics is the "root of the tree of natural philosophy." But this relationship is also part of the reason his representation theory of perception has persisted, even though its rationale is fallacious. That is, the theory of perception is the necessary correlative of an ontological view at work in modern science and scientific discourses: the ontological view that "the physical world" is not an abstract model or merely partial discourse, but *reality itself*. Once this ontological view—in fact, "onto-theological" view[38]—is assumed (as it is so spectacularly by Newton), once "the physical world" is taken as "the objective, real world," then the theory of perception as subjective representation appears to *follow* from that world rather than being that world's essential, foundational premise.

It seems clear that this vague, mistaken notion—that perceptual representation *follows from* "the physical world"—has played a key role in our intellectual culture's ongoing commitment to Descartes's theory of perception. So too has Newton's extraordinary prestige and successes. But it wasn't only post-Newtonian scientific empiricism that embraced perceptual representation; the theory is an assumed, foundational premise in philosophical empiricism as well. This can be seen in John Locke, for instance, who despite his vehement critique of Descartes's rationalism embraces wholesale the representation theory of perception and its language, drawn right out of the Sixth Meditation. As Locke puts it: "*Sensation* . . . is such an Impression or Motion, made in some part of the Body, as produces some Perception in the Understanding."[39] Locke's uncritical acceptance of this language, coupled with his insistence that perceptions are self-evident "*Ideas* in Men's Minds,"[40] yields one of philosophy's greatest, perhaps even tragic ironies: that the founding framer of philosophical empiricism uncritically adopts the dualistic perceptual ontology of Cartesian rationalism, and with it, the intractable problems of skepticism, solipsism, and idealism. Philosophical history shows that after Locke, following Descartes's lead, there seems no alternative. The representation theory of perception is the lynchpin of Berkeley's immaterialism. It is a primary device in Hume's so-called "academic skepticism." It is the assumed ontology that supports Kant's "Transcendental Aesthetic" (the arguments of which are then later used in the "Transcendental Analytic" to retroactively justify the ontology). The theory of perception is also implicit in Hegel's treatment of sense-experience in the opening arguments of the *Phenomenology of Spirit*. The theory is a tacit part of Nietzsche's late critique of perception as a value-laden power.[41] It is there, operating as a foundation in Husserl, Carnap, and the Vienna Circle; it is there in most twentieth-century empiricism and neo-pragmatism (in Quine's *Word and Object,* for instance). And the theory is there, assumed or argued on Cartesian grounds, in much contemporary philosophy of mind and cognitive studies.

It is with this legacy in mind that I quote John Cottingham: "Descartes is still rightly called the father of modern philosophy . . . [in the] sense that without Descartes's philosophy the very shape of the problems with which we wrestle, about knowledge and science, subjectivity and reality, matter and consciousness, would have been profoundly different."[42] Indeed. And by now, I hope to have shown why. For each of those clusters of problems—knowledge and science, subjectivity and reality, matter and consciousness—each is rooted in Descartes's representation theory of perception. His theory sunders our relationship to each other and to the natural world and sunders our mind's relationship to our own flesh. Until this theory of perception is abandoned, until it is understood as a fallacious abstraction, the landscape of our philosophy, psychology, and cognitive studies will remain inescapably Cartesian. Until then we will be caught in the Cartesian Theater.

It is my view that one of the most important dimensions of Merleau-Ponty's thought is his explicit, rigorous work to expose the theory of perceptual representation for the abstraction it is. He argues, with great specificity, that the internal/external dichotomy is not the reality of perception but rather a flawed and abstract model of it. For Merleau-Ponty shows that as we *live* and *breathe,* perceptual experience is more. Perception is my "opening" onto a world that is not merely a screen of ideas. It is a "synergy" between my living, embodied self and the transcendent, natural world. It is the site where other embodied selves emerge, where our perspectives meld, cross, or intertwine. No doubt, how this all works is still unclear. However, as it unfolds in the following chapters, I will show that Merleau-Ponty's perceptual ontology is no return to "naïve realism," no return to Aristotelian object-impressions. It is instead a new way of understanding our intersubjective, yet subjectively organized, perceptual experience beyond the paradigm of representation.

1 The Sensation Fallacy: Toward a Phenomenology of Perception

You have a new conception and interpret it as seeing a new object. You interpret a . . . movement made by yourself as a quasi-physical phenomenon which you are observing. (Think for example of the question: "Are sense-data the material of which the universe is made?")[1]
—LUDWIG WITTGENSTEIN

Don't think, look!
—LUDWIG WITTGENSTEIN[2]

1. Looking Beyond "Sensation"

After Descartes, wherever one looks—in science, psychology, and philosophy—one finds the *sensation*. While the word "sensation" appears only sparingly in Aristotle and Scholastic philosophy, after Descartes it becomes a master concept. It is not hard to understand why: the sensation is the key element that permits Descartes's synthesis between the subjective, ideal domain of immaterial Mind (theology) and the objective, mechanistic world of Matter (natural philosophy). *Res cogitans* and *res extensa:* two distinct worlds linked through the sensation. In the prelude, I discussed the legacy of the Cartesian project, the weird way its flawed ontology has continued to shape the thinking of philosophers, psychologists, and scientists. This influence is still evident in the way we freely wield the language of "subjective" and "objective" in our pursuits of knowledge. It is evident in our continuing efforts to understand the "objective reality" of our human nature through machines. (Descartes's favorite analogy was the clock; ours is the computer.) And it is evident in the widespread way in which thinkers, teachers, and textbooks treat sensations as the *basic matter* or *substratum* of perception. Indeed, far and wide, inside and outside intellectual culture, sensations are treated as the fundamental *objective* material, rooted in "sensory mechanisms," and perceptions are viewed as unreliable *subjective* representations.

It is weird but true: four hundred years later, Descartes's "sensation" has come to seem like common sense. But at the outset of *Phenomenology of Perception*, Merleau-Ponty argues "that nothing could in fact be more confused."[3] Nothing, he says, is more confused than our notion of the sensation and because we "accept it readily," we overlook "the phenomenon of perception" (PP 3). In the first four chapters of *Phenomenology of Perception* Merleau-Ponty argues, in extraordinary detail, that the widespread, post-Cartesian commitment to the sensation causes substantial difficulties: it blocks our ability to recognize the character and features of perceptual experience, and it smuggles along the terms and categories of Descartes's dualistic ontology. Without reconceiving the sensation (and the representation theory of perception that goes with it), we remain trapped in the Cartesian Theater, haunted by the specters of idealism, solipsism, and relativism. In my view, these arguments by Merleau-Ponty are immensely important, even though still widely unrecognized by philosophers, for what is at stake in them is a liberating new paradigm for understanding our perceptual life, embodied being, and relation to the natural world. To be sure, what is at stake is a new perceptual ontology that finally supersedes the idealistic and subjectivistic categories of Cartesian metaphysics.

My goal in this chapter is to reconstruct the central thrust of these important arguments by Merleau-Ponty, to show that this basic ontology of the sensation, for all its familiarity, keeps us blind to our own perceptual experience. Now, to be precise, I believe that the philosophy and sciences of perception have yielded not one, but two main operative meanings for "the sensation": (1) as an apparent sense quality, that is, a "sense-datum," and (2) as nerve function. With this distinction in mind, there is little question that most post-Cartesian thinkers use "sensation" in the first sense. On this view, while there is corresponding nervous excitation, "sensation" refers to basic sense-impressions or data in conscious awareness that are treated as the building blocks of internal perceptual representations. However, in recent years a number of thinkers in the philosophy of mind/cognitive science tradition have tried to put it all on the "outside," arguing for the second view: a strictly neurophysiological account of sensation (and perception). Here, then, we encounter a difficulty, for throughout his early books, Merleau-Ponty employs a strategic distinction between what he calls the "empiricist" and "intellectualist" traditions: criticizing first one, then the other, and then staking out his own position against them both. But on the subject of the sensation, dividing the views in terms of "empiricism-intellectualism" is not correct (as we will see), and it certainly doesn't fit the terms of the contemporary discussion. Thus, in what follows I will refer to the two traditions on sensation I mentioned above—the sense-data and neurophysiological views—as "empiricist" and "physicalist" respectively. I will argue in the spirit of Merleau-Ponty that each of these traditions, in distinct ways, keeps us from seeing and understanding the character of perceptual experience. Each of them keeps us at odds with ourselves, keeps us *thinking about* perception rather than studying it on its own terms. I thus conclude that whatever the state of contemporary cognitive science, we must nonetheless carry out and embrace a phenomenology of perception. That is to say, we must "return to our senses," return with Merleau-Ponty to study, explore, and elucidate the teeming, rich perceptual experience that is our opening to the natural world and other living beings (*l'ouverture au monde*).[4]

2. The Empiricist Tradition of Sensation

I mentioned above that Merleau-Ponty's strategic distinction in *Phenomenology of Perception* between "empiricism" and "intellectualism" is not correct when it comes to sensation and perception. This is because intellectualists (such as Kant) and empiricists alike have held essentially the same theory, that is, *Descartes's* theory: the view that external material objects activate one's sense organs, which cause sensations in one's mind or brain, which in turn the understanding compiles or "internally represents" as perceived objects such as a tables and chairs. Again, to use familiar terms, perception is an internal representation of an external material world built up out of sensations. In the prelude, I argued that Locke assumes Descartes's dualistic theory of perception; he imports it as the bedrock for his own empiricist theory of knowledge. Locke's commitment to the theory is evident throughout book 2 of the *Essay,* in which he also works to establish that these basic sensations are simple and relationally discrete. Consider the following passage by Locke:

> Though the Qualities that affect our Senses are, in the things themselves, so united and blended . . . yet 'tis plain, the *Ideas* they produce in the Mind, enter by the senses simple and unmixed. . . . The coldness and hardness which a Man feels in a piece of *Ice,* being as distinct *Ideas* in the Mind, as the smell and Whiteness of a Lily. . . . There is nothing can be plainer to a Man, than the clear and distinct Perception he has of those simple *Ideas;* which being each in it self uncompounded, contains in it nothing but *one uniform Appearance,* or Conception in the mind, and is not distinguishable into different *Ideas.*[5]

Here and elsewhere, Locke offers us examples of these simple sensations: "*Yellow, White, Heat, Cold, Soft, Hard, Bitter, Sweet*" (*Essay* 105). He insists that they are *ideas,* that they are "in the mind," that all our complex ideas are "*made by the mind out of them*" (*Essay* 164), and that they should be referred to as "sense-qualities." In all this, the specific definition of sensation as *sense-data* has been born.

It is hard to describe how utterly pervasive the sense-data understanding of sensation has been after Locke. It is axiomatic in traditional empiricism: in Hume, Mill, Russell, Moore, Carnap, and Ayer, to name a few. (This is why I refer to this type of view of the sensation as "empiricist.") But the view is present as a basic assumption in Kant's critical philosophy.[6] It is also implicitly or explicitly present in twentieth-century philosophies that are attempting to transcend traditional empiricism, for example, in Quine and Sellars.[7] Indeed, whenever one sees a philosopher defining sensation with a list of qualities, such as cold, hot, white, sour, hard, bitter, red, this understanding is at work. While contemporary physicalists—the second tradition, which I will discuss below—explicitly reject the notion of sense-data, the empiricist tradition has been far more pervasive in our intellectual history. Sensations are treated as *sense-data* or *sense-qualia:* they are atomistic, simple impacts or impressions of sensory information that are present to awareness; it is out of them that the mind or brain builds complex perceptual wholes such as a table, a tree, or another person.[8]

However, Merleau-Ponty shows that there is a profound problem with this empiricist view of the sensation, for "this notion corresponds to nothing in our experience" (PP 3). He shows that even our most rudimentary perceptions are not atomistic, but *relational* and *meaning-laden.* Indeed, attending closely to Merleau-Ponty's key arguments allows us to discover something rather stunning: that the empiricist theory of the sensation has absolutely no empirical confirmation. We will see that the sensation, construed as a basic sense-datum, is an artifact of second-order thinking—an abstract concept—that has been reified as ontologically basic. This entails that the accompanying theory of perception as an internal, ideal representation of an external world built up out of sense-data is equally abstract, and ultimately flawed. In any event, we will see that this empiricist theory of sensation and perception keeps us blind to the very character of perceptual experience, and our understanding of Merleau-Ponty's perceptual ontology will be well underway.

"The Sensation Fallacy"—this is my name for the notion that simple sense-qualities are fundamentally real and constitutive of perceptual wholes. Merleau-Ponty exposes the fallacy here by drawing on the central insight of the Gestalt psychologists, the insight that perceptual experience is always complex, a *figure* against a *background,* a thing amid a context.[9] Merleau-Ponty would have us put it to the test: try to identify a pure, simple sense-datum in our experience. We cannot. On the contrary, everywhere we look, or feel, or hear, we perceive some "element" *against* a differentiating field and *in virtue of* that field. For example, we see the chalk mark against the blackboard; if there were no difference at all (in color or texture) between the chalk mark and the board, we wouldn't perceive it. We hear the watch ticking only amid the silence of the room. We feel the particular warmth of the water in relation to air and body temperature. Everywhere we look, taste, and feel there is perceptual complexity—a figure identified and delineated in relation to its context, its background. Indeed, every experience, all our empirical observations, reveal that perception is not atomistic, but fundamentally complex and relational. As Wittgenstein indicates well (in the first epigram), the pure, simple, atomistic sensation is not an empirical fact, but an idea, an abstract *concept*.[10]

Perhaps someone would object here to Merleau-Ponty (and Wittgenstein) by saying that we *can* identify atomistic sensations in experience. We might, for instance, follow the procedure of Hume's famous "proof" in the *Treatise* to show that simple sense-impressions or qualities exist. As Hume puts it: "Put a spot of ink upon paper, fix your eye upon that spot, and retire to such a distance, that at last you lose sight of it; 'tis plain, that the moment before it vanish'd the image or impression was perfectly indivisible."[11] Hume's claim here, which he takes to be decisive, is that the little dot one sees just before it disappears is a pure, simple sense-datum. In fact, he is mistaken: since the spot of ink is placed on a piece of paper, and is seen only against that paper, the exercise actually confirms the figure-background character of perception. Perhaps we might try a different tactic, for example, standing before a large white wall: philosophers have claimed that here is a pure, atomic sensation, the sensation of "white."[12] However, this attempt also overlooks the conditioning background—for example, the light shining on the wall from the overhead fixture and the necessary distance between my nose and the wall so that no shadow is cast. Indeed, the conditioning "background" for a perceptual figure isn't necessarily behind it, but is often *before* and *around* it. Well, then, let's try closing our eyes tightly, or going into a sensory deprivation tank. The blackness there might be taken as a simple, context-free sensation. However, Merleau-Ponty argues that this procedure for identifying a pure sense-datum, by definition, is *to not sense:* "A really homogeneous area offering *nothing to be perceived* cannot be given to *any perception*" (PP 4). In other words, to sense is to sense something; this third tactic (sensory deprivation) tries to identify simple sensory content by eliminating all such content. The conclusion here, the empirical *facts* here, seem clear: there is no sensory "element" that doesn't presuppose a differentiating, conditioning field. The pure, atomic sensation—the alleged building-block of complex perception—is not an empirical or experiential object.

The implications of Merleau-Ponty's argument are enormous. For one thing, it seems that the empiricist ontology of the sensation has it just backward: sensations do not build up to perceptions. On the contrary, empirical experience shows that a "sensation" (or "sensible" as Merleau-Ponty puts it) is always experienced amid perceptual complexity, always identified against a larger field. If one believes that one has found a pure, context-free sense-datum, it has only been by conceptually isolating one aspect of the larger perceptual field and then forgetting the field. We see then why the sense-data ontology of traditional empiricism is abstract and fallacious: it is the result of taking sensibles perceived in context (Locke's "yellow, white, heat, cold, soft, hard, bitter, sweet"), intellectually isolating and fixing them, and then reifying those derivations as ontological objects, as the constitutive elements of perception. This is a fallacy of mistaking a second-order, conceptual process for the primary, experienced one. It is a fallacy of mistaking the abstract for the fundamental. It is the same error that would be made if one cut a loaf of bread into slices and then assumed the loaf was originally composed of just those slices.

This fallacy of forgetting primary experience for some second-order, derivative idea or concept is one frequently committed in our western intellectual tradition. As indicated in the introduction, it is the kind of fallacy that phenomenologists are keen to uncover. We will see many permutations of this fallacy as this book unfolds. However, in the case of perception, Merleau-Ponty shows that the temptation to this fallacy is particularly strong, because forgetting the perceptual background is perpetuated by the very character of perception:

> To see an object is . . . [to] become anchored in it, but this coming to rest of the gaze is merely a modality of its movement: I continue inside one object the exploration which earlier hovered over them all, and in one movement I close up the landscape and open the object. The two operations do not fortuitously coincide. . . . It is necessary to put the surroundings in abeyance the better to see the object, and to lose in background what one gains in focal figure. (PP 67)

Merleau-Ponty is reiterating here a further key insight of Gestalt psychology: that figure-background perception is a relationship that is inversely determinate. That is, the more one focuses on some perceptual figure, the less aware one becomes of the field or background. Drawing on the old adage, as I focus on this particular tree, I "lose sight" of the forest that surrounds it. To be sure, the forest is *there*—it doesn't vanish—but it is in the "background." This fact of perception, the fact of focus, is why legions of philosophers have forgotten the conditioning context for their "sense-data." Be that as it may, when we return to perception beyond this forgetting, we observe that figure-background perception (a perceptual *field*), comes first. And we thereby recognize, with

Merleau-Ponty, that "the traditional notion of the sensation" is "a late product of thought" (PP 10).

In acknowledging the sense-datum as a conceptual object, we have already been able to see some key features of perceptual experience. For example, we have seen that perception is *complex* and *relational*; it is a figure perceived against a background, a thing perceived in context. I have also suggested that perception is marked by *focus* and *background indeterminacy*. Merleau-Ponty argues that a further thing we can observe is that these basic figure-ground perceptions are charged with *meaning*:

> Already a "figure" on a "background" contains . . . much more than the [sense-]qualities presented at a given time. It has an "outline," which does not "belong" to the background and which "stands out" from it; it is "stable" and offers a "compact" area of colour, the background on the other hand having no bounds, being of indefinite colouring and "running on" under the figure. The different parts of the whole—for example, the portions of the figure nearest to the background—possess, then, besides a colour and qualities, a particular *significance* [*sens*]. (PP 13, PP-F 20)

Our basic perceptions are significant, laden with sense (*sens*: sense and direction). To use contemporary parlance: they are *intentional*. They bear meaning within and because of the complex relation between the figure and its background. Consider Merleau-Ponty's example above: there is a sense of density to the white patch, a sense of depth between patch and homogeneous background, a sense that the background "runs on" beneath the patch. But we can grasp this latent significance better by considering a chair in my living room. When I perceive the chair, amid the larger, less determinate field of the room, the perception is charged with significance, with a sense (*sens*) of open possibilities. There is the sense, for me, from my position, that it has a back to it that I do not see. I also have the sense that I *could* see the back, if I went around it, over in that direction. And I have the sense that I can sit on this thing, that it is built for my tired body, just as a glove invites the insertion of my hand. Besides these spatial and dispositional meanings, perceived things (in context) may also bear temporal and affective significance: "Here is the chair I *usually* sit on, my *favorite* chair to sit on at the end of the day." Our most basic perceptions then are not pure, atom-like *qualia*, but meaning-laden perspectives (or *Gestalten*) that open up a host of possible behavioral and affective responses on my part. "Don't think," Wittgenstein tells us, "look!" Perceptual experience at its most basic level is not merely "syntactic" (to use contemporary parlance). Rather, it is meaning-*full* in virtue of its figure-background complexity, in virtue of the fact that any given perspective radiates the sense of other perspectives, in virtue of the experiences or needs I bring to the moment.[13]

Related to this basic intentionality (*sens*) is another feature of perception that is present in our experience. This is the fact, the knowledge by direct acquaintance, that in perception I am opening onto things that *transcend* me, that go beyond me and my ideas. One aspect of this transcendence is that perception is a field of *contact with otherness*. I incessantly see and touch and smell coherent, holistic things that are distinct from me: tables, chairs, a beautiful piece of pottery, steaming hot food from the Chinese restaurant. Sometimes these things resist my explorations or limit my options ("all this furniture is in my way!"); sometimes they draw me "out of myself" ("what a fascinating sculpted bowl this is!").[14] But also I form my ideas *about* these transcendent things, things that don't vanish or become pink just because I think they do. And I open onto other perceivers perceiving *me*, touching me, and touching the things that I perceive. "Don't think, look!" Look and see what you live and experience: below the intellectual concept of pure sense-data, basic perception is "knowledge of existences." In perceptual experience "I emerge from my individual life by apprehending the object as an object for everybody" (PP 40). In it I "open to a plurality of thinking subjects" (PP 62). It is not just strange, but *contradictory to our knowledge by direct acquaintance* to say that this contact, my caress, this sculpted piece you and I perceive together, my body as felt and experienced, your perceiving body as perceived, are "merely in my mind or brain." Where precisely in my brain are you as perceived and touched? Where precisely in my mind or brain is the chair, as I perceive it with my hands, body, and eyes? Fortunately we can be saved from these absurdities by remembering what we know from experience: perception is our opening onto things that are *not oneself*. Withdraw into our thoughts or imaginations as we might, withdraw into and reify our ideas or theoretical objects as we do, perception is our perpetual deliverance from narcissism.

This transcendence in our basic perceptions has another important dimension. Yes, it is experienced as contact with things that are not oneself, but it is also experienced as an *excess*. The perceptual field is a field of excess: it spills out every which way, beyond and around the specific things one attends to. For example, I perceive my comfortable chair amid the living room, but the living room itself—with its windows, doorways, and walls—points to rooms and a yard and a neighborhood beyond it. And if I went outside to perceive my neighborhood, there would be still more beyond it. Perceptual experience as we live it always points to more: more perspectives on the perceptual figure, more beyond this surrounding room, forever more beyond the edges of my visual field. This is part of why perception takes the figure-background form that it does. Indeed, "focus" is required amid such a field. It is also part of why our perceptions themselves bear meaning, for they always point beyond themselves. And if I follow up the *sens* of something in my periphery or behind my back and turn my head to focus on it, there will again be more, spilling out beyond this new perception. What I have just indicated in spatial categories is equally true of time. I perceive, for instance, the lamp at some moment, but this focus also points to moments beyond. It bears the sense that the lamp was there before I looked (the past), and that it will be here *later* (the future). In fact while I have been maintaining my gaze, time is passing; it is already later. Our basic perceptual experience then is not a collection of sense-data given as distinct snapshots. Rather it is lived as an engagement with what is beyond me, what exceeds and transcends my gaze and caress: coherent, holistic things, other living beings, and a three-dimensional locale with temporal dimensions. To once again use Merleau-Ponty's evocative phrase, it is lived and known as our "opening onto the world" (*l'ouverture au monde*).

3. Merleau-Ponty's Experiential Realism and Some Cartesian Objections

Merleau-Ponty's early arguments against the empiricist tradition of sense-*qualia* in *Phenomenology of Perception* have led us into some of the phenomena of living perceptual experience: for example, its complexity, its fundamental *sens* (intentionality), and its transcendence. With all this in place we are now able to see a second substantial consequence of those arguments: that we must finally abandon the widespread notion that perception is "built up" by the mind as a house is built up out of bricks. To be sure, it is because thinkers such as Locke and Kant take sense-data as basic atoms, meaningless elements, the mere *matter* of perception, that they insist upon complex perceptions (of coffee cups, tables, chairs, and other people) as mental constructions that are constituted by the faculty of understanding. Far from overturning Cartesianism, these accounts of idea-based, mental construction solidify Descartes's theory of perception as a "veil of representations" and carry along all the problems of relativism, solipsism, and idealism.

However, once we realize that there are no sense-data *per se*—that the basic, pure, atomic sense-impression is an abstract concept which loses sight of living perception itself—then the theory of perception as an internal screen of ideas built upon sense-data is revealed as equally abstract. This conclusion is also confirmed on experiential grounds. Look and see: what we experience directly are precisely those coherent, holistic things that Locke calls "secondary ideas." Thirsty, I reach out for my coffee cup amid the books and papers on my table. I pass into a room, see the painting on the wall, dripping reds and burnished orange. I walk down the street and see the face of a suffering child. It is not necessary to mentally construct, constitute, or "build up" such things. They are already there in our basic perceptions, charged with significance, available to be noticed. Indeed, the internal representation theory of perception stands revealed as an abstraction layered upon abstraction, one that keeps us thinking about perception in an abstract and dualistic way while we live and know it as something quite other: an opening onto things and other living beings themselves, with the world as their natural setting.

At this point, an objection might arise: "Isn't this view about perception just naïve realism?" The short, direct answer is: "No, not in the least." My more fulsome answer begins by asking just what "naïve realism" *means.* By and large, the philosophical literature uses this label to refer to any view of perception that is not internal and representational. However, taking naïve realism in this sense simply makes this objection to Merleau-Ponty trivial rather than forceful. It becomes the following: "Isn't Merleau-Ponty's view of perception non-representational?" Well . . . yes. But that in no way makes him wrong. If, however, instead of begging the question, we take naïve realism to be the view that we perceive things *just as they are in themselves,* then this is not Merleau-Ponty's view at all. Of course Merleau-Ponty believes that the visual cortex is involved in vision. Of course he holds that the rods and cones in the eye condition the colors one perceives. Merleau-Ponty explicitly argues that the brain, central nervous system, and sensory-motor systems make essential contributions to perception. Thus, he wholeheartedly insists that we do not perceive "things as they are in themselves." However, none of this means that the mind or brain constructs perceived entities out of atomic sense-qualities and then screens them "in the brain" like a private movie.

To be very clear about this, Merleau-Ponty's phenomenology of *Gestalt* perception works against two main fronts—both of them lingering artifacts of Cartesian metaphysics. One front of his critique is against the notion that, in perception, the mind or brain creates *ideal duplicates* of things by building up atomic sense-impressions. This, Merleau-Ponty argues, is an abstract theory predicated on the sensation fallacy, a theory that ignores and contradicts what we live in perception. The second front is closely related to the first: it targets the notion that perception is located *in* my mind or brain, that perception is an *internal* screen covering the *external* reality. It is precisely these ontological elements—these artifacts of dualism—that support the whole notion and language of perception as a "subjective representation." And again, it is these elements that carry along the idealism, skepticism, and subjectivism that haunts post-Cartesian philosophy.

Instead of this representational paradigm, Merleau-Ponty's phenomenology of perception offers something different, a better way of thinking and talking: perceptual experience itself is not some *re*-presentation, but the fundamental *presentation* upon which all my conceptual abstractions and ideal duplicates are based. Perception is not "inside" me, like a beetle in a box, but rather emerges *between* my organizing, sensing body and the things of the world. It is a *synergy,* to use Merleau-Ponty's favored term. It is a working together of my living body (with its neurophysiology and sensory systems), transcendent things, other creatures, and the world as the field of their relatedness. True to the phenomenon of "synergy" (well-known, for example, among chemists), the results of this working together of body, things, others, and the world is an interactional field that emerges at the nexus of its participants and which we call *experience.*[15] Merleau-Ponty argues that this synergistic or "interactionist" account of perception is a far more promising paradigm than the age-old scheme of "representation." For one thing, it has the great advantage of being more true to the fundamental phenomena of living perception—for example, its complexity, carnality, transcendence, intersubjectivity. But it also leaves behind the conceptual and linguistic vestiges of Descartes's dualistic metaphysics.

In section 4 below, I will argue that perceptual experience reveals a further feature that makes the notion of synergy particularly appropriate: that the whole of perception cannot be analyzed or dissected without losing its dynamic qualities, that it cannot be exhausted by an *explanation.* For the moment, I hope to have settled the objection that Merleau-Ponty's perceptual ontology is naïve realism. On the contrary, one exists in the world, perceiving transcendent things and other beings, but this synergy is informed and organized in accordance with my body. That is, it is literally *organ*-ized. There is no reason but a dubious metaphysical tradition for placing the perceptual synergy *inside* me as some ideal duplicate. Instead, we can say what we knew before we read Descartes: I am interacting with the real table in my perceptual experience of it. The veil of ideas is lifted. As Merleau-Ponty puts it in *The Visible and the Invisible:*

> [T]he table before me sustains a singular relation with my eyes and my body: I see it only if it is within their radius of action; above it there is the dark mass of my forehead, beneath it the indecisive contour of my cheeks. . . . With each flutter of my eyelashes a curtain lowers and rises. . . . I would express what

takes place badly indeed in saying that here a "subjective component" . . . comes to cover over the things themselves: it is not a matter of another layer or veil that . . . pose[s] itself between them and me. The stirring of the "appearance" does not disrupt the evidence of the thing—any more than the monocular images interfere when my two eyes operate in synergy. (VI 7)

With this new kind of view in place (what we might call experiential or perceptual realism), the Cartesian Theater (with its private screenings) is finally closed. "Don't think, look!": in perception, I am at and amid real things and other people through the agency of my body. Of course there are things and features of things that I do not or cannot perceive. That doesn't mean that those things exist "out there," somewhere on the other side of a veil of ideas. Instead, they are also here, but beyond this perspective, awaiting my further exploration. Or perhaps they are beyond my organism altogether, but not beyond these other perceivers who act in ways that reveal them to me.

"But how about perceptual error, optical illusion, and the like? Don't these occurrences prove that perception is merely subjective? Don't they prove that perceptions are appearances that veil the objective truth?" In this objection, we confront a way of thinking that has seduced many people to Cartesian representationalism. Pointing to perceptual error or optical illusions to establish that perception is a "subjective appearance" is a familiar strategy in the historical traditions of philosophy and psychology, but also in the most contemporary of writings.[16] The problem is that this type of argument is fallacious. This is because the facts of perceptual error and illusion do not establish Descartes's dualistic perceptual ontology. We can begin to see this by considering a famous, textbook example of an optical illusion, the Müller-Lyer illusion:

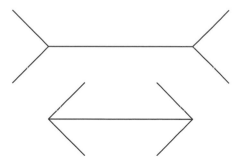

It is not unusual to see writers use this illusion to conclude that perception is a merely subjective event: "The two lines appear to be different lengths, when objectively they are the same; therefore, perception is subjective appearance, which hides objective reality." This reasoning is specious, common though it may be. Just because one can construct (with a ruler) some numerically determinate figure that we perceive indeterminately, does not entail the ontological claim that fundamental reality is a collection of fully determinate objects and perception a mere subjective appearance. That ontological conclusion simply doesn't follow. Indeed, as Kant shows in the first *Critique* (against, for example, Leibniz and Zeno),[17] just because we can conceive (or construct) a line as an infinity of points doesn't entail that the points *really come first*. Further, the fact that I have to *construct* my fully determinate figure, implies the correctness of Merleau-Ponty's different, better interpretation of the Müller-Lyer illusion: that perceptual indeterminacy is ontologically basic, that things such as ambiguity, illusions, and mirages, are fundamental aspects of the perceptual synergy out of which our so-called "objective" constructions are built.[18]

I believe these insights answer this specific attempt to reassert that perception is "mere appearance" that hides objective reality: the argument by optical illusion begs the question by assuming the ontology it is seeking to establish. These insights also begin to answer the claim that perception is "merely subjective." For when we return to perception as we actually live it, when we open our eyes and ears to phenomena, we remember that illusions, mirages, perceptual errors are distinctly different than subjective. Everyone in the audience, from a wide variety of perspectives, sees the magician's assistant cut in half. Everybody in the car sees the image of shimmering water on the hot pavement in the distance. Anyone standing in this place, at this distance, would see the tower as round when it is really square. To be sure, differences in the sensory organs, such as blindness, can create exceptions, but as we know, "exceptions don't disprove a rule." Look and see, hear and touch: perceptual errors, illusions, and mirages, are not ephemera. Instead, they are coherent, stable, predictable phenomena. They are not intellectual acts of assertion or judgment; I can't will them into being or will them away. Far from "merely subjective," they have an intersubjective dimension to them: the illusion I see is the illusion you see from a different perspective, or the one you *would* see if you were standing where I stand.

These considerations begin to show that we need a new way of understanding and talking about the phenomena of illusion. The traditional terms—"subjective appearance" versus "objective reality"—simply do not fit the phenomena. And at this point in the book, this result ought not be surprising: those terms are the categories of the representational paradigm. They are artifacts of a post-Cartesian intellectual culture that keeps us blind to perceptual experience through adherence to an abstract, conceptual model of it. When, however, we set aside those traditional categories, when we return to perception as we live it rather than conceptualize it, we remember that perceptual experience is complex and relational; it does not give us a "collection of atomistic objects," but things continually emerging amid a transcendent field. This figure-background complexity allows us to understand perceptual anomalies not as "internal subjective appearances," but as phenomena that occur in a larger perceptual, intersubjective context that also involves non-illusion. For example, the magician's assistant is cut in half amid a stable theatrical context that "foregrounds" the event and makes it convincing. The mirage is "strange" because it continues to appear at the same place on the horizon of the road even though the car is moving. Or some illusion stands revealed in terms of a later dis-illusion, such as when I suddenly recognize those branches as actually belonging to the tree *next* to the one I thought. Rather than disqualifying perception as an internal veil of appearances, these observations attest to the excess or abundance of the real world in every perceptual perspective. As Merleau-Ponty puts it:

> I thought I saw on the sands a piece of wood polished by the sea, and *it was* a clayey rock. The breakup and destruction of the first appearance do not authorize me to define henceforth the "real" as simply probable. . . . The disillusion is the loss of one evidence only because it is the acquisition of *another evidence*. . . . What I can conclude from these disillusions or deceptions, therefore, is that perhaps "reality" does not belong definitively to any particular perception, that in this sense it lies *always further on;* but this does not authorize me to break or ignore the bond that joins them one after the other to the real. . . . Each perception is mutable . . . but what is not . . . what each perception, even if false, verifies, is the belongingness of each experience to the same world. (VI 40–41)

While more could be developed about perceptual errors, illusions, and hallucinations, I believe I have said enough to support my claim that perceptual anomalies do not establish the dualistic subjective-objective, appearance-reality categories of Cartesian empiricism. On the contrary, we have seen in a preliminary way that those anomalies can and ought to be re-interpreted in terms of Merleau-Ponty's experiential realism. They can plausibly be accounted for as phenomena that can emerge in the synergy between sensing bodies and things with the world as their field of relatedness.

Perhaps finally, in the face of all these Merleau-Pontian arguments, the representational theorist of perception will retreat to radical skepticism to save their dualistic perceptual ontology. "Look," he or she might say, "I am able to doubt that these table and chairs exist. I am able to doubt that all of it exists. I am able to doubt that the world exists. Therefore, my perceptions of such things are internal, subjective, and essentially mental." It should not surprise us to hear this final skeptical defense. For, indeed, the ontology of internal representation has always been Cartesian. Among philosophers this skeptical argument has enjoyed incredible prestige; it is a most familiar refrain. What *is* surprising is the reflexive insistence on the skeptical argument when it is so manifestly problematic. To paraphrase an argument made by Leibniz three hundred and fifty years ago,[19] if one is *really, honestly* going to throw everything in doubt, then a priori one can't hold *anything*—least of all, a dualistic ontology. Indeed, as Leibniz sees, the Cartesian method of doubt either smuggles in truths it doesn't doubt or it leaves you with nothing. We have already seen a permutation of Leibniz's argument in the prelude, when I argued that granting Descartes's skeptical arguments disqualifies the basic premise of his wax argument. I argued that Descartes can only muster this argument for perceptual representation by shifting the meaning of "perceptual error" in a way that undoes the skeptical arguments. Again, be skeptical if you will, it does not legitimately follow that perception is an internal, mental representation.

But there is more to say to my philosophical skeptic. For even framing the doubt—putting it in language, offering it as an argument to persuade other people—presupposes (as a necessary condition of possibility) the transcendent social world that is experienced through perception and the language through which it is expressed. To be sure, it is only by living in a social-linguistic field, by having a body with which to write and speak, by being in perceptual relations with other people, that I have the resources to articulate skeptical arguments that seek to persuade others to call it all into doubt. Radical skepticism cannot legitimately eliminate perceptual, worldly, social experience; it is the intersubjective field upon which skepticism is predicated. "Don't think, look!" When philosophers try to persuade you of radical skepticism, you can see the living truth that underlies and belies the content of their claim. You can see these skeptics in physical, corporeal relation with you, speaking with their mouths, gesturing with their hands. You hear them use a specific, culturally sedimented language. You can see their frustration as you continue to point out that their constant refrain, "But you can also doubt *that* . . ." also presupposes the social-perceptual field. In this recognition I believe we discover a new, more fundamental permutation of the *cogito* argument: "I raise radical skepticism within *language*; therefore I already exist in the world." Indeed, it is only by being blinded by the post-hoc content of one's doubt that one is able to ignore the prior worldly and social conditions of its possibility.

There are other arguments against the gambit of Cartesian doubt, for instance, that the skeptical argument depends upon assuming the very theory of perception one concludes from the argument—another Cartesian Circle.[20]

But I believe we have seen enough. I believe I have said enough to show that the post-Cartesian empiricist tradition of perception does not reveal perceptual experience, but actively conceals it. The discrete sensation that this tradition extols as the building-block of perceptual experience is an abstract, problematic concept, not a fact. So too is the picture of perception as a screen of ideas, as an internal representation of some external presentation. It seems clear, then, that our basic approach for understanding perception must not start with "the atomic sensation," but by really studying and attending to this experience on its own terms—the project of phenomenology. However, before we can do that we must address the physicalist way of treating the sensation. While my specific concerns with the physicalist tradition are different, my conclusion is not: carrying out a phenomenology of perception is not optional or "intuitionistic," but imperative. For the phenomenological approach offers important correctives to the lingering ontological and linguistic sediments of the Cartesian tradition, and it also keeps us alive to our rich perceptual life in the world and with others.

4. Contemporary Physicalism

In the nearly fifty years since Merleau-Ponty's death, a new tradition for understanding the sensation has emerged and solidified, the tradition I will refer to as "physicalism."[21] Generally speaking, the contemporary physicalist movement has developed in and around what is known as "the cognitive revolution"—the recent breakthroughs in cognitive science to explain the processes of mind in neurobiological and evolutionary terms. While there are vast differences and live debates among thinkers in this rapidly expanding movement—for instance, about which explanatory model to accept for conscious processes, or about the fate of folk-psychological concepts such as belief and desire—they share a kind of quiet, widespread consensus against the empiricist account of sense-data or sense-*qualia*.[22] In fact, physicalists would surely applaud Merleau-Ponty's critical arguments that such sensations are abstract concepts, artifacts of a dubious philosophical tradition. Daniel C. Dennett, for example, has consistently argued that there are no sense-*qualia*, that is, no "inner figment[s] that could be colored in some special, subjective . . . sense."[23] For Dennett, the Lockean picture of inner *qualia* is part of the Cartesian Theater and must be rejected. With a different purpose in mind, Paul M. Churchland argues that: "The *objective* qualia (redness, warmth, etc.) should never have been 'kicked inwards to the minds of observers' in the first place. They should be confronted squarely where they stand: *out*side the human observer."[24]

For such physicalist thinkers, sensations then are simply neural excitations, neural functions, "the physical features of our psychological states."[25] With this view comes a whole research program to explain perception as a result of (top-down) cognitive processing over the (bottom-up) neural information that is sensation.

Now, in truth, Merleau-Ponty does not foresee the physicalist tradition on sensation and perception. While he was extremely attentive to the developments of psychology, evolutionary biology, and ethology during his lifetime, he simply does not foresee the force with which the neuro-scientific tradition would take hold in psychology and philosophy, nor the fluidity of its concepts and models. Honestly, how could he? Who could have? Even so, this lack of clairvoyance becomes evident to contemporary readers in the early chapters of *Phenomenology of Perception*. Here Merleau-Ponty does briefly consider what he calls the "physiological" attempt to define the sensation and argues that it is committed to the untenable "constancy hypothesis." That is, it is committed to an account of nervous function cashed out in terms of mechanistic, linear, point-by-point correspondences between a stimulus and a perception.[26] However, this is an utterly unconvincing argument against contemporary physicalism, because most physicalists have long abandoned (Newtonian) mechanistic causality as the pattern for understanding neural function.[27] It seems then, that in this argument Merleau-Ponty has confused a general schema for defining the sensation (that is, in neurological terms) with a specific way of characterizing the relations in that schema (Newtonian, mechanistic causality).

Having said that, it is important to see that Merleau-Ponty's thought shares with contemporary physicalism an insistence that nervous and brain function are essential to perception. In both *The Structure of Behavior* and *Phenomenology of Perception*, for example, he frequently articulates perception in terms of "peripheral" and "central" functioning, and makes many of his arguments by drawing upon case studies of patients whose behavior and experiences are shaped by nervous-system disorders or brain damage.[28] However, it is also clear that Merleau-Ponty would have deep reservations about the physicalist tradition on sensation and perception. He would argue, I believe, that this contemporary effort to *explain* consciousness or perception in neurophysiological terms doesn't exhaust everything that can be said—and *needs* to be said—about perception. He would say that no matter how successful these explanations become, we still must embrace and carry out a phenomenology of living perceptual experience. In this section, my task is to make these arguments in relation to physicalism—arguments that Merleau-Ponty does not explicitly make, but which I believe he would find congenial. I will attempt to show that Merleau-Ponty's phenomenology of perception is not rendered obsolete by physicalism, but, on the contrary, remains crucially important to support these explanatory efforts, and to help us live well and richly in the world with others.

A first way to appreciate the continuing importance of Merleau-Ponty's phenomenology of perception is by recognizing that the new physicalist tradition has never entirely been able to leave the Cartesian, empiricist tradition behind. In this chapter, I have treated the physicalist and empiricist traditions as distinct because I think in principle they can be rigorously separated; but in historical fact, despite all good intentions, most physicalists still think and speak "Cartesian." It is rather typical, for instance, to see such philosophers and psychologists insist upon perceptions as "representations," and refer to such representations as "inside" rather than "outside." It is not uncommon for them to still treat perceptual experience as essentially "subjectivistic" and "intuitionistic." They still often talk about experience as "*qualia*" and do so in more or less atomistic terms, rather than complex figure-background organizations. We have already seen that these terms and concepts are constitutive of Descartes's thought, and they carry along all the sediments of the dualistic ontology that these physicalists are aiming to overturn. For example, a careful, consistent physicalist theory should work to reject the whole notion that perception is a representation. For this concept in its meaning (as a *re*-presentation or copy) and history (rooted in the ancient Greek sense of *mimēsis*) supports the Cartesian image that perception is an *ideal duplication* inside one's mind, distinct from the physical world "out there." "Well," physicalists might reply, "we don't mean it that way; we simply use 'representation' to refer to the complex physical interaction between body, brain, and world that we are aiming to explain in neurobiological terms." Nonetheless, I would answer that language and language-use is rarely arbitrary in this way. We can rarely just stipulate new meanings to old words in natural language: our words and concepts, their meanings and implications, their conceptual baggage, are always rooted in history, in a cultural, social, and intellectual heritage. The words we choose, the words we use, have sediments, and so far contemporary physicalists have insisted upon using language that is historically loaded with dualism.

We already see, then, one crucial way in which Merleau-Ponty's phenomenology supports contemporary efforts to explain perception (and consciousness) as a natural and physical phenomenon. Given the rigor of his critique of Cartesianism (and indeed, all dualisms), Merleau-Ponty's phenomenology can help us get our concepts, terms, and ontology in order. It offers what in one passage he calls "ontological rehabilitation."[29] For example, studying and elucidating living perception on its own terms, we see that it is experienced as a complex, fluid field-relation, involving focus and indeterminacy. We see that the atomic sense-datum is an abstract concept. We see and remember to see that perception is not some internal screen of ideas, but our very access to and contact with what transcends us every which way. We see and remember to see that this opening onto what is *not us* is badly conceived as an "internal representation" or "subjective appearance" and is better understood as a *synergy* between organisms and the world. In short, Merleau-Ponty's philosophy not only exposes and aims to correct the hidden ontological framework that still radiates through the language of much contemporary physicalism, but also offers new, decidedly non-Cartesian language and concepts through which we might better describe and model the neurophysiological processes of consciousness and perception.

However, it isn't just that Merleau-Ponty's phenomenology of perception supports the physicalist project to explain perception through "ontological rehabilitation." It also reminds us of the *limits* of such explanations. Let me say at the outset of these arguments that I believe the efforts to explain consciousness and perception in neurophysiological and evolutionary terms, without any appeal to an immaterial soul-substance, is tremendously important. It has been claimed by several thinkers that the recent advances made in this regard—in neurophysiology, cognitive psychology and philosophy, ethology, and evolutionary theory—constitute an intellectual revolution of the first order (such as the Copernican and Darwinian revolutions). I agree with this strong assessment, and I believe that this explanatory work should be greeted and pursued with great enthusiasm. So my concerns are not about the fact or successes of this work to explain perception. Rather, they are about the subtle, but widespread assumptions that this explanatory mode of discourse can *exhaust the reality* of perception, and that the neuro-scientific way of thinking about perception is the *fundamental* way to understand it.

To show that these assumptions are mistaken will take a bit of work. It requires that I argue against some of the deepest, reflexive habits in our western intellectual and pedagogical tradition. It also requires the reader to constantly bear in mind that this is not a rejection of scientific explanation.[30] Rather, these arguments aim toward a fair assessment of the limits of explanatory discourse—a project that, I believe, ultimately strengthens this discourse by circumscribing its proper domain.[31] Imagine, for instance, trying to build a house without fully appreciating the limits of some important tool: indeed, one might try to pound nails with a cross-cut saw! And conversely, imagine how much more effective the building work becomes when you precisely understand the proper uses and limits of each of the tools at one's disposal. I think it is correct and important to understand the phenomenological circumscription of science or explanatory discourse in exactly this way.

I want to begin my argument by focusing on a blindingly familiar, essential process in explanatory work: the process of *analysis*. Simply put, analysis is a way of understanding something by breaking it up into its component parts; it is a process of intellectually dividing or dissecting a complex whole so that the whole can be understood through its parts. This is why Robert M. Pirsig has famously compared this process to a knife (the analytic knife), "an intellectual scalpel" that moves so quickly and reflexively we often don't see it at work.[32] While it is clear that analysis is a cognitive ability that humans have and use, it is equally evident that analysis has a special prestige in the western intellectual tradition, a prestige that dates back to the Greeks and their influence. Indeed, "the analytic method" is Aristotle's great departure from Plato's dialogical dialectic; it is Aristotle's innovative method for revealing the truth of things by uncovering and examining their *details,* the parts of the parts. A first thing to be acknowledged about the analytic way of thinking and proceeding is that it is extraordinarily powerful. We *do* get detailed, clear understanding of complex things by tracing out their parts, the parts of these parts, and the functional relationships among them. We do, for example, gain clarity about a football play by "breaking it down" into the various positions and studying the action at each position. (It is no accident that these commentators are called "analysts.") We do get clear, detailed understanding of the human body in anatomy class by dissecting it into different systems and studying the parts proper to those systems (circulatory, muscular, nervous, and so forth). Analysis is an indispensable, powerful tool for knowing about things in the world and how they work.

But as Thoreau wisely says, "Nothing has a gain that doesn't have a cost." And the "cost," the *limit* of analysis and analytic explanation (that is, the attempt to explain something in terms of its parts), is that analyzing a complex phenomenon is achieved a priori through sacrifice. The analyst makes a decision, literally a *de-cision*—a cut—to break up the complex whole in a certain way, and this decision necessarily precludes other heterogeneous ways of analyzing the thing. It also precludes another equally important kind of understanding: an understanding of the thing's dynamic life *as a whole*. To illustrate the first of these limits (that is, precluding other analyses), consider sitting in a faculty meeting, listening to an administrator describe the organization of the university. What she puts up on the screen and describes might be something such as the following:

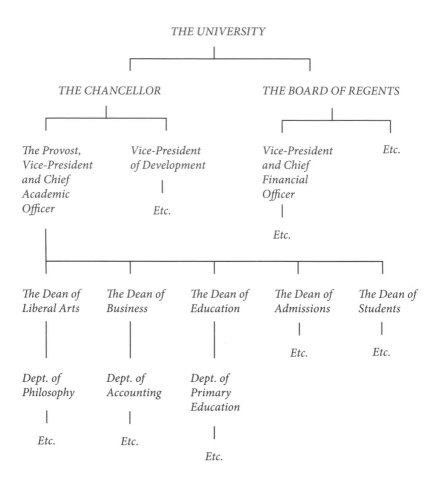

What we have here is a much-abbreviated analytic description of a university, one that shows some parts and the hierarchy of their functional relations. On one level, such a description is highly informative: one gains detailed understanding of the complex whole, "The University," by seeing the different offices and their hierarchical relations. But on another level, *it is only one way of breaking it up*. It is, frankly, the way an administrator would break it up. Students, for example, would surely break things up differently, perhaps with themselves at the top, with different lines of functional dependence, and other elements (such as the Student Activity Council) more highly emphasized. "For after all," many students would argue, "without the students there is no university, no way to justify the existence of all those administrators and faculty members." My point here is that an analysis always takes shape from a *perspective* on the complex whole, and through the values that flow from that perspective. Also, I am arguing that to analyze the complex whole from one perspective entails that other, different perspectives and ways of analyzing the whole are precluded. This is, a priori, the cost of having *a perspective*. Indeed, as cartographers are keenly aware, representing a set of territories to reflect their actual shape is only achieved by neglecting their relative size. In short, even though most analysts, including Aristotle, typically act as though an analytic description of something is a "God's-eye view," a "view from nowhere," in fact it is not. Any given analytic description takes shape from a perspective and from often hidden values that limit what it is able to represent. This, then, is a first way in which analytic descriptions or explanations, for all their clarifying power, are not exhaustive.

However, as indicated previously, my concern about analytic description and explanation isn't merely that they cannot exhaust all the salient perspectives on a phenomenon. It is also that they *cannot exhaust the phenomenon*. To see that this is so, and that this limitation really matters, consider a famous scene from *Hamlet,* act 3, scene 3, which contains "the play within the play." Here, of course, Hamlet has recruited a group of traveling players to re-enact the poisoning of a king to see if this "pricks the conscience" of Claudius and confirms him as the murderer of Hamlet's father. In theatrical terms, the scene is a tour de force with at least three overlapping points of action: Hamlet's and Horatio's ongoing discussion of the situation, Claudius' and Gertrude's reactions, and the players themselves enacting the murder. What is essential to this scene is the overlapping inter-relationship of these points of action. Indeed, to focus on only one of them, or each in succession, is to misunderstand the scene: it is to miss its dynamic *Gestalt*. While a person might certainly "analyze" this scene (clarifying the parts of the parts and their functional relationships), no such analysis would be equivalent to the *experience* of seeing the whole dynamic scene performed. The dynamic experience of the parts amid the whole is analogous to going the theater to experience Hamlet on a Saturday night, rather than sitting home reading an analysis of the parts of the parts. I hope my conclusion is clear: analytic understanding is useful and clarifying; it can enrich our experiences in certain ways, it can reveal new things to us, but there is *always more* going on in experience, *always more* than any analysis can capture. There is always more left behind a decision to intellectually dissect something in a certain way. In a phrase, what one gets with dissection (whether it is physical or intellectual) is the loss of *life*.

I have argued, then, that it is a mistake to assume that having and labeling and identifying all the parts of something and their functional relationships "just is equivalent to" or "amounts to" or "exhausts" the complex, whole, dynamic phenomenon.[33] This error is analogous to believing that the dissected cadaver is "equivalent" to or "amounts to" or "exhausts" a living, pulsing body. What is true of living behavior is equally true of living perception: there will always be more than any true and compelling explanation of it in terms of neurons, dendrites, axons, and central, modular processing can exhaust. There is the overlapping dynamism of perception—the way I perceive things and other beings in a larger, stable context. There is the experiential meaning (*sens*) in perception: the overflowing positional, dispositional, and affective meanings that infuse every perspective. There is the lived space and time of perceptual experience that cannot be reduced to atomic points on a Newtonian grid. And there is the experience itself, for instance, of a deep blue that no radiation wavelength number can ever capture. Far from "epiphenomenal," or "irrelevant," these features are the very fabric of our perceptual life and they *really matter*. Consider, for one example, the recent neurological research that has demonstrated the relative lack of communication, in people with dyslexia, between the three regions of the brain that are involved in reading.[34] This discovery is important for diagnosis and compensatory treatment, and it is certainly explanatory: it tells us a lot we did not know about how the brain functions and dysfunctions. But having this explanatory data cannot tell us about the profound frustration people with dyslexia *feel*. It cannot tell us what the living experience of those who see letters reversed is like, cannot illuminate all the social and pedagogical obstacles such students have to live through. There is always more to experience than any neurophysiological analysis can capture. To be sure, we do not live and breathe, suffer and succeed in our explanatory models.

We see then a deeper reason why it is more appropriate to conceive perceptual experience as a synergy. For in living perception we really do have "a whole that is greater than the sum of its parts." Here, my arguments join up with one made by Merleau-Ponty in *The Visible and the Invisible,* as he articulates the synergy of perception by analogy to binocular vision:

> The binocular perception is not made up of two monocular perceptions surmounted; it is of another order. The monocular images *are* not in the same sense that the thing perceived with both eyes is. . . . [T]hey vanish when we pass to normal vision and re-enter into the things as into their daylight truth. They are too far from having its density to enter into competition with it: they are . . . drafts for . . . the true vision, which accomplishes them by reabsorbing them. (VI 7–8)

What is said here about monocular images might well be said about the "elements" of the perceptual synergy, that is, the neurophysiological body, transcendent things, and the world: each of them offers "drafts" that are absorbed and transformed in living perception. Just as binocular vision has a depth and density that monocular images do not, because its two images overlap, so too does the interaction of our sensing body, things, and the world give rise to living perception as we know it. This perceptual synergy cannot be analytically dissected or explained without losing it, because it is not built up piece-by-piece as a house is built up out of bricks. Instead, it emerges full-blown, at the nexus of its participants. Thus Merleau-Ponty finishes his analogy by saying: "The monocular images cannot be *compared* with the synergic perception: one cannot put them side by side. . . . We can effect the passage [from monocular to binocular vision] by *looking*, by awakening to the world; we cannot witness it as spectators. . . . Thus in perception we witness the miracle of a totality that surpasses what one thinks to be its conditions or its parts" (VI 8).

Having given these arguments about the limits of analytic explanation, and its inability to *exhaust* living perception, it is important to say that such explanation *may well* uncover real things and real relations. Indeed, it does not follow from these arguments that analytic explanations of perception (or consciousness) are problematically *abstract*. On this point, I reject a line of argument occasionally made by Merleau-Ponty. He says, for example: "every scientific schematization is an abstract and derivative sign-language, as is geography in relation to the countryside" (PP ix). His basic claim in such passages seems to be that scientific explanations are second-order representations in the way a map is to a landscape. But this isn't quite correct. Analytic explanations *are* "second-order" in the sense that one must have an experience of the whole, complex thing before one can proceed to analyze it. (This recognition is important, for it reminds us that analytic explanation is always a way of thinking *about* experience.) But it does not follow from this that the parts and relations uncovered through analysis are ideal constructions of a more original reality (such as a map to a landscape). Not at all: unlike empiricism's sense-data and screen-of-ideas theory of perception (which *is* such an ideal construction), the nerves, synaptic functions, and modular brain processes that contemporary science uncovers are all real. My arguments in this section, then, are not trying to establish that analytic explanation fails to tell us about the real. On the contrary, it certainly does. Rather, my conclusion is that this discourse—this way of thinking, speaking, and working—is always *partial*, always *limited*, always bound to a perspective.

At the same time, however, it is important to underscore that the neurophysiological level is not "more real" than living perception. To be sure, the person with dyslexia has a brain that lacks connection among the three sectors involved in reading—this is real. But equally real, at another level, are the frustration, the social and pedagogical obstacles, the phenomenon of seeing letters reversed. To think that these phenomena of life are "less real" is to smuggle along the Cartesian view of experience as "internal, subjective appearance," or to mistakenly think of analytic explanation as a "God's-eye view." The phenomena of living experience are neither less real nor more real than the neurophysiological processes: they are different aspects of the same reality, gotten at through a different order of discourse and observation.[35]

I also want to stress that the arguments I have made here about the limits of analytic explanation do not make perceptual experience "mysterious" or "ineffable." In my view, the way this kind of language gets tossed around in contemporary philosophy of mind—often as a "whipping boy" for physicalists—actively obscures important distinctions that need to be drawn. True, I have argued that living perception cannot be *exhausted* by analytic explanation, but not that we should refuse or block the efforts to explain perception in neurophysiological terms. There is, however, a larger reason for rejecting the language of mystery: it obscures the important fact that perceptual experience *is* knowable in another, different way. It is knowable through a *phenomenological* approach that seeks to rigorously study and articulate other real aspects of living experience, aspects that cannot be captured by analytic explanation (for example, the dynamic, *Gestalt*-like, meaning-laden character of perception). Far from "epiphenomenal," "intuitionistic," or "subjectivistic," the phenomenological way of knowing by direct acquaintance reveals living perception as our opening onto the world and others. It reveals phenomena and experiences that have what William James called "cash-value," that is, real effects and pragmatic importance as we live our lives. Indeed, Merleau-Ponty's phenomenology seeks to illuminate and enrich experience as it is lived. I must say, at the beginning of the twenty-first century it really is time for philosophers to stop denigrating phenomenological understanding as a tactic to justify their explanatory programs. It is far more productive to understand these approaches each as they are: as different orders of discourse and observation; different, fundamental ways of knowing.

In this section, I have tried to establish that contemporary physicalism, for all its revolutionary power, all its sophisticated understanding of our sensations in terms of neural function, cannot exhaust the phenomena of living perception. It is rather fascinating to reflect upon how such thinkers—philosophers, scientists, and psychologists—ever came to assume that it could. I suspect that the seduction here has something to do with the great prestige of Newtonian "objectivity," its promise of a complete and total knowledge. But it also has to do with the ways in which this desire for an absolute discourse has been fostered in some of our academic disciplines. Be that as it may, it is time to wake up from this post-Cartesian fantasy, time to accept what we already know is true: that there is, in fact and in principle, no perspectiveless perspective, no discourse or "form of life" that can exhaust all others. As Merleau-Ponty puts this very point:

> The question which [contemporary phenomenological] philosophy asks in relation to science is not intended to contest its right to exist or to close off any particular avenue to its inquiries. Rather, the question is whether science does, or ever could, present us with a picture of the world that is complete, self-sufficient and somehow closed in upon itself, such that there could no longer be any meaningful questions outside this picture. (WP 43)

To be sure, we need our analytic explanations of perception and consciousness; this work is important and revelatory. But we are also creatures who live and love. We are beings who feel joy or despair or frustration, who paint or sing to express ourselves. We are beings who have the power to imagine new possibilities, to soar in daydreams and plunge into fictions. We are beings who cherish experience. Thus we also need a philosophy that speaks to our experiences as living beings.

Fortunately, we already have such a philosophy, and its name is phenomenology. Not only does this philosophy contain the resources to criticize and rehabilitate the flawed ontological traditions that muddle our vision and thinking, but it also keeps us alive to something that analytic explanation draws upon and then forgets: the dynamic, meaningful, excessive, qualitative, intersubjective field of worldly experience.

5. Conclusion

In this chapter I have sought to explicate two powerful, influential traditions on sensation and perception, and the distinct ways in which they both obscure our living perception. The first tradition—Cartesian-based empiricism—starts with atomic sense-data and ends with perception as an internal veil of ideas. Casting mind and world in a strictly dualistic, essentially theological framework, this tradition layers over the deeper fact that perception is lived and known as our opening onto a world that transcends oneself, that is *not oneself.* The second tradition, contemporary physicalism, seeks to avoid that dualism, but ends up reducing perceptual experience to neurophysiological processes. While these processes are clearly one essential aspect of it, perceptual synergy always gives us more. It seems, then, that if we are concerned to understand our living experiences we have little choice. We cannot afford to keep duplicating those oversights or compounding them through further intellectual machinations. Instead, we must return with Merleau-Ponty to perceptual experience as it is lived. We must bring to light its overlapping, dynamic character and become reacquainted with its carnality and intersubjectivity. As Merleau-Ponty puts it: "We believed we knew what feeling, seeing and hearing were, and now these words raise problems. We are invited to go back to the experiences to which they refer in order to redefine them" (PP 10). In the next chapters we will "go back" with Merleau-Ponty to some crucially important dimensions of living experience. Only then, in the later chapters of this book, can we understand his account of how expressive cognition (thinking, language, and knowledge) grows out of that experience.

2 The Secret Life of Things

> Experience in its immediacy seems perfectly fluent. The active sense of living which we all enjoy, before reflection shatters our instinctive world for us, is self-luminous and suggests no paradoxes. Its difficulties . . . are uncertainties. They are not intellectual contradictions.
> —William James[1]

> Nothing is more difficult than to know precisely *what we see*.
> —Merleau-Ponty[2]

1. Phenomenology, Ontology, Symbiosis

In the previous chapter I argued that our intellectual efforts to understand ourselves, our relations with the natural world, and with others require that we carry out a phenomenological study of living perceptual experience. I have suggested that this is not really optional: no matter how extensive or fine-grained our neurophysiological explanations of perception become, there is a priori always more than they can capture. This "always more" that analytic explanation leaves behind is not minor or irrelevant, but immensely significant. It is the dynamic experience that we live in every moment of our lives. It is also the distinctive knowledge of ourselves, the world, and others that we get from that experience—knowledge by direct acquaintance. Indeed, I have argued that living experience isn't some screen of ideas inside the mind or a veil of subjective appearances. For Merleau-Ponty, quite the contrary: it is a continual opening to and immersion in a natural world that is not oneself; it is the field in which we live, breathe, think, and love. Understanding this experience on its own terms—studying and articulating its unique features—isn't some retrograde mysticism, but rather part of an important intellectual movement toward enriched understanding and integrated living. I am convinced that these goals are part of the enduring legacy of phenomenology, part of the reason Merleau-Ponty's thought has remained vital and productive for many philosophers and theorists around the world.

Nonetheless, I have also shown how easy it can be to overlook living experience. As we have seen by considering the Cartesian-empiricist tradition—and even the contemporary physicalist movement—there is an extraordinary tendency to miss the complex characteristics of living perception. There is a profound temptation to intellectually reify some one aspect of the experiential field as *constitutive* of the field. All this is why Merleau-Ponty says (in the above epigram) that "nothing is harder than to know what we see." As he puts it in a public radio address in 1948:

> The world of perception, or in other words the world which is revealed to us by our senses and in everyday life, seems at first sight to be the one we know best of all. . . . Yet this is a delusion. In these lectures, I hope to show that the world of perception is, to a great extent, unknown territory. . . . I shall suggest that much time and effort, as well as culture, have been needed in order to lay this world bare and that one of the great achievements of modern art and philosophy . . . has been to allow us to rediscover the world in which we live, yet which we are always prone to forget. (WP 39)

Again, this cultural work of "rediscovering the world" is called phenomenology. For the philosopher, as distinct from the artist, it involves studying living experience on its own terms, criticizing abstract accounts and models of reality that hide and deform it, and trying to find language that will reveal this elusive experience to others for their confirmation or criticism. This understanding of phenomenological method permits some insights that may be illuminating. First, it allows us to see what I believe is an enduring distinction between Merleau-Ponty's method and Wittgenstein's "grammatical investigations." For despite many similarities in their views and arguments (to an uncanny degree for thinkers who did not know each other's work), Merleau-Ponty has little confidence that grammatical studies into the proper content and boundaries of language regions can let experience come alive. For him (following Heidegger), bringing the subtleties of experience to light and life requires extremely intentional, strategic acts of showing (saying to show). Further, these acts of showing may well require the creation of new language, new forms of expressive and evocative language, rather than Wittgenstein's reliance on existing and "ordinary" language.

A second thing I should say about Merleau-Ponty's phenomenological method is that it has substantial ontological intentions. To show this, I want to mention an old, malingering criticism that "phenomenology is all well and good, but its results and insights are merely psychological." At this point we are able to identify the error in this effort to contain or minimize phenomenology: it depends upon the notion that perceptual experience is essentially subjective ("merely psychological") rather than *real*. However, once we have abandoned the Cartesian theory of perception as abstract and illegitimate, once we give up the traditional notion that experience is a "screen" hiding reality (the Cartesian Theater), then Merleau-Ponty's efforts to study, uncover, and show the elusive features of living experience *just is the study of reality*—reality as it is lived and directly known (by acquaintance). In a phrase, for Merleau-Ponty (as it was for Heidegger), phenomenology *is* ontology. It is the rigorous philosophical effort to articulate human reality as it is lived and directly known (by acquaintance).

Thus, in a rather famous passage, Merleau-Ponty indicates the primary task and orientation of his *Phenomenology of Perception*:

> The first philosophical act would appear to be to return to the world of actual experience which is prior to the world of pure objects, since it is in it that we shall be able to grasp the theoretical basis no less than the limits of that objective world, restore to things their concrete physiognomy, to organisms their individual ways of dealing with the world, and to subjectivity its inherence in history. Our task will be, moreover, to rediscover . . . the layer of living experience through which other people and things are first given to us, the system "self-others-things" as it comes into being. (PP 57, translation modified)

There is a lot going on here. Merleau-Ponty announces that his project is a "return to the world of actual, living experience." He tells us that he seeks to restore to things and organisms "their concrete physiognomy" and their "inherence in history." His task is to "rediscover" and *uncover* the "system 'self-others-things.'" This last phrase provides a template for how I will proceed: in this and the next two chapters I will follow Merleau-Ponty's written efforts to illuminate the different components of the "system 'self-others-things.'" This chapter will explore his phenomenological arguments about "the secret life of things"—his efforts to say and show the distinct, but elusive features of perceptual experience as it unfolds all around. In chapter 3, I will elucidate Merleau-Ponty's groundbreaking work on the living body (self); and chapter 4 will address his equally novel view of intersubjectivity (others).

Before plunging into the details, however, there are still some overarching insights to be gleaned. In the previous chapter, I discussed Merleau-Ponty's account of living perception as a synergy and "interaction." And in the above quote we see him emphasize this characterization; he says that "self-others-things" is a "system" that creates experience *together*. But his use of "system" (*le système*) here is less helpful than the word he typically employs: *symbiosis*. Indeed, at the deepest, even constitutive level of Merleau-Ponty's philosophy, the embodied self, other selves, and the world are symbiotic, interwoven, entangled—with each "component" contributing to the synergy of living experience. This insight allows for a preliminary look at the character of Merleau-Ponty's ontology, his account of lived reality:

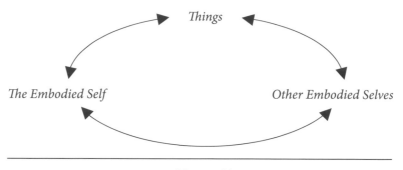

The World

There are of course limits to every model or diagram, and this is no exception. For example, it is impossible for a diagram or words on a page to respect the dynamic interactivity of the components in living experience. This observation points to a pressing difficulty for Merleau-Ponty's project (and my own efforts to elucidate it). How is any writer to discuss living experience if it is a "dynamic, interwoven fabric"? How can any writer honor the movement of living reality? To be sure, our customary, sedimented ways of speaking (in and out of the academy) are the stuff of mechanism: "discrete units," "force causality," "hardware," "binary systems." And our acts of predication, our assertions and the arguments built up out of them, freeze the interactive flow of experience: they pick out this or that thing (the *subject* of the judgment) and then make claims about it (the *objects* of it). How are we in thought and language to do justice to this perpetual movement in experience, this perceptual symbiosis?

This is a primary challenge for Merleau-Ponty (as it is for Heidegger as well). However, seeing this challenge also helps us appreciate their sense of the promise of phenomenology, for its very nature is not to *represent* (copy, *mimēsis*) "subjects" and their predicates (objects). Rather, it is to find and even create language that illuminates the dynamic life that is unfolding all around, human reality as it is lived. There is, quite literally, no end to Merleau-Ponty's efforts to find and create new felicitous language for better showing. Often the reader detects his "birthing pangs," his struggle to find more expressive language—language that better honors and respects the elusive complexities of living experience. One can see this struggle play out over the course of Merleau-Ponty's entire career, for example, as he moves from his early language of "symbiosis," "reciprocity," and "the living body" (in *Structure of Behavior* and *Phenomenology of Perception*) to his later expressions of "interweaving," "reversibility," "chiasmatic intertwining," and "the flesh." There is no question that his creative, evocative re-deployment of language makes Merleau-Ponty's writings often difficult to grasp—at least initially. But it is crucially important to see that it is not the result of "muddled thinking," lack of rigor, or unrestrained style (fairly common complaints about Merleau-Ponty from Anglo-American philosophers). On the contrary, these aspects of his writing are there by painstaking decision and struggle; they are strategically chosen for their potential power to illuminate the symbiosis of primary experience, the interweaving of "self-others-things" as it plays out in living experience.

In the pages and chapters that follow I will be working with considerable care to respect the symbiotic, mutually interactive dynamic throughout our perceptual life. In this chapter focused on "the secret life of things," my task is to reveal the synergistic involvement of the living body and the world-field in our perceptual experience of things. My efforts at care won't always make for easy reading (although I will do my best). But this dynamic involvement is an important part of what phenomenology tries to respect. And once again, this struggle with language helps us appreciate why "understanding what we see" is so hard. It helps us understand why, as Merleau-Ponty says, it has taken a great deal of time, labor, and culture to bring living experience to our richer awareness.

2. Features of the Field: Things, World, Intentionality

Any new reader of Merleau-Ponty's works will quickly grasp that his thought offers an extraordinary meditation upon "the secret life of things." Indeed, his work as a whole contains a philosophical study of our experience of perceived things that is arguably unsurpassed in the western world for its breadth and sensitivity. However, I do not think his insights have been well understood among philosophers, a situation that this chapter hopes to help redress. To this end, my discussion will center around key elements of his account in some early chapters of *Phenomenology of Perception,* as well as the later chapters on "Sense Experience" and "The Thing and the Natural World." As things proceed, I will also draw upon key ideas and formulations from his late writings (such as "Eye and Mind" and "The Philosopher and His Shadow"). In general terms, Merleau-Ponty's work on the subject of perceived things is consistent between his early and late texts. But in chapter 5 (and beyond), I will elaborate my sense of important ways in which his later thinking develops beyond the ideas and formulations of the *Phenomenology of Perception.*

The good news is that we do not have to begin from scratch: in the previous chapter we started to uncover some features of our perceptual life. Following Merleau-Ponty, I argued there that living perception doesn't arrive as a collection of atomic sense-qualities. It doesn't occur as a collection of monadic objects arrayed before the gaze, connected by external, mechanical force relations. On the contrary, we saw that living perception opens up as a complex *Gestalt*, as a figure perceived against and amid a background. Again, look and see: everywhere we look, listen, and touch, perception involves a detailed focus on one part of the field while the rest of it recedes into a less determinate background. In this chapter, it is time to emphasize something that Merleau-Ponty is exquisitely clear about: what we "figure" upon in our *Gestalten* are the things of the natural and cultural world. Living perception opens upon tables and chairs, trees and trucks, loaves of bread, and wildflowers. It opens us to artworks and pottery, roads and forest pathways. At the level of our lives, sense experience doesn't give us, for example, "sour" and "yellow" to be assembled by one's acts of intellectual judgment; rather these "simple" sensibles ("yellow" and "sour") are analytically derived from the bowl of lemons on the kitchen counter.[3] In the throes of our day, we don't hear isolated notes that the mind labors intellectually to compile; rather we hear a *song* or *melody* from which distinct notes can later be discerned. Indeed, as Merleau-Ponty himself comes to see, it is a bit too formal to continue using the language of "figure-background": living perception offers us coherent and consistent things, entities, beings. It offers us natural things and cultural artifacts. It offers up both delightful and startling experiences of other living creatures who perceive us (as we will see in chapter 4). And, importantly, it always offers them up in a natural-cultural context or background that Merleau-Ponty (following Heidegger) calls *world*.

Coherent, consistent things amid a world of things: this is a first look at what living perception offers up. It is important to recognize that it is not experienced as a collection of pure objects, each in its own place. On the contrary, it opens up in perspective, with things presenting one side and hiding other sides. It comes overflowing with half-hidden things that overlap, hide, and allude to other things. Indeed, the world of living perception is utterly *abundant*. It is excessive. And it is this abundant excess of the world that demands my focus on this one thing or that, while the rest of the field recedes. For example, I focus on the vase of flowers on the table: it has other sides that I cannot see; it hides most of the chair behind it and part of the wall beyond. Further, as I attend to the red roses, the table, chair, and wall become blurry each to its own degree, as do my hands before me. Equally certain, however, is that in a moment I can shift my focus to a painting on the wall and the scene will become reorganized. Or I can walk around the table to see the flowers from the other side. Far from a sequence of snapshots, living perception is experienced as an ongoing flow of perspectives on coherent things amid an over-spilling world.

Already, we can see that the living body is essentially involved in the perceptual symbiosis. First, this is because one's body is amid this landscape: perspectives—*Gestalt* organizations and reorganizations—emerge in relation to one's position and attention in the abundant field. But also, we focus on things that are about the right size and right distance for our bodies. Things too big, too small, or too far away cannot appear for our eyes; they defy exploration with our hands. Sounds too high-pitched elude our ears (a dog whistle, for example). Thus, Merleau-Ponty argues that things emerge (amid the world-field) at an "optimum distance" from the living body: its position and distance creates a zone of "maximum visibility" that is intrinsic to the experience of things.[4] Of course, humans can enhance or shift that zone through movement and focus, and they have the ability to augment their sense-modalities with instruments: microscopes, binoculars, hearings aids. In chapter 3, I will discuss the fascinating extent to which we are able to incorporate such instruments into our living bodies and expand our perceptual powers. Be that as it may, the fluid array of consistent, coherent things that "figure" in our perceptual landscape does not reveal a collection of pure objects before a mind, but rather the body's perpetual involvement. As Merleau-Ponty puts it:

> The fact is that if we want to describe it, we must say that my experience breaks forth into things and transcends itself in them, because it always comes into being within the framework of a certain setting in relation to the world which is the definition of my body. . . . The thing is big if my gaze cannot fully take it in, small if it does so easily, and intermediate sizes are distinguishable according as, when placed at equal distance from me, they cause a smaller or greater dilation of my eye. . . . It is therefore quite true that any perception of a thing . . . refers back to the positing of a world and of a system of experience in which my body is inescapably [involved]. (PP 303–304)

Another aspect of our body's necessary involvement in the perception of things-in-context is the sheer carnality of it. Perceived things are not experienced as abstractions or wisps of thought. Rather, they have a density and thickness to them: the inviting ceramic of the cup, the cool, smooth surface of the Corvette, the fascinating layers of line and color in a Van Gogh. These carnal textures are often inviting, yes, but they also have a density and thickness that resists appropriation by our gaze or caress. For one thing, as already discussed, these coherent carnal beings we perceive have "other sides" than the ones that are present to us; they have hidden depths. And all around these beings is a world that keeps spilling out: earth beneath my feet, landscape beyond the car, sky above my head. There is an interesting paradox here which Merleau-Ponty never gets tired of trying to evoke: that perceptual experience is a field of *contact* with things, but it is a contact with things and a world that opens up, eludes, and limits our explorations. Further, it provides experiences of certain beings who demand a different kind of approach altogether: other perceiving creatures who perceive *me* and perceive things *with* me. Carnal contact, coherent things in an open context, radical otherness: once again, these are all experiences that emerge for one's living body; they are all experiences we have of the world's transcendence.[5]

So far we have seen the way that living experience offers up transcendent things (rather than "sense-data" or mere "*qualia*") amid a surrounding, overspilling environment, and we have seen the way the living body's capacities shape them into *Gestalt* organizations. These insights allow us to revisit and expand upon a further claim discussed in the previous chapter: Merleau-Ponty's insight that our living experiences of things are infused with meaning-direction (*sens*, intentionality) in virtue of these configurations. We have already seen that post-Cartesian empiricism cannot respect the fundamentality of these sense-meanings. Since empiricism followed Descartes's theory of sensation by positing pure, discrete, atomistic sense-data as the building-blocks of perception, that tradition thereby followed him in positing that all meaning must reside in mental, intellectual acts of association and judgment—that "all meaning is in the mind." However, as Merleau-Ponty argues, this intellectualist view of perceptual meaning overlooks the extent to which the "the lines of meaning" in our perception of things inform and resist our acts of intellection. He invites us to consider, for instance, the Zöellner illusion (PP 35):

Merleau-Ponty gives us here a fairly formal example. Even so, we can see that this perceived figure-background organization is charged with sense. The auxiliary lines *mean,* to my eyes, that the long diagonals bend. The alternation of the horizontal and vertical lines (on the diagonals) makes every other line appear hazy. The white spaces between the lines ripple with depth. This meaning-direction (*sens*) is not the result of explicit acts of judgment, but rather the prior condition for such judgments. It makes possible, for example, my false judgment that the diagonals converge at some of the ends. Further, no act of interpretation, willpower, or judgment can make me see those lines as parallel. In short, the meanings that emerge in living perception are already there as part of "the secret life of things." They emerge in the symbiosis between the living body and the things of the world.[6]

One distinct way these sense-directions unfold is built into the very fact of perspective: to focus on a thing from one perspective *means* that there are other spatial and temporal perspectives I might adopt. Seeing the sculpture from this side and position just *is* for me to have the sense-directions of other sides and positions I could take up; it also bears the temporal sense that I might come back later. The sofa in my family room opens up several distinct possibilities: for example, I can lay on it, move behind it, or look under it. The coffee cup on the counter bears the sense of how my hand might hold it. Every thing we perceive in the world opens up these possibilities and directions for my behavior. Even so, it would be a mistake to say that these meaning-directions are *given*. They are not present as the things are present to my hands and eyes. Rather, these sense-directions are "non-things": they hover around the things and charge them with possibility. This is why living perception is not experienced as a static spectacle, but rather as a "vital communication" with things in the world.[7]

A further point to grasp about this living intentionality is that it contributes to a certain kind of open indeterminacy that is characteristic of perceptual life. I have just discussed how focusing upon some one specific thing in the field holds open other meaning-directions for my future behaviors. This means that I am never quite settled in any perspective: no sooner do I focus on a thing in the world, than other things and perspectives start vying for my attention. For example, a student walks into class on the first day and a subtle process goes on: "Which desk do I want? That one in the front? But that spot means I am more likely to be called on, and I can't see the rest of the class. How about that desk in the back row? But then I won't be able to see as well. Perhaps a desk in the middle. But which one?" To be sure, the student perceives coherent things in the context of the classroom, but the multiplicity of meaning-directions that emerges creates open indecision. This open indecision is so not because the experience of things offers no options, but because it provides so *many* options; not because experience is meaningless, but because it is brimming with sense-directions. As William James observes in the first epigram to this chapter, living experience involves a "difficult" dynamic that is not "contradiction" but "uncertainty," a charged indeterminacy. This open, expectant tension is what Merleau-Ponty is referring to when he famously stresses that living perception is *ambiguous.*

It is imperative to understand that Merleau-Ponty's view of the "ambiguity" of living perception is not for him to say it is meaningless or vague (as some critics have suggested). On the contrary, he uses the word literally to denote that our experience of the world is pregnant with multiple meaning-directions for our living bodies, with multiple things calling for our attention. To focus on one thing (for whatever reason) brings a momentary resolution to the open tensions of the abundant world. To see this dynamic schematically, we might consider the figure known as the Necker cube:

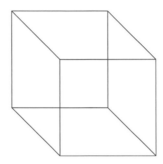

At first, the image is ambiguous; it oscillates between different possibilities, but then the ambiguity resolves and we suddenly see a box from above opening to the lower right, or a box from below opening to the upper left. Whichever way we resolve it, the other possibility doesn't vanish, but remains alive as part of a beckoning horizon.

Or consider a more fleshed-out example of this resolution dynamic, from Merleau-Ponty:

> If I walk along a shore towards a ship which has run aground, and the funnel or masts merge into the forest bordering on the sand dune, there will be a moment when these details suddenly become part of the ship, and indissolubly fused with it. As I approached . . . I . . . felt that the look of the object was on the point of altering, that something was imminent in this tension, as a storm is imminent in storm clouds. Suddenly the sight before me was recast in a manner satisfying to my vague expectation. (PP 17)

Our perception of things amid the world involves these "ambiguity relations," these moments in which the plurality of meanings and things is resolved into a particular configuration (figure amid background). But these resolutions are never final, because they too open up other meanings that call for our attention. What we have, then, as part of our secret life with things is a movement from indeterminacy to configuration and back again. This dynamic is a sort of pulse that beats as we move through and engage things in the world. It is why we experience living perception as an ongoing, meaningful flow rather than static snapshots or discrete objects. And it is the rather natural outgrowth of our living body's insertion in a world of natural and cultural things that go beyond it every-which-way.

In this section, we have seen a number of things about living perception that our western philosophical traditions on perception have been unable to honor. Far from being "a collection of bare particulars," a set of pure, discrete *qualia,* or total chaos, Merleau-Ponty's phenomenological approach tries to show that living experience is an "intentional tissue" (PP 53). It is the living body's ongoing organization of coherent things into sense-laden configurations. Again, this is not a "merely psychological claim," but an ontological recognition—an account of what we actually, truly live as we open our eyes and move through the world. What is already starting to emerge, then, is that Merleau-Ponty's symbiotic account of perceptual experience is opening up a new grasp of *sensibility,* a new promise for human sensitivity. There is no way to understand this fluid, sense-laden experience by analytic dissection, no way to explain or objectify "the secret life of things" without tearing apart the tissue or freezing the flow. Instead, we must open our eyes and ears and hands to this carnal world.

3. Color, "Non-Things," Synaesthetic Perception

In this chapter we are considering key elements of Merleau-Ponty's account of living perception. So far we have seen his claims that it involves a persistent encounter with things amid the over-spilling world, and that these encounters open up meanings that keep our lives vital and fluent. But no account of our living experience of things would be complete without addressing color. If there is anything we know about perception, visual perception at least, it is that it comes in hues. The problem has been to find a philosophy of perception that does justice to the complexities of our experiences with color.[8] We have already addressed the Cartesian-empiricist-Kantian tradition for which colors are pure, discrete atoms which our acts of judgment assemble into coherent wholes. Paradoxically enough, this tradition also flirts with the notion that colors are "secondary qualities," contents added by the mind to the real, existing *forms* of things.[9] The problem is that neither of these fairly widespread notions of color respects the subtle ways that color is lived; they both involve highly abstract, overly dissected images of color. That is, in each-their-own way, they turn color into a kind of object. But Merleau-Ponty shows in many writings throughout his career that this is not how colors are fundamentally experienced. They are not experienced as objects or things themselves, but as "a way into the things" (PP 305), or as "functions" in the field of experience (PP 306). How are we to understand these somewhat oblique expressions?

A first thing to stress is that color is never lived in the singular: our living experience of things always involves *colors;* it involves things and background fields of many different hues. Indeed, colors (along with spatiality and temporality) are one of the primary ways in which we experience differentiation in the world. For example, I perceive the green grass amid and against the brown of the tree trunks and the deeper green of the bushes. Things stand out in the world through their rich differences in color, and we are able to see that our experience of the world's abundance takes shape through these multiple, mosaic "fields" of color. Another aspect of this differentiated relationship is that the colors are what they are in virtue of other colors. For instance, I experience the green of the grass not only through the surrounding colors, but also through the lighter and darker greens (and light browns) that ripple within it. This is why it is so abstract to think of a color as a pure *quale*: in living experience there is no green that is independent of other greens, browns, and blues. As Merleau-Ponty puts this point in *The Visible and the Invisible:*

> The color is yet a variant in another dimension of variation, that of its relations with the surroundings: this red is what it is only by connecting up from its place with other reds about it . . . or with other colors it dominates or that dominate it, that it attracts or that attract it, that it repels or that repel it. In short, [this red] is a certain node in the woof of the simultaneous and the successive. It is a concretion of visibility, it is not an atom. (VI 132)

We see then that in living reality color too has a symbiotic life: colors are what they are in relation to the capacities of my eyes, of course, but also in virtue of the other colors that oscillate around them. They are not discrete *qualia,* but emerge at a nexus of relations. This is a first way in which colors are more like a "function" than an object. But colors also have a subtle relationship with the things of the world. First, they are peculiarly resistant to perceptual figuration. Try it and see: try to focus on the white of a coffee cup as a perceptual figure. It doesn't really work: there is a brief moment when it feels as though the whiteness might come forth, but then the cup itself reasserts itself in the scene. I almost grasp the green on the book cover as a thing, but then the contours of the book take over. It would appear then that we see the things of the world *through* their colors, but do not really see those colors as things.[10] I must say, this is a weird dimension of perceptual life: colors are absolutely manifest in our perception of things in the world, and yet are not themselves things. Indeed, they indeed seem to be a "way into the things," or a kind of *threshold* for them (PP 306).

However, it must also be stressed that colors are not experienced as something separate from the things that bear them. On the contrary, colors seem to emanate from the depths of things.[11] After all, where is the white of a page in a book? The white is not experienced as layered on top of the page like some shellac, but rather as running throughout it, constituting its form. The same is true with the all natural and cultural things, and other people as well: they stand out as distinct where their colors come to an end. Look and see: there are virtually no black lines around the things of the world. The prosaic black line only happens in cartoons or comics. Instead of that, things in experience are separate from others, "delineated," precisely at those places where colors break off. The Cartesian-Kantian view that color is separable from form (and later added by the mind) is an abstraction that arises from tearing color out of its living context and turning it into a separate and separable ideal object (which is what I have called the sensation fallacy).

It seems then that our living experiences of color present a distinctive, manifest, but deeply unusual dynamic. Color is a primary way that living perception (vision, at least) is differentiated; it gives both content and form to the things of the world. Yet, the colors themselves are not experienced as things; they recede as the things stand forth. This is a rather weird feature of our "secret life with things," but there are others as well. For Merleau-Ponty shows that living experience as we know it is constituted by phenomena even more elusive than color. Yes, there are coherent things in context that radiate sense-directions for my body. And there are colors that subtly inform and differentiate the visual field of things. But there is also the play of light, reflection, and shadows. A first thing to notice about these things is that they are not experienced as "things" at all. They are non-things. They hover around as vagaries. They haunt the things of the world. Look again and see: the white coffee cup isn't simply white. It is white with a halo of shadow on the inside rim; there is also diffuse shadow on the counter beneath it. And there are several areas where the light reflects back, glossy and bright. To be sure, we overlook this play of light, reflections, and shadows as we focus on things. But equally certain is the fact that we couldn't perceive as we do without them. In "Eye and Mind," Merleau-Ponty illustrates this point by referring to one of Rembrandt's most famous paintings:

> We see that the hand pointing toward us in *The Nightwatch* [*sic*] is truly there only when we see that its shadow on the captain's body presents it simultaneously in profile. . . . Everyone with eyes has at some time or other wit-

Figure 2.4.
"The Night Watch."

Rembrandt Harmensz. van Rijn. 1642.

Copyright © Rijksmuseum Amsterdam.

nessed this play of shadows, or something like it, and has been made by it to see things and a space. But it worked in them without them; it hid to make the object visible. To see the object, it is necessary *not* to see the play of light and shadows around it. (EM 128)

Following Merleau-Ponty's reading, notice that directly in the center of the painting is the interplay (to which Merleau-Ponty refers) of the lighted hand and its shadow on the captain's chest. Once we notice this shadow, which is typically not noticed, we become aware how essential it is, for without it the hand has no reach, the painting has no *depth*. And what is true of this great

Figure 2.5.
Detail of "The Night Watch."

Rembrandt Harmensz. van Rijn. 1642.

Copyright © Rijksmuseum Amsterdam.

painting is doubly so of our life experiences. There are shadows all around my chair, behind the door, beside and under the things on my desk, draped across my lap. It wouldn't be life without these shadows; once again, it would be a cartoon or a comic.

What has just been said about shadows is also true of light and reflections: the yellow light behind us makes the page come alive, but is not itself seen. We are always seeing the natural and cultural things with light and through light, but the light itself is not experienced as a thing. Also there are those shimmering reflections on the coffee cup, the vague duplicates of my room on the window, the glare on my computer screen. As we move through our days, we either notice these secret ciphers or not, but they are inseparable from experience as we live it. To paraphrase Merleau-Ponty: they are not seen themselves, but cause us to see the rest.[12] Even so, it is important to appreciate that ordinarily they don't trump the density and coherency of colors and things. As Merleau-Ponty argues in considerable detail, colors have a remarkable constancy, despite the play of shadows and light. Drawing upon research by the Gestalt psychologists, when people look at sheets of white paper, some in the light from the window, others in the shadow from the wall, people report that they are all white. A wall appears white even though it is feebly lighted and bathed in shadow. How can this be? Merleau-Ponty's answer is that the coherence of things and the constancy of their colors is part and parcel of the holistic, *Gestalt* organization of the field.[13] This answer, he argues, is supported by the fact that viewing things through a screen (or with half-closed eyes) suddenly changes their color: the wall or some of the pages become bluish-grey. In other words, we see once again what we have been seeing all along: that the coherent things and colors of the world emerge and have the character they do in the synergistic relation between one's living body, features of the world-context, the things themselves, and the non-things that highlight them: "The object which presents itself to the gaze . . . hardness and softness, roughness and smoothness, moonlight and sunlight, present themselves . . . not pre-eminently as sensory contents, but as certain kinds of symbiosis, certain ways the outside has of invading us and certain ways we have of meeting this invasion" (PP 317).

The insights and results of this section allow us to illuminate one other important aspect of the living symbiosis. So far in this section I have been stressing color, light, and shadow—elements that give strong emphasis to perceptual modality of vision. There is no question that this emphasis follows Merleau-Ponty's own disposition to emphasize visibility and painting, an emphasis that has come under a fair amount of critical scrutiny.[14] But it is important to appreciate Merleau-Ponty's explicit arguments that once we overturn the *qualia* view of sensation and return perceived things to their place in a symbiotic field, then we immediately open up to the *inter-sensorial* life of perception. Indeed, in the flow of living perception, prior to abstract analysis, one doesn't see something as though one is looking through a tube. One opens onto the thing with one's whole body, with all the sensory modalities that the body brings to bear. Seeing the coffee cup on the table before me brings with it the possibility of touching it and smelling its contents. Hearing the fist "thud" on the table tells me the table is hard. Smelling the Indian food enhances its taste. In virtually every experience of things in the world, there is an overlapping of at least some of our sense modalities, just as there is an overlapping of views in binocular vision.[15] And just as binocular vision yields an experience of the world's depth, the overlapping of sense modalities gives the things we perceive depth, consistency, and density. Merleau-Ponty says:

> If a phenomenon—for example, a reflection or a light gust of wind—strikes only one of my senses, it is a mere phantom, and it will come to near to real existence only if . . . it becomes capable of speaking to my other senses, as does the wind when, for example, it blows strongly and can be seen in the tumult it causes in the surrounding countryside. Cézanne declared that a picture contains within itself even the smell of the landscape. He meant . . . that a thing would not have this color had it not also this shape, these tactile properties, this resonance, this odour. (PP 319)

At this point it should be pretty clear how abstract it becomes to talk about "five separate senses." This kind of talk derives from the analytic textbook, not *life*. Quite the contrary, the return to experience shows that we perceive coherent, consistent things in the world (tables, chairs, paintings, other people) with all the sense-modalities that grace has given. And since one's body is never lived as a collection of discrete objects or mechanisms (as we will see in chapter 3), the extraordinary, sense-laden things in the abundant world are utterly free to arise as inter-sensorial beings. A great virtue of Merleau-Ponty's account of inter-sensorial perception is that it coheres with phenomena we know perfectly well from the flow of life. For instance, it explains why seeing the blue water of the bay calms our bodies, and conversely, how red or pink brings arousal (PP 209–211). It explains how one can see the brittleness of glass, the hardness of an airplane blade, or the dryness of linen from a certain fold in it (PP 229). It explains how one hears the hardness and unevenness of cobbles in the rattle of a carriage (PP 230)—how the viscosity of syrup is present to sight, how the sweetness of honey radiates from its stickiness (PP 230). Further, it explains why our everyday language is full of expressions where the senses crisscross: we say that sounds are "sharp" or "dull," that tastes are "thick" or "dense"; we talk about music as "hard" or "soft," "light" or "heavy." There is no shortage of examples that demonstrate the overlapping of our sense-modalities: it is as common and constant in living experience as the beating of one's heart. As a result, we need to embrace the fact that "synaesthesia" is not some weird laboratory condition, but quite the opposite: "Synaesthetic perception is the rule, and we are unaware of it only because scientific knowledge [that is, objectifying analysis] shifts the centre of gravity of experience, so that we have unlearned how to see, hear, and generally speaking, feel" (PP 229).

Multiple, subtle, embodied, overlapping, symbiotic: all of these terms get involved when attention is rigorously turned to our living experience of things. The complex facts here require a new language for talking about the world that we live. Far from a collection of "objects," or a "blooming, buzzing confusion," Merleau-Ponty tells us that things in the world emerge at the nexus of *levels*—an operation that has its own logic to it.[16] Thus, drawing on a superb discussion of this aspect of Merleau-Ponty's work by Alphonso Lingis, we can say that specific things emerge for us at the intersection of: (1) levels of light, sonority, and tangibility set by the world, (2) levels of receptivity set by the body's capacities, (3) levels of accessibility set by the body's size, orientation, and position in the world, and (4) levels of density and availability set by the things themselves.[17] Understanding the world in these terms—as a nexus of levels—is not necessarily easy, but at least it aspires to "sing the world" in a way that honors rather than deforms it. To be sure, it is not very helpful or illuminating for people to demand that the "system" and "logic" of living experience conform to some other logic, such as syllogistic or predicative logic. Instead of that, it should be clear by now that enriched, deepened engagement with the world requires that we carry out and follow a *phenomeno-logic*. As Lingis says: "The world is not a framework, an order, or an arrangement. . . . The levels are not dimensions we can survey from above; we find them not by moving toward them *but by moving with them*."[18]

4. The Virtue of Sensibility

In this chapter, I have sought to return to experience as it is directly lived, to move with the "secret life of things." I have tried to show (through "saying") its flow of *Gestalt* organizations and sense-directions, its interplay of color, light, and shadow, its synaesthetic richness. I have sought to uncover the body's inseparable involvement in this extraordinary experience of the world—a world that is *not* oneself, yet which arises at a nexus of levels some of which one's body sets. Merleau-Ponty reminds us, time and again, that these insights about our lives are not obvious or transparent: "Nothing is more difficult than to know precisely *what we see*." For just as we forget the blinking of our eyes and the rhythm of our hearts, so too do we lose sight of our perceptual life. But it should also be underscored that it doesn't help to grow up in a culture wherein philosophy, theology, and science often denigrate that life as subjective, mechanistic, illusory, or the very principle of sin. As Merleau-Ponty puts it, in much of our lives vision has become "profane" (EM 128), unaware of its synergistic life. Learning to see, taste, and touch, learning to feel and sense, to respond to the world all around takes "time," "effort," and "culture" (WP 39). It is, he says, a "gift earned by exercise" (EM 127).

To illustrate this challenge, but also its promise, I want to recount a story from one of my students.[19] He told me how on the first day of his drawing class the students were instructed to sketch an apple that was sitting before them on the table. They did so, with my student feeling quite proud of his work. Then, however, the professor surveyed the various pieces: *this* drawing shows the apple with a stem and a leaf on it, when no such stem exists; *that* drawing has the apple floating in space (where's the table surface?); *these* drawings ignore the light reflecting on the surface of the apple, or depict its form with a black outline. In short, the teacher showed the students that they hadn't drawn the apple at all, but rather their *ideas* of the apple. And now, he told them . . . now they could begin the real work of drawing—the work of learning *how to see.*

It is evident that human beings can enact this deepened, transformed perception. After all, by the end of the semester my student was creating superb drawings. In a similar way, if my phenomenological arguments in this chapter have been successful, the complex, symbiotic character of living experience should be starting to emerge. However, leaving "profane" vision (abstract ideas of seeing) behind requires that we understand the specific forms of thinking that block our sensibilities. It requires patience and caring—a commitment to study our experiences as they unfold. Stop and listen. Listen in the silence. There is the wren singing her delicate song. Here is this complex of flavors in a glass of wine (how extraordinary!). Or there, notice how the sunlight and shadows play through the trees. These are the things and non-things that make our experience possible, and they are easily forgotten. Even so, this chapter has sought to show that we can become alive to our perceptual landscape. As does the artist, we can become more aware of its sense-directions and interplay of levels. The more aware we become, the more we live and think *in keeping with it,* the less intellectually autistic we are. Once again we can see that Merleau-Ponty's phenomenological "return to our senses" is no mysticism. Quite the contrary, it is a *virtue,* in Aristotle's sense of the word. This is to say, sensibility is an excellence realized through proper training, exercise, and practical reason (*phronēsis*).[20] This virtue of sensibility has the potential to save us from environmental disaster by illuminating the natural world and exposing the abstractions that have supported its mindless appropriation and abuse.[21] Less globally, this virtue is also about our health and wellbeing, about thinking in consonance with what we live, rather than in contradiction to it.

In these final reflections, I have started to uncover some of the rather profound *ethical* content in Merleau-Ponty's phenomenological project (more of which will be seen in chapter 4). Nonetheless, it has become somewhat common for philosophers to assert or assume that "Merleau-Ponty has no ethics." Some of the impetus for this mistaken assertion has to do with the fact that Merleau-Ponty did not write a book that blazons itself as an ethics, such as *Nicomachean Ethics* or *Groundwork for the Metaphysics of Morals*. But I also believe some of this sentiment has to do with the contemporary influence of the important ethical philosophy of Emmanuel Levinas. In the first of his two major works, *Totality and Infinity,* Levinas develops a provocative critique of phenomenology (and Merleau-Ponty by implication) in terms of what he calls *sojourning*. Sojourning, Levinas suggests, is "the way of the I against the 'other,'" it is the process of identifying and maintaining oneself by being "at home" in the world. As Levinas puts it: "The 'at home' is not a container, but a site where I *can*, where . . . I am . . . free. It is enough to walk, to *do*, in order to grasp anything, to take. In a sense everything is in the site . . . everything is at my disposal, even the stars, if I but reckon them. . . . Everything is here, everything belongs to me . . . everything is com-prehended."[22] For Levinas, sojourning is a mode of appropriation, a mode of violence, in which we remake the world and others to reflect ourselves. It is a consumption of others' transcendence. To use one of his most famous phrases, it is "a reduction of the other to the same." Further, Levinas specifically argues (in a way that has been influential) that phenomenology is a philosophy which preeminently legitimates and promotes this appropriation of the other. No doubt: this has the makings of a serious critique.

There is a lot that needs to be said about the agonistic relationship between Levinas and Merleau-Ponty. There are many lines of argument, and the issues get deep and complex (as we will see in chapter 4). However, at this point in the book I believe we are able to understand that Levinas's "sojourning" criticism is unjust to Merleau-Ponty's thought. For, setting aside the question of whether it is a fair criticism of Heidegger (and there are arguments to be made on both sides), it seems reasonably clear that Merleau-Ponty's "return to our senses," his virtue of sensibility, does not amount to a consummation or a comprehension of the other. Rather, in his philosophy, living experience emerges as a symbiosis, as a synergistic nexus of widely divergent levels, as an opening (*ouverture*) to transcendence. Indeed: things, the world, and others (we will later see) transcend me in living experience. They are incomparably here, present. But, Merleau-Ponty also insists, they are "inexhaustible," "irreducibly other," and "alien."[23] For Merleau-Ponty, one's experiential relationship with the world is far different from totalizing appropriation: "my perceptual opening to the world, which is *more dispossession than possession*, claims no monopoly of being and institutes no death struggle of consciousness" (PS 170, emphasis added). Thus, while Levinas has some effective criticisms which will be discussed in the next chapter, we have already uncovered enough to deny that Merleau-Ponty's account of perceptual experience itself is a "reduction of the other to the same." On the contrary, it is an "ontological rehabilitation" of the sensible that has rather deep ethical resonance. It is about exercising the "virtue of sensibility." It is about reawakening our wonder in the natural-cultural world and with others all around.

5. Conclusion

In this chapter, I have sought to follow Merleau-Ponty's writings into "the secret life of things." What life there is! We perceive coherent things in the context of an excessive world; we perceive them at a "nexus of levels" that are set through the things themselves, "non-things," the over-spilling world, and the capacities and synaesthetic potentialities of our living bodies. Further, because the world of things is "inexhaustibly rich" (PS 167), spilling out every which way, our perceptual experience is ambiguous, shot through with a multiplicity of sense-directions. This is the flow of our lives below the level of predication, acts of judgment, and textbook analyses. Already the reader might be starting to wonder: what does *knowledge* become on such an account? This is an excellent question, I think, because the history of philosophy reveals that most philosophers root their epistemology in their ontology. For an illustrative, pertinent example, consider Aristotle's metaphysics of substance. In Aristotle's ontology, reality is the collection of all substances, that is, the collection of natural kinds defined and differentiated in terms of objective properties. Upon this objectivist understanding of the real, Aristotle casts knowledge as the process of representing those pure kinds and properties in thought and language. Thus is born, in western mind, the prestige of analysis and logical analysis. Thus is born the Syllogistic.

However, the arguments in my first two chapters have shown that all this objectivism forgets the fluid richness of living reality. It forgets that the "object" is an abstraction of some aspect of the symbiotic field—an abstraction that severs the things from their dynamic, meaningful contexts. So again we ask: what must the processes of thinking, speaking, and knowing be if living reality is a fluid synergy? What else could they possibly be, if not *mimēsis*? In a word, Merleau-Ponty argues that these processes must be *expression*. He argues that thinking, speaking, and knowing have always involved expression, but that this cognitive process has been obscured by the idols of representation. I believe that these are big, important arguments in Merleau-Ponty's philosophy and I will spend considerable time on them in later chapters. But first, we must continue our study of Merleau-Ponty's ontological system, "self-others-things." In doing so, we will next consider his philosophy of the "self" as a living body. And this is not, as we will see, a detour, for in the phenomena of embodied subjectivity we will discover the seeds of the expressive act.

3   Singing the Living Body Electric

I sing the body electric,
The armies of those I love engirth me and I engirth them,
  They will not let me off till I go with them . . .
    . . . and charge them full with the charge of the soul.
—WALT WHITMAN[1]

I want to speak to the despisers of the body. . . . "I," you say, and are proud of the word. But greater is that in which you do not wish to have faith—your body and its great reason: that does not say "I," but does "I."
—FRIEDRICH NIETZSCHE[2]

1. Toward a Philosophy of Living Embodiment

It is well known that the mind-body problem is defined by a blatant contradiction in Descartes's *Meditations*. On one hand, Descartes argues time and again that the mind is immaterial: he establishes mind as *res cogitans* by its *not* being material; he insists that mind and body are "completely different" substances. Yet at the end of the Sixth Meditation, Descartes also argues that mind and body are "very closely joined" and "intermingled," that they form a "single unit." How is this union possible? How is it possible for the immaterial mind to be "connected" with the material body? After this problem in the *Meditations* became evident, many philosophical attempts have been made to explain the mind-body relation, starting already with Descartes's own thesis of the pineal gland. But what is never far from the discussion (and often assumed by it), is Descartes's way of casting one's body as an *object* "out there," physically and metaphysically closer to a rock than to *me*. This radical, objectivist view of the body was true for Descartes on principle. Since matter is defined as extension in force relations ("the subject matter of pure mathematics"), the organic, material body becomes *partes extra partes*. That is, each part of it is externally related to the other parts with all action occurring through mechanical force. I hasten to add that this is how, say, a toaster works; and Descartes embraces this kind of analogy, comparing our bodies to "a clock constructed with wheels and weights."[3] Thus is born in western intellectual history what Michel Foucault has called "the age of man-the-machine."[4]

It is not particularly difficult to trace out the continuing legacy of the Cartesian body-machine. It is legitimized by Newton's "natural philosophy" which ignores the "subjective-mind" half of Descartes's ontology and casts the universe as "a great object" (once again like a clock). It is subtly carried through Locke's empiricism, in which the "passive" body is "forced" to receive "impressions" from the objects around it.[5] Foucault has argued that this mechanical image of the body both supported and gained support from the rise of industrialism with its need for a productive and efficient work force.[6] In intellectual culture, the body-machine pervades nineteenth and twentieth-century behaviorism, in which all actions are cashed out by theories of the "reflex" and "stimulated response." And it persists well after behaviorism in our contemporary talk of the body and cognition in terms of "computational systems," "hardware," "software," "mechanisms," and "networks." Be all this as it may, one thing is sure: so long as we continue to understand, discuss, and model the body as a machine—as an inanimate object constructed of independent systems—we will never understand its *life*. That is to say, we will never understand the phenomena of living embodiment. As long as this happens we will be forever "out of step" with our bodily experiences, dislocated from our myriad ways of comportment, and unaware of phenomena that our scientific models and explanations need to respect. Indeed, the virtue of sensibility I discussed in chapter 2 requires that we thoroughly study and articulate, rather than ignore, our embodiment as it is lived. It requires that we *celebrate* embodied experience and not despise it: that we learn, with Whitman, how to "sing the body electric."

In the philosophical effort to rigorously study embodied experience there is probably no better place to start than with Merleau-Ponty. Merleau-Ponty is widely known among philosophers and theorists as "The Philosopher of the Body." Some people have claimed that his phenomenology of embodied experience and agency is his genius and legacy.[7] I must say at the outset of this chapter that I don't share this view. Of course I agree that embodiment is a central dimension of Merleau-Ponty's thought, and it is one that offers promising solutions for some traditional philosophical problems. However, I believe that Merleau-Ponty's "legacy" (as it were) is considerably broader, resting also on his late elemental ontology and his account of expressive cognition. Also, I believe that some deeply pressing objections to his philosophy emerge because of important features of living embodiment that he fails to recognize. I will articulate these problems in section 5 of this chapter, but first and foremost my task is to elucidate key features of Merleau-Ponty's phenomenological account of the living body—features that should be revelatory of our experiences.

We will recall that Merleau-Ponty's phenomenology aims to "return to the world of actual experience . . . to rediscover the system 'self-others-things' as it comes into being" (PP 57). In the last chapter we explored the third part of this symbiotic triad, "the secret life of things." In this chapter we plunge into his account of the first part, Merleau-Ponty's ontology of the embodied self. The arguments for this chapter are drawn primarily from his earlier work—*Phenomenology of Perception* and *The Structure of Behavior*. I am reserving discussion of his later, radicalized treatment of the living body as "flesh," for chapter 5.

2. Beyond the Body as Thing

A deep irony can be discerned in Aristotle's great work of psychology, *De Anima*. In its title and design, the text sets out to understand *life*. But as a work in Aristotle's "theoretical philosophy," it proceeds by analysis: he seeks to understand organic life by dividing it into four functions—nutrition, locomotion, perception, and thought. Devoting a lengthy discussion to each of these, Aristotle further analyses the parts of these parts, along with *their* parts. Indeed, despite many important insights, by the end of the work the dissected organism seems more dead than alive. Similar problems hold for many contemporary discussions in biology, psychology, and neurophysiology. That is, we get rich, revealing analyses of genetic formations, nervous functions, and brain processing, but (as I argued in chapter 1) these explanations don't exhaust the whole of embodied life. They do not and cannot, for methodological reasons, articulate and honor the dynamic, synergistic features of embodied experience. They don't speak to us as we live and breathe. Thus, Merleau-Ponty's phenomenology of the living body is not rendered moot or "merely psychological" by the extraordinary advances in these scientific domains. Rather, it is a different order of discourse, one that seeks to uncover real features of living a body. Again: phenomenology is ontology. These features purport to be ones that we know by direct acquaintance, but which have become obscured through analytic method or other abstract models. As we proceed into Merleau-Ponty's account, we will very quickly discover how badly the Cartesian image of the object-body violates this life, how it obscures and even contradicts our embodied experiences.

For example, when we "return to our senses" one of the first things we notice is that one's body is not lived as one thing among many. On the contrary, we experience our bodies as a "necessary condition" for perceiving things, as a vital, dynamic source before which things in the world surge up and recede. Beyond the arguments of the previous chapter, Merleau-Ponty stresses several aspects of this unique relation. First, our very concept and experience of a worldly thing is that one can take up a multiplicity of perspectives upon it.

The chair, the sofa, the house across the street: these are all things that I can *survey*. Also, the things around me in the world can be left behind: their coming to be present in my perceptual field involves their possible absence. However, neither of these two features—the ability to openly explore things and to abandon them—holds true for my living, perceiving body. The living body has a permanent, relatively stable structure that is fundamentally different. As Merleau-Ponty puts it: "the permanence of my own body is entirely different in kind [from objects]: it is not at the extremity of some indefinite exploration; it defies exploration and is always presented to me from the same angle. Its permanence is not a permanence in the world, but a permanence on my part" (PP 90). Indeed, I cannot walk around my body. On the contrary, my body is that with which I walk around the things of the world. I cannot leave it behind. One's living, dynamic body is always there as a subtle sentinel, more or less present to awareness while one perceives, thinks, dreams, and imagines. It is also there in a relatively stable way: my eyes open onto the world at the height of about six feet; my body bends forward at the waist and backwards at the knees to sit on a chair; my hands are particularly adept at exploring what is in front of me. Merleau-Ponty argues that things appear to us in a perspective because the relative stability of our bodies both grounds and resists all variation of perspective.[8]

Thus one's living body is involved in all experiences of things in the world, but it cannot be surveyed in the way they can. Merleau-Ponty argues that one's living body resists exploration in other ways as well. For one thing, humans (and virtually all perceiving animals) are "built" with their sensory "systems" on the *outside*, aiming outward toward the world. Evolutionary theorists argue that this fact is well-explained through natural replication: organisms with this outward arrangement are likely to survive longer and reproduce. Be that as it may, this outwardness helps us understand why it is so easy to overlook one's own body, why it is easy to forget about it as the constant pole in one's experience: we are, in a sense, configured to forget the body as we perceive things in the world. This outward arrangement also imposes structural limits on my self-explorations. I can't see the back of my head (without two mirrors). I can't get the manipulative surfaces of my hand, the palm and fingers, up past the small of my back. I can't see very far inside myself. More radically, Merleau-Ponty argues that I can't even perceive myself perceiving. I may, of course, partially "objectify" parts of my living body (my foot or my hand or my thigh) and partially examine those parts from different perspectives—but I cannot objectify myself as a perceiver. Try it by looking in a mirror: one can either focus on one's perceiving eyes, in which case the mirror image recedes into the background; or one can focus on the reflected image, at the cost of awareness of one's perceiving. Merleau-Ponty argues that the same disjunction is true of one hand touching one's other hand or other parts of one's body: there is always a "gap" between the animating intention of the one hand and the passivity of what is being touched.[9] Thus he says: "Insofar as it sees or touches the world, my body can therefore be neither seen nor touched" (PP 92). Indeed, one's living, perceiving body is part of the synergy with things and the world, but is not reducible to one's experience of them.[10] It is lived instead as a stably structured, carnal being that nonetheless organizes the world around it.

There are other features that distinguish the living body from the things of the world, other features that, contrary to Descartes, place it on the side of *me* rather than the side of things. For one, there is the living experience of its spatiality. To be sure, one's body is not experienced as "beside" things as, say, the chair is next to the couch (PP 98). On the contrary, the body's position in the room determines the "beside" relation in the first place. For instance, if one looks at the chair from the side rather than the front, the couch is "*behind*" the chair, and not "beside" it. Up, down, beside, behind, inside, outside, left, right, concave, convex, vertical, horizontal, between, above, below: these are all spatial relations that draw their very meaning and intelligibility from my body lived as an organizing whole. As Merleau-Ponty puts this: "The outline of my body is a frontier that ordinary space relations do not cross. This is because its parts . . . are not spread out side by side, but enveloped in each other" (PP 98). That the living body's "enveloped" wholeness creates a "frontier" can also be seen in our emotions. For instance, the sadness of a death or a betrayal radiates throughout my whole body: "I can't speak; I can't even move." Nonetheless, we wouldn't dream of saying that the inanimate things of the world feel some sadness or joy, or the delirium of falling in love. And the pain in my foot doesn't cause me to be in pain "from the outside"; rather "my foot hurts!" or "the pain is in my foot!" (PP 93). There is much that will be said about this subtle separation between body and world, but for now these examples remind us that the corporeal background for "the secret life of things" is not merely positional, but affective through and through.

So far I have followed Merleau-Ponty's arguments to show that one's living, breathing, "electric" body is not well understood as one thing among others in the world, that it is simply not experienced as "a thing among things." At the same time, it is important to stress Merleau-Ponty's insistence that the living body is not *opposed* to those things either. There is no dichotomy between my embodied self and the things. I am of the same "stuff": there is constant contact between my living body and things because we share surfaces, contours, material densities, and depths. While experienced as different, the things and I are in a "reciprocal relation," to use Merleau-Ponty's early language for now.

We are in a particular inter-relationship—to and fro—that is marked and organized by my receptivity. As Merleau-Ponty stresses: "My body is not only a nexus of sensible qualities among others, but an object that is *sensitive* to all the rest, that reverberates to all sounds, vibrates to all colours" (PP 236). This internal, reciprocal relationship is underscored by the fact that living, human bodies (and those of some animals, to some degree) have the power to *incorporate* inanimate things into their operations: the blind person's cane, the clothes we wear, a prosthetic hand, the musician's instrument, an animal's tool. These "auxiliaries" are drawn into one's self and lived as part of one's active body. We feel, act, and make music through these auxiliaries in a very full sense of the word (PP 152). In section 4, below, I will elaborate Merleau-Ponty's account of how these everyday incorporations are possible; the point for now is that the living body and inanimate things are experienced as different, yet also in fluid, internal relations, with distinctive dynamics that must be studied and articulated.

Already in this chapter we have uncovered seeds for dissolving Cartesian dualism. That dualism meshes with a longstanding theological tradition and underwrites a dream of pure material objectivity purged from subjective bias, but it has nothing to do with what we experience as embodied agents in the world. My body is not lived as a thing, but as a vital power among the things, as a mobile, relatively stable, receptive creature that organizes the world as it goes. Contrary to Cartesianism, my body is closer to my "self" than to objects, or perhaps it is better to say that my embodied self and the things of the world are closer together than Descartes's dualistic thought can possibly imagine. They are bound up in the same synergy, yet experienced as remarkably different. It is true that this fluid, differentiated, yet reciprocal relationship of embodied self and world is difficult to conceive. It is easier by far to bifurcate "subject" and "object," and let the body be damned. But the Cartesian and post-Cartesian body-object is an abstraction and a dangerous one at that. It contradicts what we know of our living bodies in the flow of life, and it suppresses our sensibilities.

3. Beyond the Body as Machine

For Descartes the body is not just a thing or an object. More specifically, it is a mechanistic object. This is to say, it is a collection of externally related parts that operates through direct, linear causal force. As Descartes puts it: "nerves are like chords which go from the foot right up to the brain. When the nerves are pulled in the foot, they in turn pull on inner parts of the brain to which they are attached, and produce a certain motion in them."[11] In our age scientists would certainly substitute electrical impulses for the "pulling" of the nerves, but this update by itself wouldn't change the underlying ontology: if we visualize the body as a strictly linear system, parts A to B to C, each activated in turn by a force that starts from without, then we essentially conceive the body as a machine. As I have already suggested, this image had tremendous uptake after Descartes through traditional empiricism to its nadir in behaviorism: throughout this heritage the body is essentially passive, activated by forces on the peripheral "receptors" that go on to trigger a global response. Indeed, on this image all body activity is truly only *re-activity*; it is a complex sum of reflexes and conditioned responses to the "environment."

By the middle of the twentieth century it was already becoming clear that this image of the body-machine could not be sustained. Already philosophers such as John Dewey had undermined the mechanistic "reflex arc."[12] Already psychologists had acknowledged the lack of determinate, linear relations between material stimulation (on the periphery), and sensory contents and global response. Merleau-Ponty's early work was certainly inspired by and contributed to that growing awareness. His first book, *The Structure of Behavior,* is a trenchant critique of Watsonian behaviorism that utilizes then current experimental research and the Gestalt psychologists' concept of form. One of his lines of argument is particularly useful here as we seek to undo the image of the body-machine, and that is how much the living body actively contributes to the stimulations it receives. Drawing on the research of Weisäcker, Merleau-Ponty argues:

> The organism cannot properly be compared to a keyboard on which the external stimuli would play . . . for the simple reason that the organism contributes to the constitution of [the form of stimuli]. When my hand follows each effort of a struggling animal while holding an instrument for capturing it, it is clear that each of my movements responds to external stimulation; but it is also clear that these stimulations could not be received without the movements by which I expose my receptors to their influence. . . . Thus the form of the excitant is created by [the organism's] proper manner of offering itself to actions from the outside.[13]

Indeed, as Merleau-Ponty puts it in *Phenomenology of Perception*, the body must be *attuned* to stimulations in order to receive them (PP 75). It must be organized as a whole and actively prepared for the stimulations it encounters, and all of this challenges the abstract image of the body as a fundamentally passive recipient of external forces.[14]

We can see this point more fully through the commonplace example of having one's reflexes tested. It is self-evident that a reflex response in my leg occurs when the doctor taps my knee. But it is equally evident that for the "kick" to occur, I have to be set up "just so." I have to relax my leg, let it dangle, and "not think about it." In short, I have to *make myself* a sort of object. To use Merleau-Ponty's terms, my leg and body as a whole must be attuned to the goal of the test for the mechanistic reflex to manifest. If I straighten my leg, walk around the room or otherwise engage in the operations of life, then there can be no test. Similar attitudinal preconditions can be found behind all reflex behavior: for example, my eyes need to be open for the doctor's light to cause them to dilate. This recognition shows, first, that the living body's position and dispositions, its global orientation, its attunement to a situation, all provide antecedent preparation for the reception of stimulations and the body's subsequent responses. In this sense, the living body *greets* the world that has influence on it. It also shows that behaviorism is flawed in its most basic premise: behavior can't be reduced to the sum of reflexes and inculcated responses because, as we have seen, those reflexes and responses are conditioned by behavior. In short, behaviorists commit a reification fallacy. They mistake derivative, conditioned, partial phenomena—that is, the reflex and conditioned response—for an unconditioned, fundamental bedrock. The living body isn't a fundamentally passive machine, activated merely by external triggers. It only appears as one if theorists confuse the highly "controlled" (abstract) conditions of the laboratory or the examination room for the conditions of life.

Returning to the conditions of life, we have begun to see that the living body is actively attuned to the world around it. It symbiotically greets the world. It sets itself up in advance to receive and act in relation to things. As Merleau-Ponty puts it: our body as "the potentiality of this or that part of the world, surges toward objects to be grasped and perceives them" (PP 106). But what does this more precisely mean? In what sense is the body a "potentiality"? What is this "surging toward" things that we are about to grasp, this "preparation" for soon-to-be-received stimulations? In this idea we are at the threshold of an essential element in Merleau-Ponty's phenomenology of the living body: his account of "body" or "motor" intentionality. In the previous chapters we have already seen Merleau-Ponty's view that our *Gestalt* organizations of things in the world are laden with multiple sense-directions, or what is now commonly called "intentionality." What is important to emphasize in this chapter is the way in which this intentionality radiates from and to the living body. There is a long tradition in philosophy that has treated intentionality as equivalent to states of belief, desire, or volition, and so the notion of body-intentionality might seem strange. But as Daniel Dennett has argued, intentionality is best understood in a more basic, less rarified sense: it is about *aiming* or *directedness*.[15] With this relaxed, less abstract sense in mind, we can see that in *Phenomenology of Perception* (particularly in the chapter, "The Spatiality of One's Own Body"), Merleau-Ponty shows that embodied life has a distinct, extensive "directedness" to it, below the level of intellectual judgments. That is to say, it has an intentional life that is well known (by direct acquaintance), but the recognition of which requires abandoning the image of the body-machine.

Already we have seen that figure-background perceptions are shot through with meaning-directions (*sens*). Again, they are sense-directions for my body: perceiving something in perspective holds open a host of meaning-directions for other possible perspectives and behaviors. For example, I can walk around the chair, try to see it from your perspective, or sit on it if I am tired. Further, while the arrangement and character of things in the world plays a constitutive role in shaping these meaning-directions, Merleau-Ponty emphasizes that my living body is the pole around which these possibilities galvanize. To show this, Merleau-Ponty draws at length upon Gelb and Goldstein's case study of a neurological patient named Schneider—a World War One veteran who suffered considerable damage to the occipital lobe from shell fragments.[16] Schneider's post-traumatic behavior is marked by a tragic "disconnect": he can grasp things, but not point to them; he can move his body with great speed to fulfill concrete tasks, but with his eyes shut he cannot touch parts of his body on command. When everyday objects and familiar tasks are given him, he readily takes them up and performs with great skill. However, if Schneider is asked to identify a simple object held up before him, he gets confused: "It is black, blue, and shiny. There is a white patch on it, and it is rather long. It reflects light." But only after being shown it in working position, does he recognize the object: "It's a pen!" (PP 131). Schneider easily swats the mosquito that is stinging him, but if asked to point to the part of his body that is being touched he starts by moving his entire body, then swinging the specific limb, in order to zero-in on the spot (PP 107).

The things that Schneider is able to do might appear to lend themselves to mechanistic analysis: he can swat a mosquito, fulfill simple tasks on command, and pick up a tool he requires. However, it is what Schneider *cannot* do that is so revealing of the living embodiment most of us enjoy and take for granted. Again, he cannot point to things in front of him or to parts of his own body. He is incapable of play-acting with his body or rehearsing movements. He does not recognize that people can look in other directions than the one are already looking in. He understands that triangles fit inside squares, but not if the triangles have to be rotated. If an object is placed in front of him, he is unable to wonder where it came from. The list goes on, but it is clear, Merleau-Ponty argues, that what Schneider and similarly affected patients are lacking is an *intentional arc* (PP 111). They are trapped in the actual. They are unable to perceive the zone around them as a *virtual* space (PP 111), as an area of open possibilities, other perspectives, and imaginative variation. As Merleau-Ponty puts it:

> Whereas in the normal person every event related to movement or sense of touch causes consciousness to put up a host of intentions that run from the body as the centre of potential action either toward the body or toward the object, in the case of the patient, on the other hand, the tactile impression remains opaque and sealed up. [A key] may well draw the grasping hand toward itself, but does not stand in front of it in the manner of a thing that can be pointed out. The normal person *reckons with* the possible. (PP 109)

This "reckoning with the possible," this opening up lines of force and possibility beyond the concrete, is the very fabric of our everyday experience. My living body's intentional arc makes possible the abstract act of pointing to one thing among many. It lays down an open zone in which I can rehearse movements in the absence of a concrete task. It opens up and "directs" me to objects and perspectives, spaces and times, beyond those I presently hold; that is, it yields awareness of my being in a "global situation" (PP 79). Through it, my body prepares for the stimulations it is about to receive. It holds open space and time for my imagination. Indeed, Schneider understands neither analogies, metaphors, nor stories. He has sadly diminished sexual function, for he has no sense of the erotic. In short, the life-world (for most of us) has a *physiognomy*.[17] This physiognomy, radiating from our intentional arc, is not merely "psychological." It is lived at the roots of non-pathological embodied experience and is witnessed in the simplest operations that we take for granted. It isn't some "intuitionistic" shellac painted over what is really mechanistic function: the body's apparently mechanistic actions are either derivative upon the intentional arc, or result from its loss. Once again we see that the living body is not fundamentally an agglomeration of dead parts activated from without, but rather an active, sense-making, organizing power. It is, Merleau-Ponty stresses, a living *conscious* body, for in the intentional arc "the consciousness of the body invades the body, the soul spreads over all its parts" (PP 75). I hasten to add that this formulation is not, for Merleau-Ponty, a slide back to Cartesianism by placing consciousness on the far side of a metaphysical divide. On the contrary, it is for him to direct our sensibilities to the embodied-cognitive life we enjoy below the level of Cartesian dualism and mechanism: "The union of soul and body is not an amalgamation between two mutually external terms, subject and object, brought about by arbitrary decree. It is enacted at every instant in the movement of existence" (PP 88–89).

We are able to see then, once and for all, that Merleau-Ponty is no behaviorist. It is worth underscoring this point, for his emphasis on "behavior" and "the body" has led a number of commentators astray. As the previous quotes convey, Merleau-Ponty is really a cognitivist—with the proviso and emphasis that cognition be understood as thoroughly embodied and situated. In this way Merleau-Ponty should be understood, and has been explicitly recognized, as anticipating the "embodied consciousness" movement that has caught fire recently through the works of people such as Francisco Varela, Andy Clark, George Lakoff, and Mark Johnson.[18] Having recognized this cognitivism in his philosophy of mind, it is important to underscore that Merleau-Ponty is no Kantian in these matters. On one hand, his radical distance from Kant is seen in his arguments that the consciousness which infuses living behavior must not be understood as a *positing* consciousness. For Kant (and many after him) positing consciousness, with its judgments and representations of discrete categorical objects, is quite literally "constitutive" of experience; but for Merleau-Ponty such positing and representing is second-order and derivative upon living experience.[19] Further, Merleau-Ponty is emphatic that the living body is not to be grasped as a transcendental subject. For while the living body does set up in advance a field of meanings and a global situation in keeping with its possible movements and projects, this carnal power is not divorced from existence and contingency.[20] On the contrary, this power can be disrupted by illness or shattered by trauma, as in Schneider's case. As Merleau-Ponty puts it: "Bodily experience forces us to acknowledge an imposition of meaning [*sens*] that is not the work of a universal constituting consciousness. . . . My body is that significant core which behaves like a general function, but which nevertheless exists and is susceptible to disease" (PP 147).

Merleau-Ponty has a good deal yet to show us about the workings of the living body, but already it should be clear how deeply the categories of Cartesianism violate the real, fundamental experiences of our bodies. The body as we live it is no thing among things, but the pulsing, carnal condition for perceiving things; it is the stable, yet elusive being around which things and the world take shape. Nor is the body well understood as a machine, for it is enjoyed as an "intentional system," as a "significant core" that has the ability to pursue the possibilities that radiate from and before it. And this shows that consciousness infuses the body from the get-go. As I live and breathe, act and flow through my day, I am not a machine with a ghost attached at the pineal gland. Instead, I am a living-conscious body.

Therefore, I would assert that there can be no solution to the mind-body problem as it is traditionally cast, and this is true in principle. For once the organism is cut into mutually exclusive terms—once an apple is cut in half—

there is no way to put it back together as it was. Nor will it do for one to accept the post-Cartesian, abstract definitions of mind and matter and then disprove one side of the binary or the other (the basic strategy of reductive materialism and idealism). Instead of all that, what is required is renewed study and sensitivity to the phenomena of embodiment that are lived prior to abstract, dualistic concepts. What is called for, then, is a phenomenological return to our situated, embodied minds so that we can think more consonantly with what we live. In the next section we will take further steps down this path.

4. Further Features of Embodied Life

Cases of severe physical trauma negatively indicate, as we have seen, that a living body typically sends waves of significance round about. Its bearing on coherent things in the world holds open, or *means,* other possible perspectives. Its flowing movements spin out "intentional threads" that connect the body to things as poles of potential action and response. As Merleau-Ponty says, body-consciousness is "in the first place not a matter of 'I think that' but of 'I can'" (PP 137). Its projects open up a "milieu," an intentional space where things are marked in relation to the living body's practices, capacities, and powers. For instance, I go into my kitchen, not as "one object-point among many in Newtonian space," but as a place where I am at home, a place where I go often and love to be, where I prepare the food that brings my family together. While cooking, I soar through this place like an eagle: I know where the pans and utensils are without looking; my body knows the distance between the counter, the stove, and the sink. However, it isn't just the world around me that can have this physiognomy, so too does my own living body. Indeed, Merleau-Ponty's account of motor intentionality illuminates another deeply familiar feature of embodied life that is easily overlooked: the experience of *body image* or corporeal schema.[21]

Sitting at my desk, working on my papers, I reach back and scratch my shoulder; I dangle my right leg over my left knee, I cross my arms over my stomach. That is, thrown into a project, I nonetheless know where the other parts and regions of my body are. How are we to understand this? Under classical empiricism and behaviorism, the body image is nothing but a fortuitous association of isolated reflexes and conditioned responses. As we saw before, this ignores the fact that behavior, and with it the corporeal schema, preconditions the manifestation of reflexes: the body image is already there surrounding and attuning my conditioned responses; thus, it cannot be a sum of them. But having made this rather Kantian argument, it is also important to stress that the body image is not constituted by positing consciousness, for I live through my body image before and below the level of intellectual acts of judgment. I don't judge or mentally posit where my shoulder is before I scratch it; it is in the "background" of my current project, part of the living system that is my body, part of an intentional web that I am able to trace without explicit reflection. The body image is at once more global than behaviorism can see and less "intellectual," less "representational" than Kant could conceive.[22] The body image is, Merleau-Ponty says, a "vague power against which the gesture and its aim stand out" (PP 101), and "a global awareness of my posture in the intersensory world" (PP 100). In fact, Merleau-Ponty is clear that our synaesthetic perception of the world as an inter-sensory field (see chapter 2) is achieved through the body image: one's senses are connected and overlap through it. Eye is to seeing as ear is to hearing as hand is to touch: these simple analogies, which Schneider could not comprehend, are rooted in most people's ability to graph parts of themselves onto each other through the body image, and similarly, to graph parts of themselves onto the world all around.

The body image or corporeal schema is a deep, constant feature of our embodied life, and it is easy to take for granted. Nonetheless, we can learn more about it and the dynamics of embodied life by considering acute cases of its disruption. For example, Merleau-Ponty discusses at length the phenomena of phantom limb and anosagnosia: the first is the experience of still having a limb after it has been amputated; conversely, the second is the refusal to acknowledge some disability or debilitating illness. In relation to these lived phenomena and others like them, Merleau-Ponty argues that the bifurcated categories of post-Cartesian thought are singularly unhelpful. Phantom limb, for instance, is not merely some confused nervous discharge: local anesthetic by itself does not eliminate the phenomenon. And typically, the missing hand, arm, or leg is experienced in the same position as it was at the time of injury.[23] At the same time, the phenomenon isn't merely psychological or "in the head," because severing the nerves that connect the stump to the brain extinguishes it. Instead, Merleau-Ponty says that we need to see living experience as the place where the physiological and psychic "gear into each other" (PP 77), where—to use better, less Cartesian terms—the *biological* and the *personal,* while different, nonetheless overlap and implicate one another. For Merleau-Ponty this differentiated overlapping is well accounted for by the living body and the intentional arc. To be sure, I am a biological being with a genetic inheritance which develops in certain patterns, which is prey to disease, trauma, and contingency. Yet I am also the cognitive-carnal power to throw myself into possibilities as personal projects, to organize the world as a situation, to cast it as a familiar setting. It is in terms of these two intertwined layers or modalities of embodied life (the biological and the personal) that phantom limb and anosagnosia (among other disorders) can be understood in a promising way:

> What it is in us that refuses mutilation and disablement is an *I* committed to a certain physical and inter-human world, who continues to tend toward his world despite handicaps and amputations and who, to this extent, does not recognize them. . . . The refusal of the deficiency is . . . the implicit negation of what runs counter to the natural momentum which throws us into our tasks, our cares, our situation, our familiar horizons. To have a phantom arm is to remain open to all the actions of which the arm alone is capable; it is to retain the practical field that one enjoyed before mutilation. In the self-evidence of this complete world in which . . . is still present the project of writing or playing the piano, the cripple [*le malade*] still finds the guarantee of his wholeness. But in concealing his deficiency from him, the world cannot fail simultaneously to reveal it to him . . . [for] I can no longer, if I have lost a limb, be effectively drawn into it. (PP 81–82, PP-F 97)

In short, phantom limb and other disruptions of the body image occur because of the overlap and, in these specific cases, the conflicts between one's biological life and one's personal projects. In fact, these conflicts are typically more acute directly after a trauma: with time and practice these two "spheres" tend to synchronize. While Merleau-Ponty's discussions focus on rather extreme examples, the above passages should make clear that none of us is immune to such disruptions. When we are ill, when we travel, when we were toilet training, for instance—these are all times at which our biological and personal lives are in conflict. And debilitating trauma or illness is always a horizon of our lives. Be that as it may, Merleau-Ponty's recognition of these two layers, modalities, or "folds" of embodied experience is central to his work on the living body. Above, I named these layers as the biological and the personal, but throughout *Phenomenology of Perception* Merleau-Ponty uses a number of different terms to talk about them: (1) the habit body and the personal body, (2) the impersonal and the personal, (3) the biological and the individual, (4) the sedimented and the spontaneous, (5) the organic and the existential. He is abundantly clear that this two-fold dynamic does not constitute a new dualism, for both "sides" of the dynamic are aspects of the same living body, sustained in and directed toward the natural world. Rather than a dualism or reductive monism, the biological and personal layers are in a distinctive interrelation: the first (the biological) enables the second (the personal) by providing "stable organs and pre-established circuits," and the second "sublimates" and transforms the first into a "situation" (PP 87, 84). The last clause provides our first look at a dynamic that is central to Merleau-Ponty's account of expressive cognition: the living body's ability to transform sedimented structure into new, meaningful forms. I will elucidate this ability in great detail in chapter 6 (and beyond). At this point, it is enough to see Merleau-Ponty's view that our lives dance in the ebb and flow of these two powers—the biological and the personal—in the self-same body. As he puts it:

> [M]y organism, as a prepersonal cleaving to the general form of the world . . . plays, beneath my personal life, the part of an *inborn complex*. It is not some kind of inert thing; it too has . . . the momentum of existence. It may even happen when I am in danger that my biological situation abolishes my human one, that my body lends itself without reserve to action. But these moments can be no more than moments, and for most of the time personal existence represses the organism without being able either to go beyond it or renounce itself. . . . While I am overcome by some grief and wholly given over to my distress, my eyes already stray in front of me, and are drawn, despite everything, to some shining object. (PP 84)

As living (human) bodies, we are at once a sedimented-biological life and a personal, intentional, projective power. To-and-fro, overlapping one another, sometimes in conflict . . . For Merleau-Ponty, seeing these two modalities and the various relations between them is crucial for understanding our embodied lives. For one thing, the inter-dynamic between the biological and the personal makes sense of our experiences of time—of past, present, and future. Time is literally in my joints; it is marked in and on my biological body. I don't bend over these days as freely as I once did. There is a spreading dash of gray at my temples. There is this ugly scar on my leg where I gashed it when I was six years old. Indeed, time isn't some transcendental "form" of intuition applied to experiences of one's body from outside. On the contrary, time is lived through one's body: one's body "belongs" to time and "combines" with it (PP 140). Yet time is not lived as a collection of separate instants either, for one has the personal power to integrate one's past into one's present, or throw one's present toward a future. For instance, we rather typically view past events as "leading up" to our present one, and even long-gone traumas can inform or disrupt our projects for the future. Even so, all it takes is the flu to shatter my world: I suddenly find myself thrown back into the viscera of my body—marking time by the stages of illness rather than by my aspirations. And every night my personal life slips away in the restorative vagaries of sleep. Embodied life has this strange and wonderful temporal rhythm: a weaving back, forth, and through the demands of my organism and the integrative horizons of intentional life. "Such is the lot of a being who is born" (PP 347).

Merleau-Ponty's two-fold dynamic between the biological and the personal layers of embodied life also recognizes a set of familiar psychological phenomena that typically cause problems for orthodox behaviorist and Cartesian-Kantian accounts. A first, the phenomenon of repression, was already alluded to above: when we are committed to a certain situation, a certain course of action or project, we don't "want" to acknowledge what will disrupt it (for example, one's injured hand, one's illness, or the growing conflict in a friendship). Conversely, we can become so absorbed in our bodies (in chronic pain, for instance) or some sedimented pattern of behavior, that we repress our spontaneous possibilities. In short, Merleau-Ponty's account here can explain one of Freud's most enduring insights: that repression is a fundamental experience of the living body.[24] For Merleau-Ponty, repression emerges at the level of the living body, not between a positing consciousness and a material substrate. It emerges in the relation and conflict between our impersonal operations and our intentional arc (and, to be sure, our relations with others). Repression is itself "organic," embodied: this is why "positing consciousness" can be so surprised to discover it.

Beyond repression, the two-fold body also helps us understand the emotions. For Descartes, emotions are strictly states of the mind, analogous to volitions and judgments—something he explicitly asserts in the Third Meditation. This intellectualist treatment is tacitly embraced by Kant and finds its contemporary analogue in accounts that place the emotions into some box in a schematic of cognitive states. There is, of course, no question that emotions are related to consciousness, but it is living-body-consciousness: emotions surge up at the intersection of impersonal and intentional life. As Merleau-Ponty says: "To feel emotion is to be involved in a situation that one is not managing to face and from which, nevertheless, one does not want to escape" (PP 86). Although terse, this sentence does begin to illuminate our emotional experiences. Joy, sadness, excitement, anger, obsession, ennui: in them (and others) we are "overwhelmed." Below the level of intellectual judgments and positions, we experience something that one's conscious-body cannot personalize and yet from which it cannot turn away: for instance, the death of a friend, the soaring burst of new-found love, the dreariness of the Sunday night blues. Given their shared place in pre-positing embodied-conscious life, and the similarity of their dynamic, is it any wonder that what we so often repress is our emotions?

The above discussions of repression and emotion are only preliminary: they are indications of how Merleau-Ponty's accounts of these important embodied phenomena will go. And there are other features of embodied existence that Merleau-Ponty discusses, such as the imagination and the erotic, which could be explored in great detail.[25] However, my primary concern has merely been to elucidate some of the explanatory promise of his account of the dynamic overlapping between these layers of the living body—the impersonal, biological and the intending, projective, personal.

We have seen, then, Merleau-Ponty's view that the biological layer of embodiment sustains the personal layer, and yet the personal folds back on the biological—weaving through and around it a field of personalized action, or a *situation*. We have also seen that one layer or the other can receive emphasis, but also that we flow between these emphases or that they come into conflict. The last thing I want to address here is Merleau-Ponty's further recognition that the impersonal can become part of the personal, that one's living body is able to incorporate things and new behaviors into its sedimented structure. He refers to this phenomenon with the term "habit acquisition" (PP 142). We might see this phenomenon with own Merleau-Ponty's example of learning to dance (PP 142–147). At first I stumble and feel like a clod. My feet just won't go that way; my already sedimented habits (and perhaps physiology) resist this new behavior. Yet these strange movements are a *possibility* for my body, and if I practice long and hard the fire may catch and they may become part of my sedimented body. This process of "incorporation" is not foreign to most of us (although for people suffering like Schneider it would be). It is how we learned to swim, play an instrument, or ride a bike. Even more basically, it is how we learned to walk, climb the stairs, and write cursive. It is at the roots of language-learning, for after all, language is a behavior (as I will argue in chapter 7). It is how "auxiliaries" such as musical instruments, prostheses, canes, and other tools become part of one's corporeal schema. At first, the impersonal, sedimented body resists; indeed, because of its habits and structures, that layer of the body *is* resistance. But when I take up these possibilities, "bend" my body to them, they can pass over from a potentiality to an actuality. They can become a deep part of my repertoire, not to be forgotten, "just like riding a bike." As Merleau-Ponty puts it, habit acquisition (or "incorporation") is "a rearrangement and renewal" of our living body; it is "our power to dilate our being-in-the-world, or change our existence by [appropriation, *annexant*]" (PP 142–143, PP-F 168).

Again, there is so much more we might develop about the features of our living bodies. This area is one of the most fecund dimensions of Merleau-Ponty's philosophy. Rather than carry out an exhaustive analysis, which would require a book of its own, I have attempted here to illuminate some central themes in his phenomenology of embodied experience and show their promise. Hopefully by now you have found some of yourself and your embodied life reflected in his discussion—more, I suspect, than you found in the lists of body parts and Latinate words you probably had to memorize in biology class. Don't get me wrong: those lists, parts, and words may well be essential if we are concerned to repair bodies (as does a doctor) or provide analytic explanations of their functions (as does an anatomist), but they don't do much to reveal how we *live* the body—sensitive, rich, and electric.

There are, indeed, many different ways to "despise" the living body, as Nietzsche put it. We can denounce it as the "prison of the soul" or the principle of sin. We can insist that our analyses exhaust it. We can dismiss it from the penumbra of "legitimate" philosophy as "not intellectual enough" or "touchy-feely." We can, in our everyday lives, ignore, forget, or overlook it, and as we saw, these tendencies are supported by the outward structure of the body itself. Yet this carnality is what we live, and as Merleau-Ponty's philosophy shows, we are in fact able to know it and articulate its features so that whole sectors of our experience become intelligible. We can see and study, for example, the way perspectives pivot around the living body. We can explore the body's intentionality and affectivity. We can elucidate the marvelous ability to incorporate gestures, habits, and activities, to make some new possible behavior a deep part of one's incarnate being. To be sure, one's living-conscious body is not a machine and it is the height of abstraction to insist that it is. Instead, it is a *style* of being—a way of being a biological creature—that is at once individual and general, at once dynamic, affective, intentional, incorporative, and contingent. It is, as Merleau-Ponty puts it in his final writings, neither substance nor matter nor machine, but *flesh*.[26]

5. Three Problems for Merleau-Ponty's Account of Living Embodiment

So far in this chapter, I have been expressing appreciation for Merleau-Ponty's work on the living body. As should be clear from what I have said, I believe this work is a singular contribution to contemporary philosophy. It is one that opens vistas for understanding our lives beyond the framework of "man the-machine," and it is one that has had a great deal of influence (acknowledged and not) on later thinkers. However, I also mentioned at the outset of the chapter that some of the most pressing difficulties for Merleau-Ponty's philosophy cluster around his account of the living body. As a coda to this chapter I think it is important to acknowledge and discuss these difficulties. I myself believe that these problems are substantial; they imply that Merleau-Ponty's account, for all its power and promise, is only an early chapter in the effort to understand and articulate living embodied experience.

A first problem for Merleau-Ponty's phenomenology of embodiment arises out of Michel Foucault's explorations of the political genealogy of the living body. At the outset, let me say that the relationship between Merleau-Ponty's and Foucault's philosophies is complex and vexed. Foucault's philosophical career really begins around the time of Merleau-Ponty's death, and so Merleau-Ponty's thought is frequently under interrogation by Foucault. At the same time, Merleau-Ponty's phenomenology and ontology of living embodiment is rich and subtle enough to challenge some of Foucault's views as well. It is because of this interesting, critical complexity that I want to move toward Foucault's most successful criticism by first circumscribing a significant problem or weakness in the so-called genealogical phase of Foucault's thought. That is, I think we can better appreciate Foucault's strongest criticism by setting out of play an aspect of his genealogical project that Merleau-Ponty would have vigorously and I believe correctly challenged: Foucault's insistence that the self, the body, and its behavior are, to use his exact terms, strictly "constituted" by societal norms and coercive practices; that the body receives all "definition," "form," and "meaning" from these social forces.

Later referred to by scholars as "social constructionism," this view has been a focus of intense research, discussion, and controversy in the last twenty-five years, and thus it has seen much modification and amelioration. As a result, my following arguments are specifically directed against the strongest, most reductive version of the view—the version that Foucault seems content to suggest in his genealogical books: "The body is the surface of the inscription of events (traced by language and dissolved by ideas). . . . Genealogy, as an analysis of descent, is thus situated within the articulation of the body and history. Its task is to expose *a body totally imprinted by history*."[27] Consider also this, from *The History of Sexuality, Volume 1*:

> This new persecution of the peripheral sexualities entailed an *incorporation of perversions* and a new *specification of individuals*. . . . The machinery of power that focused on this whole alien strain [of peripheral sexualities] did not aim to suppress it, but rather to give it . . . permanent reality: it was *implanted in bodies, slipped in beneath modes of conduct*. . . . The strategy behind this dissemination was . . . to incorporate them into the individual.[28]

In light of these passages (and many others) it would seem that "social *constructionism*" is the perfect name for Foucault's strong position on the "production" and "fabrication" of selves. For just as a builder constructs a house out of raw materials—imposing a design upon them—so too, Foucault says, does society *totally inform* or "constitute" the raw materials that make us selves. Society's orders of discourse "inscribe" and "differentiate" our bodies; its practices of knowledge and power "infiltrate" and "define" them; norms are "implanted beneath modes of conduct"; the body is "totally imprinted" by society and history.

Again, I have attempted extra care in presenting my target so that we can soon appreciate Foucault's far better challenge to Merleau-Ponty. But first we need to grasp why Foucault's strong social constructionism is implausible from a Merleau-Pontian perspective. Indeed, Foucault's explicit insistence that society is "*totally* constitutive" of one's body, imposing *all* form and definition, renders the body essentially passive and formless, a contentless material substrate, a "blank slate." However, we have already seen in this chapter that the living body is *not* essentially passive and empty of content. It surges up toward the world and (by extension) the social-cultural world through its "stable organs and pre-established circuits" (PP 87). It is an organic being, with a basic structure that makes certain actions possible and other actions utterly impossible. It has a genetic inheritance that literally *in-forms,* to some extent, the body and behavior. It has a brain and central nervous system that develop, function, and dysfunction in identifiable patterns. It is also, we have seen, a habituating system that is able to incorporate new behaviors and cultural forms, such as dancing and bike riding. Incorporation transpires not by external imposition of form, but by repetition and application in relation to social practices and norms. Whatever else we want to say about the living body, at this point it should be evident that it is no "blank slate" or "formless substrate." This conclusion requires that cultural theorists offer a more supple, inter-dynamic, and carnal account of the relationship between body and culture than a kind of social Kantianism in which the noumenal body is "constituted" by the categories of society. It requires an account that elucidates the incorporation and imposition of social forms, but also acknowledges the ways and extent to which the living body *resists* such forms—as Foucault himself comes to see.[29] And it suggests that we talk about the performance or enactment (or, as Judith Butler argues, the materialization) of such things as subjectivity, sexuality, gender, and race, rather than their "construction" or "constitution."[30]

Having made this argument that we must study the performance and materialization of such things as subjectivity, sexuality, gender, and race in living bodies, I must also say that Merleau-Ponty doesn't himself offer such a study. At best, I think we could only say he offers fragments toward such a study. This is where Foucault's genealogical project correctly bears in on Merleau-Ponty. For setting aside his reductive tendency, Foucault's thought is powerfully revealing of the coercive influence of cultural forces, systems, and norms on living bodies—and this orientation is simply not present in Merleau-Ponty's thought. For Merleau-Ponty, the experiential field is a largely happy place. For him, the body "surges" and "rises" to the world, it is our "potentiality" and "anchorage" in a field of possibilities, it is our "soaring power," and these things, I have argued, are all true. But Foucault has shown very well that there is another dimension which it would be folly to forget: the experiential field is also *political*. It is a site of force relations and coercive structures. Foucault's famous example is, of course, disciplinary power: over the last three hundred years, we living body-subjects have been increasingly subjected to tactics that aspire to render us "docile," that is, more obedient and more efficiently productive.[31] In workplaces, schools, hospitals, and prisons, in the military and in family life, he argues, we see mechanisms and practices that actively coerce our behavior, from panoptic observation to normalizing, hierarchical examinations. Although, in my view, Foucault's strong social constructionism is untenable, his insights on the political character of these familiar mechanisms and practices is utterly compelling, and there is little or no recognition by Merleau-Ponty that culture coerces our bodies in a political way. This is not to say Merleau-Ponty doesn't have a political theory, for he does.[32] What he doesn't have is a political theory *of the body*. That is, he is missing a "body politics"—and this is a serious omission.

This political-cultural lacuna in Merleau-Ponty's phenomenology has been the site of an extensive body of critical scholarship, particularly by feminist philosophers and theorists. It is not possible in this chapter to survey, much less study, the many writings, thinkers, and debates in this important movement.[33] But I do want to indicate some of its key moments. Early work on the problem of "body politics" in Merleau-Ponty's thought was done by Iris Marion Young in her classic essay, "Throwing Like a Girl."[34] Young argues that a phenomenology of feminine body comportment and motility reveals the kinds of features Merleau-Ponty has brought to light—such as projective intentionality and open, organizing motility in the field. However, she argues that these features are conflicted, negatively impacted, and disrupted by the situation women typically find themselves in. As Young puts it:

> Women in sexist society are physically handicapped. Insofar as we learn to live our existence in accordance with the definition that patriarchal culture assigns to us, we are physically inhibited, confined, positioned, and objectified. As lived bodies we are not open and unambiguous transcendences which move out to master a world that belongs to us, a world constituted by our own intentions and projections.[35]

Young reveals, in great phenomenological detail, the body politics that impact the living embodied experiences of women. For instance, the pressure for women to inhibit their body space and motion in keeping with a normalizing vision of femininity: sitting like a "lady," standing like a "girl," having "poise" rather than free and open comportment. All this comes with and perpetuates the "ever present possibility that [a woman] will be gazed upon as a mere body, as shape and flesh that presents itself as the potential object of *another subject's intentions* and manipulations."[36] In a similar way, and with a critical edge toward Foucault himself, Sandra Lee Bartky has articulated the disciplinary regimes that relentlessly target women: the weight-loss, starvation programs, the skin care and makeup programs, the dictates of deferential posture.[37] These are all aspects of body politics that women experience and about which Merleau-Ponty's phenomenology of the living body is silent.

Building upon these early insights and arguments, more recent and extended work on the cultural investments of the body has been carried out by thinkers such as Judith Butler, Elizabeth Grosz, and Gail Weiss. In some early essays, Butler argues that Merleau-Ponty's treatment of sexuality in *Phenomenology of Perception* reveals masculine and heterosexist biases and thereby reproduces certain cultural structures of normalizing sexuality.[38] In *Bodies That Matter,* Butler shows that embodied sexuality itself (and not merely gender) is an effect of power dynamics, regulatory norms, and discursive practices. Working within this general domain, Gail Weiss has shown that Merleau-Ponty's insights about the body image are only a rough and partial beginning.[39] In *Body Images: Embodiment as Intercorporeality,* Weiss argues convincingly that a person does not have a body image, per se, but several body *images,* which are thoroughly informed by social and cultural structures, such as sex, race, gender, ethnicity, social class, and religion, among others. Further, Weiss elucidates, well beyond Merleau-Ponty, the fluid spontaneity of our body images, and also the ways in which those images can be in conflict and even self-destructive. In a somewhat different direction, Elizabeth Grosz has demonstrated the inordinate difficulties that emerge for any effort to think about the body, and women's bodies in particular.[40] These difficulties emerge from profound, masculine biases in the discourses of philosophy and the natural sciences, but also from the fluid and multiple (and not binary) forms of lived embodiment that exist. What we get then from these diverse accounts of body politics, and others as well, is a fairly decisive recognition of a problematic limit in Merleau-Ponty's account of the living body. That is: there is a far more complex involvement between the living body and culture than he was able to imagine, much less recognize. The upshot is that his philosophy is more or less silent on this crucial issue and, to some extent, it thus becomes complicit in supporting cultural norms that have had deleterious effects on many people.

The above discussion of the problem of politicization-enculturation already points to a second major problem in Merleau-Ponty's phenomenology of the living body: that it is wholly incognizant of *sexual difference.* This is to say, his philosophy doesn't acknowledge, respect, or even seem to notice profound differences between men and women in the living experiences of their bodies. All of the feminist theorists named above press this point against Merleau-Ponty, but it has been dramatically underscored and elaborated by Luce Irigaray.[41] For Irigaray, sexual difference isn't just one concern among many. Rather, she argues, it is "one of the major philosophical issues, if not the issue, of our age."[42] For her, the ability to think through and celebrate sexual difference is the pathway for a radically transformed culture, epistemology, and ontology. It is also, she says, the threshold for a new understanding of the passions and desire, and thus, the possibility of a new ethics (of sexual difference).

I would say that the vast body of Irigaray's writings has been in the service of rigorously thinking through sexual difference, and she has utilized a number of different strategies to do so. In one mode, she is engaged in critical interrogation with the dominant philosophers of the western tradition, including her contemporaries. She also engages in the practice of retrieving and illuminating the works of influential women whom the masculinist tradition has left behind. Most important for my discussion is her ongoing effort to carry out a phenomenology of female embodiment. For example, Irigaray expresses time and again that women have sex organs—organs for pleasure—on the outside and the inside. They have multiple sets of lips for caressing and enveloping a sexual partner. They have inter-uterine folds that shed blood and tissue in a monthly cycle, that can open up to conceive, carry, and give birth to a child. No phenomenology of the body will be satisfactory that doesn't recognize these and other fundamental differences and experiences women live in their bodies. As a result, Irigaray argues that Merleau-Ponty participates in what is endemic among (male) philosophers of the tradition: he presents as *universal* what is really a reflection of his male experiences; he commits "the fallacy of the masculine universal."[43] Ignoring the fundamental differences and experiences women live in their bodies—failing to even recognize there might be differences that qualify his assertive voice—he speaks too easily of "*the* living body." As Elizabeth Grosz has put this point, with extra reference to culture and race: "there is no [living] body as such: there are only *bodies*—male or female, black, brown, white, large or small—and the gradations in between."[44]

It might be wondered, what does the recognition of this fallacy, the masculine universal, imply for Merleau-Ponty's phenomenological claims about the living body? What does it imply for our efforts to think universally at all, to create general theories and accounts? With regard to the second question, it does not imply that we must collapse thought into nothing but specificity (as if we could!), but that we need to create a new, genuinely post-Platonic account of generality and specificity that recognizes the contingent, historical, limited, creative, and embodied character of generality. In my view, important work toward such an account has been done by Irigaray and Wittgenstein, but also—it must be said—by Merleau-Ponty himself.[45] With regard to the first question— the implications of Merleau-Ponty's fallacy of the masculine universal in his phenomenology of the body—one important thing which it underscores is that phenomenological claims are not subjective pronouncements or impositions of truth. As with any form of reasoning, saying, or showing, phenomenological claims (including those in this book) are insights that require a process of confirmation: upon discussion and examination some of them will need to be abandoned, revised, or limited in scope. As a general rule of phenomenological practice, this reminder implies that we need to be more self-consciously circumspect about our general claims and attentive to their limits. It also means we need heightened sensitivity—and more than Merleau-Ponty displays—to the embodied differences between men and women. It means we need to be more vigilant about the ways sedimented language and traditions efface those differences and continue to resist their recognition. And it means, as Irigaray says, that we need to create a space for women and men to think through sexual difference, celebrating it as a site of wonder, desire, and fecundity. At the end of this second set of criticisms, I do not think Merleau-Ponty's thought contradicts the contemporary efforts by philosophers and theorists to think in more pluralistic ways about living bodies, nor Irigaray's call for a "new age" of sexual difference. Rather, the problem is that Merleau-Ponty has no apparent sensitivity to its need—no awareness of the phenomena that his phenomenology is effacing.

We have seen the problem of body politics and the problem of sexual difference. A third problem in Merleau-Ponty's phenomenology of living embodiment is closely related to these: the problem of *desire*. Close textual study reveals, in a rather shocking way, that the word appears rarely in Merleau-Ponty's books,[46] and this has led theorists to pressing questions about his account of the body. For one, what even is desire for Merleau-Ponty? Certainly he would deny the traditional dichotomy between a merely biological account of desire and one that is pure enculturation. In keeping with his other work on the living body, it is virtually certain he would argue that desire is both biological and cultural, both impersonal and incorporated. But what are the nuances of this account? A generous study of the vexed "Sexuality" chapter of *Phenomenology of Perception* yields an interpretation that Merleau-Ponty views desire (or sexuality at least) as a mode of body intentionality. Indeed, we have already seen Merleau-Ponty's view that Schneider's lack of diminished sexual function is tied to the impairment of his intentional arc. However, Alphonso Lingis has argued that this view of desire as "significance" is insufficient.[47] For one thing, Lingis argues, it ignores the living experience of the affective force and drive of desire. But he also says it overlooks the extent to which desire, sexual desire, at least, seeks a kind of orgasmic disintegration and disorganization of self. Clearly, Merleau-Ponty's rather vague suggestions in this chapter cannot be a sufficient phenomenological account of desire.

Dorothea Olkowski, for her part, has pressed this objection further.[48] She argues that Merleau-Ponty's "Sexuality" chapter isn't about sexuality at all. At best, it is a partial account of *sensuality*: eros, and not libido. Olkowski further argues that his omission is no accident: it is a direct implication of his inability to recognize sexual difference which, she says, is fueled by his inability to think space as the "interval" in Bergson's (and Deleuze's) sense of the word. I believe that these are important, forceful challenges to Merleau-Ponty's work on the living body, for in the absence of a satisfactory theory of desire, he has bypassed a central, pervasive feature of human embodied life. And it is a feature that would seem to have an important role in any sufficient theory of *motivation*.

Body politics, sexual difference, desire: I believe that these are three gaping holes in Merleau-Ponty's work on the living body and I haven't pulled any punches in presenting them. At the same time, I do not believe that any of them *shipwreck* his phenomenology of embodiment. Instead, these lacunae call for further elaboration, for deeper sensitivity, for recognition in different directions than Merleau-Ponty was able to give. In fact, they have to some extent inadvertently inspired a fecund, energized body of research by theorists that has become a major movement in contemporary thought. In this section, then, I have uncovered some ways in which Merleau-Ponty's phenomenology of the living body is dated. Nonetheless, I would also say that if theorists have been able to demand and carry out treatment of these features of embodiment, it is to some extent because Merleau-Ponty, following Nietzsche, brought our carnal lives to philosophical significance in the first place. It is also a measure of how far so many philosophers and theorists have come from the Cartesian image of the body-object-machine. Viewed in this light, the work in feminist philosophy and theory I have indicated here is not wholly alien to the spirit of Merleau-Ponty's philosophical work on the body, even while, in diverse important ways, it goes beyond it.

In the next chapter my arguments will go beyond the body too, for as Merleau-Ponty insists, embodied subjectivity is also *intersubjectivity:* living bodies are involved with other living bodies from the start, and the perceptual field is social through and through. No presentation of Merleau-Ponty's ontology of living reality would be complete without elucidating this crucial aspect of his thought and exploring its powerful implications.

4 Elemental Alterity: Self and Others

The face of another is a surface of the elemental, the place where the elemental addresses, appeals and requires the involution in enjoyment which makes my eyes luminous, my hands warm, my posture supportive . . . my face ardent.
—ALPHONSO LINGIS[1]

1. Toward Elemental Alterity

In the course of my previous arguments, Descartes's philosophy has been essentially dismantled. The Cartesian theory of perception as an internal, subjective veil of ideas hiding objective reality is rooted in fallacies; his method of doubt presupposes the very worldly experience it aims to call into question; he violates our experiences of the world so that he can depict the world as an object or a collection of objects; and he reduces our living flesh to mechanistic function. By now it should be clear that Merleau-Ponty's ontology offers a whole new paradigm for understanding ourselves and our relations with the world. With this new ontology, we finally have a way to abandon a deeply influential, but flawed paradigm of the self and worldly experience that is based on an abstract, dualistic metaphysics. By now it should also be clear that Merleau-Ponty's ontology of living experience is not opposed to science; it is not "anti-scientific." Merleau-Ponty's phenomenology is not some romantic subjectivism, intuitionism, or mysticism, but on the contrary, *another way of knowing*—a worldly, empirical way of knowing about ourselves and reality, about life and life experiences, that neither replaces nor can be replaced by the explanatory operations of science. This is a far cry indeed from Descartes's programmatic claim that experience is "merely subjective" and that physical science is "purely objective." It is a new, promising way to understand the relationship between life and science beyond the Cartesian paradigm.

But perhaps some readers will be thinking: "Alright, yes, I accept the deficiencies in the Cartesian picture. Let's move on." If this is one's response, then a major, early line of argument in this book has been successful: the Cartesian ontology that sustains Newton, classical empiricism, Kantianism, behaviorism, and notions about the "total objectivity" of science has been undermined. It is indeed time to think anew. However, even if the reader is persuaded, there is one final domain in which we must measure Merleau-Ponty's ontology against the Cartesian paradigm, and that is its ability to illuminate the fact and character of our relationships with others. This aspect of Merleau-Ponty's philosophy is particularly promising and has energized a great deal of scholarly work. I must also stress that for Merleau-Ponty our relationships with others—other perceivers, other living bodies—are not secondary to our embodied subjectivity and our relations with things in the world. As we saw earlier, his ontological triad "self-others-things" is a synergy, and the three modalities must be appreciated as symbiotically interwoven:

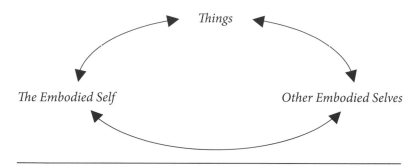

The Natural and Cultural World

If my presentation of Merleau-Ponty's ontology (chapters 2–4) treats his accounts of the perceived world, the embodied self, and others somewhat separately, this is only for the convenience of presentation. These modalities all have equal weight and must be understood as co-original in the fabric of living experience.

My present task, then, is to elucidate Merleau-Ponty's account of intersubjectivity, his phenomenology of the living relations between self and others. To do this I think it will be particularly fruitful to elaborate his account in relation to two much-discussed philosophical problems: the traditional problem of other minds and the contemporary problem of alterity. The first of these is a problem of knowledge: "How do we *know* other minds exist beside our own? What justifies our concept of other minds?" The second is an ontological problem that has irrupted around the philosophy of Emmanuel Levinas: "What *precisely* is the nature of the relationship between self and other? How is this relationship fundamentally experienced? What is the point of contact between self and other?" In relation to the first of these problems, Merleau-Ponty's philosophy contains an explicit, decisive response. Frankly, I believe that he has solved the epistemological problem of other minds once and for all, and this is no small feat. In response to the second, ontological problem, I think that Levinas has identified important features of the alterity relationship that Merleau-Ponty did not recognize. I will elaborate those features and show why they really matter. Nonetheless, I think there are some difficulties, some vexed aspects in Levinas's account of the relationship between self and other that Merleau-Ponty's philosophy effectively corrects. If my arguments to these conclusions are persuasive, I will have shown that—far from being superseded—Merleau-Ponty's thought remains indispensable for contemporary philosophical efforts to do justice to "the other of the other." Further, we will see that it provides important resources for an account of alterity that remains *elemental:* that is, one that is rooted in embodied life and nature. Since Merleau-Ponty's work on this subject remains notably uniform throughout his career, in what follows I will draw on early and late writings alike, particularly from the chapter "Other Selves and the Human World" (in *Phenomenology of Perception*), and the essays "The Child's Relations With Others" and "The Philosopher and His Shadow."

2. The Epistemological Problem of Other Minds

The ancient Greek and medieval philosophers never wondered if solipsism was true. They never wrestled with how to prove that other people exist. Indeed, the problem of other minds is a distinctly *modern* philosophical problem, forged in the fires of Descartes's Second Meditation. Recall that at this juncture in his argument Descartes has called the world and all materiality into radical question. The only thing he can know with certainty, he alleges, is that he exists as a thinking being, a mind. Recall also that to defend this result from paradox, he offers the wax argument to show that his perceptions of what seem to be material things are truly only mental ideas of such things that are laid down by the faculty of judgment. At that point, working to shore up this representation theory of perception, Descartes speculates:

> But then if I look out of the window and see men crossing the square . . . I normally say that I see the men themselves, just as I say that I see the wax. Yet do I see any more than hats and coats which could conceal automatons? I *judge* that they are men. And so something which I thought I was seeing with my eyes is in fact grasped solely by the faculty of judgment.[2]

Descartes's question is clear: How do we know that there are minds behind these behaving bodies? They could be, he says, machines or "automata" and not people. Technically, it must be admitted that Descartes's problem is worse than he recognizes, for at this point in his reasoning he can't even know that behaving bodies exist beyond his mental ideas of them. But even in the way he raises it, the problem is pressing, although it seems apparently absurd. In fact, it seems so absurd that most people ridicule philosophers for raising it. For, on one hand, we *know* other minds, other people exist; if there is *anything* people would say they know for a fact, it is this. Yet, given the operations of Cartesian doubt, is it really knowledge or mere assumption? Put another way, how we can justify our certain knowledge that other people exist?

Historically, this problem is ignored for some time. There is no awareness of the problem of other minds in Spinoza, Leibniz, Locke, or Hume. Even Descartes lets the question drop and does not feel compelled to revisit it in the Sixth Meditation. However, Berkeley (to his credit) understands the force of the problem and offers a widely accepted solution: that our knowledge of others is a "judgment by analogy." As Berkeley says:

> A human spirit or person is not perceived by sense, [since the mind is not] an idea. . . . Hence it is plain, we do not see a man, if by *man* is meant that which lives, moves, perceives, and thinks as we do: but only such a certain collection of ideas, as directs us to think there is a distinct principle of thought and motion like to ourselves, accompanying and representing it.[3]

In other words, setting aside his problematic notion that the body is a set of ideas, Berkeley is arguing that others are known by the following rationale: "I am a mind and have a body. Here is another body analogous to mine. Thus, there is another mind or person over there." Other minds exist, and this is how our knowledge of them is justified. *Quod erat demonstrandum.*

After Berkeley, this "analogical judgment" solution will become relatively standard, the fallback solution whenever the problem comes up. For instance, in the first *Critique* Kant embraces this solution without question, defense, or credit.[4] And it must be acknowledged that this analogical judgment solution has a superficial plausibility; it seems like "common sense." The difficulty, however, is that careful examination reveals the solution to be totally unacceptable. First, it doesn't solve the problem: even granting that this reasoning process is what we do, as an analogy it is an inductive argument and thus only yields more or less probable results. Thus, it doesn't explain the confidence we have that other people exist. In short, confronting the paradox that generates the problem, this solution in effect agrees that we *cannot* justify our certainty that other minds exist, and solipsism remains a possibility. Second, as Max Scheler argues (a point Merleau-Ponty will take up from him), it is well confirmed by empirical studies that infants respond to other people before they even react to color stimuli and long before they develop the ability to reason or judge by analogy.[5] Third, it seems clear that the ability to judge some entity as another mind or person presupposes the very knowledge it seeks to explain. As Merleau-Ponty puts this point (again following Scheler):

In the last resort, the actions of others are, according to this [analogy] theory, always understood through my own; the "one" or the "we" through the "I." But this is precisely the question: how can the word "I" be put into the plural, how can a general idea of the *I* be formed, how can I speak of an *I* other than my own . . . how can consciousness which, by its nature and as self-knowledge, is in the mode of the *I,* be grasped in the mode of the Thou, and through this, in the world of the "One"? (PP 348)

Indeed, I must already have the concept of "other person" in order to use it to formulate my analogical conclusion. So from where do I get knowledge of the concept? If one says previous analogical judgments, then one has begged the question. I should also mention that the recent temptation to solve this problem by claiming that others are "an inference to the best explanation" is in the same situation: to infer by best explanation that others exist is to presuppose the very concept for which we need to account. In sum, the analogical judgment solution is no solution to the problem of other minds, and it is not clear that any attempt to account for this knowledge through the use of *reasoning* can avoid these three decisive objections.

Jean-Paul Sartre also saw the difficulties in knowing other minds through reasoning, and in *Being and Nothingness* he offers an experiential solution to the problem.[6] It is important to briefly visit Sartre's well-known solution because the nature and force of Merleau-Ponty's alternative will emerge by contrast to it. In the section titled "The Look," Sartre begins by countenancing the problem: when I look at others, when I objectify them, even when they appear as a "drain hole" in being, sucking in experience, the other's subjectivity remains only probable.[7] To be sure, as an object for me, the other's subjectivity cannot in principle be present, and therefore any inference to "other subject" presupposes our knowledge of otherness. So where does that knowledge come from? Sartre says that there is only one possible answer: if I cannot encounter the other's subjectivity when I objectify him or her, I must know other subjectivities through my experiences of *becoming objectified.* Imagine, Sartre says, that while I am peering through a keyhole, I hear a sound behind me—a step or a creak: in that moment I am frozen in my tracks; I am caught before the gaze of another. In that moment, that experience, I become an object and this could only happen if I experientially know other subjectivities. Even if I turn around and there is no one there in this case, becoming an object is only possible for me if I have already lived the experience of "being seen by an Other." As Sartre puts it: "It is shame or pride which reveals to me the Other's look and myself at the end of that look."[8] Shame is the proof that other minds exist.

There is no question that Sartre's solution to the problem of other minds is ingenious. He recognizes that the problem won't be legitimately solved through reasoning and that one must go below or outside the predicative level to the experiences that inform those judgments. Further, he bases his argument on experiences that are impossible to deny: we all have the experiences of shame or pride, and these do seem to involve knowledge of the other. The question, however, is "What price green pastures?" For Sartre's "dialectic" of personal relationships—the oppositions of myself as subject with you as object (and vice versa)—offers a theoretically possible justification of our *knowledge* of others, but only by making *inter-relationships* impossible in principle. That is, I am either subject or object to you, and there is no in-between, no relationship. In grand existentialist style, Sartre embraces this impossibility by insisting "The Other, on principle, is my alienation," "The Other is my danger," "The Other is the hidden death of my possibilities," and of course, "Hell is other people!"

However, this result seems as flawed as the problem it purports to solve. As Merleau-Ponty puts it in an early essay: "In our opinion [*Being and Nothingness*] remains too exclusively antithetic: the antithesis of my view of myself and another's view of me and the antithesis of the *for itself* and the *in itself* often seem to be alternatives instead of being described as the living bond and communication between one term and the other."[9] Clearly, for Merleau-Ponty, we need a different experiential solution to the problem of other minds. We need a solution that illuminates the "living bond and communication" between the self and others that underlies our reasoning about them, as well as one that respects the fact that some relationships do decay into polarized opposition. How will this go? How do we come to know others as such in experience? How do we communicate, self and others?

The first approach Merleau-Ponty takes is less a solution to the problem of other minds than a *dissolution:* he stresses that the problem is itself predicated on a dualistic, subject-object ontology. He argues that it is only because the self is treated as a Cartesian *mind* or, in Sartre's hands, a Hegelian negativity (outside of being, outside the body, dualistically opposed to it) that the problem seems intractable. For then seeing a mere body, an *object* in this ontology, is *by definition* not to see the other's subjectivity. Under this subject-object dualism, the other's body is defined essentially the same as a rock or a toaster (matter, object, being) and the other's self can have no place there. However, we have seen that this kind of dualism is abstract and fallacious. It is an abstract conceptual schema that is built upon, and then covers over, important ontological facts: for example, the fact that the living body is badly understood as a merely material object. Moreover, this dualism cannot account for a fact that we live and know perfectly well by acquaintance: that the self is fundamentally embodied. While this inherence in the flesh means that one's self is enmeshed in the over-spilling world and is not purely self-transparent, it also means that the selves of others need not be "outside" the living world, on the other side of some metaphysical divide. As Merleau-Ponty says:

> If I experience this inhering of my consciousness in its body and its world, the perception of other people and the plurality of consciousnesses no longer present any difficulty. If, for myself who am reflecting on perception, the perceiving subject [draws] in its train that bodily thing in the absence of which there would be no other things for it, then why should other bodies that I perceive not be similarly inhabited by consciousnesses? If my consciousness has a body, why should other bodies not "have" consciousnesses? (PP 351)

In effect, knowledge of other minds only seems impossible when we start with Cartesian (or Sartrean) dualism. Thus, to abandon that prejudice is, as Wittgenstein says, "to show the fly the way out of the fly-bottle."[10]

Yet this dissolution of the impossibility is only a first step, as Merleau-Ponty is well aware. For even abandoning that dualism, we still need to understand the basis of our knowledge of other selves. How do I know that this entity facing me is another perceiving self? Can't I be mistaken? How do we get the idea of an "other self" in the first place? Merleau-Ponty's answers to these questions—his positive solution to the problem of other minds—center around his account of *behavior*. Indeed, I am not just "a body"—this way of putting it is still too static, too objectified, too Cartesian. As incarnate, I am a *behaving* body, a fleshly being who flows through the world. I am incessantly dynamic, with my heart and lungs pumping, my eyes and hands surfing the depths and riches of things. I am, in effect, a "self-moved mover," a being who is responsive to the world all around. Further, just as my body organizes perceptual *Gestalten* around it—that is, sense-laden things amid a background field—so too are my behaviors sense-laden, holistic organizations:

> If I stand out in front of my desk and lean on it with both hands, only my hands are stressed and the whole of my body trails behind them like the tail of a comet. It is not that I am unaware of the whereabouts of my shoulders or back, but these are simply swallowed up in the position of my hands, and my whole posture can be read so to speak from the pressure they exert on the table. (PP 100)

Indeed, a living, behaving body is a *projective* being: it projects out of itself, from itself as it moves through the world. These projective behaviors (for example, putting my hands on the table), involve a specific orientation of my hands and also a global reconfiguration of the rest of my body. Because my behavior is a symbiotic system and not a mechanistic collection of independent parts, I have a corporeal schema (body image) and pre-predicatively know my way around my body. It is as a symbiotic *Gestalt* that "my whole posture can be read" from the pressure of my hands: those hands gripping this way *mean* that my shoulders are extended and my torso is inclined forward. To be sure, sense and schema are bound up in my projective behaviors.

For Merleau-Ponty, it is the rich, dynamic phenomena of behavior that yield our experiential knowledge of other selves. Here I am, flowing through space, opening up an array of intentional vectors through my projects and perspectives, mapping parts of myself onto things, leaving artifacts in my wake, gesturing with my hands and eyes. But wait: here are some other beings who are also . . . *behaving*. These beings too are similarly locomotive. They project themselves in the world. They take up those possibilities I might have pursued; they look at me, gesture toward me, and reach out to grasp my hand in theirs. In the flow of life, these beings are not experienced as objects on the opposite side of some conceptual bifurcation, but as extensions of my own carnal powers. As Merleau-Ponty says:

> I experience my own body as the power of adopting certain forms of behaviour and a certain world . . . now, it is precisely my body that perceives the body of another, and discovers in that other body a miraculous prolongation of my own intentions, a familiar way of dealing with the world. . . . [T]he anonymous existence of which my body is the ever-renewed trace henceforth inhabits both bodies simultaneously. (PP 354)

In other words, through our behaviors we become paired—self and other. More precisely, since you "prolong" my intentions through your projective behavior, since you caress the things with hands not unlike mine, since you look at me with gleaming eyes, I *extend* my *self* to you. My corporeal schema and perceptual powers reflexively transfer; your resonant behavior *means* that you are "Another." Indeed, Merleau-Ponty shows that our knowledge of other minds or selves is rooted in this experiential coupling of flesh-to-flesh that is lived through our behavior.[11]

A first important thing to see about Merleau-Ponty's solution to the epistemological problem of other minds is that the knowledge or awareness of otherness through behavior is not an inference by analogy. His view isn't that one looks at one's own behavior, then looks at this other behavior, and then reasons to the conclusion that another self is there. For Merleau-Ponty, the transfer or extension of corporeal schema and intentionality is fundamentally not an intellectual *judgment*, but a lived coupling before predication. He says:

A baby of fifteen months opens its mouth if I playfully take one of its fingers between my teeth and pretend to bite it. And yet it has scarcely looked at its face in a glass, and its teeth are not in any case like mine. The fact is that its own mouth and teeth, as it feels them from the inside, are immediately, for it, an apparatus to bite with, and my jaw, as the baby sees it from the outside, is immediately, for it, capable of the same intentions. "Biting" has immediately, for it, an intersubjective significance. (PP 352)

Notice: the infant at fifteen months is not able to reason and does not perceive its own body in the same way it perceives the body of another; there is no rational inference and no perceived analogy. Instead, the baby lives its mouth from the inside as an approach to pleasure and eating. The baby sees the other mouth smiling, feels the pretense of eating on its fingers, and "couples up," mouthing along. There is here what Merleau-Ponty, following psychologist Henri Wallon, calls a *syncretic sociality,* a blurring together or overlapping of self and other than is not synthetic.[12] I hasten to add that this phenomenon isn't an abstract fiction: again, psychogenetic research confirms this kind of "syncretic" interaction with infants as early as six weeks old.[13] These empirical facts emphasize something that we all know perfectly well but forget in our Cartesian or Sartrean musings: that we literally *find ourselves* in an intersubjective world, that we have been "coupling" with other selves long before we come to explicit self-consciousness. It is in this world, amid these behaving others that we come to distinguish ourselves from them. Indeed, my very concept of "I"—as in "I think" or "I can doubt"—attests to a sociality older than me, and this finally explains why we are so confident that solipsism can't be true.

So in living experience we couple with others *as others:* the fact of their behavior *means* other selves are here and I *respond.* Below the level of judgments, subject-object dualism, radical doubt, and wondering about solipsism, I am already bound up and communicating with others in the flow of life. A second thing to appreciate about this solution to the problem of other minds is that it doesn't beg the question. For one does not need to already know some moving thing is a self in order to perceive it as behavior. On the contrary, behavior is a unique type, a "basic category" of movement that is present in our experience as such: clearly rocks don't behave, trees don't behave, toasters and waving wheat fields don't behave; they don't manifest the symbiotic, gestural, intentionality of behavior. Look and see. This being isn't a toaster or a chair; here in front of me is a "self-moved mover," a being who throws itself forward into projects with the rest of its body rippling into place, an intentional being who aims and directs as it goes. I thereby extend my own perceptual powers, and respond to this being as a self. Indeed, this extension of self to other through behavior doesn't beg the question, for it is rooted in discriminations made at the level of experience and developed over the course of our early lives.

One important strength of Merleau-Ponty's account here is that it stresses and explains our continuity with the animal world. For clearly, when we aren't slaughtering them, we can and do syncretize with animals. We extend corporeal schemata and perceptual powers to them through their organizing behavior, and even young children easily identify parts of their own bodies in the bodies of animals.[14] Recognizing that embodied behavior is central to the self and to intersubjectivity dissolves any radical bifurcation between humans and animals. Instead, as living experience amply reveals, there is a wild plurality of organic, behaving forms. Humans are animals and animals are Others, conjoined and known through their bodies in the power to behave.[15]

But almost certainly someone will object: "Isn't it possible to make mistakes on Merleau-Ponty's account? Isn't it *possible* to make mistaken 'extensions' of self to other in living experience? Doesn't this possibility entail that solipsism might be true?" The answers to these questions are "Yes, yes, and no." Yes, it is always possible to extend one's self to something that is not another self, or to fail to do so to someone who is. Yes, it is always possible to be insufficiently sensitive to the experiential characteristics that distinguish Other from thing, and this explains our deep potential for cruelty to other people and animals. However, the possibility of making mistakes in no way entails that "solipsism might be true," for one's mistaken attributions always occur in a perceptual field and psychogenetic history that is already inter-social through and through. We have been surrounded and engaged by other selves our entire lives; we develop and apply the concepts of "I" and "Other" through that ongoing engagement. Indeed, the ability to make a *mistake* in our attributions doesn't eliminate the general fact of sociality, but presupposes it.

If, in reply, one seeks to call the general fact of sociality into doubt through the evil demon argument (or some such skeptical hypothesis), then the objection—about the "possibility of mistakes"—has actually slid into a different objection. For then it isn't any longer the "possibility of mistakes" that keeps solipsism open, but radical skepticism—an approach to perception, experience, and philosophy that I set aside in chapter 1. But perhaps a third concern about mistakes could be raised which is slightly different. Perhaps this objection doesn't stem from mistakes in sensitivity (which I discussed above), but from, for example, the thought-experiment of a robot that is so *perfect* that its movements are indistinguishable from behavior. The critic says: "In this case, we would attribute otherness to a machine and be none the wiser; everyone around me could be a machine!" However, as is true of many thought-experiments, the problem with this one is that the stated conditions prevent the intended conclusion. That is, if we *really* have an entity that *is utterly indistinguishable* from living flesh, then, *ex hypothesi,* it *is* living flesh and *not* a machine. If, in reply, the thought-experimenter starts to indicate features that nonetheless make it a machine, then he/she has given up the establishing premise of "utter indistinguishability," and the process of distinguishing Other from thing once again becomes a matter of sensitivity. In short, this third version of the objection by mistakes (the "thought-experiment" version) either defeats itself or reduces to the first—which has already been answered.

Indeed, there is no escaping our sociality. Not through the most radical doubt or the wildest thought-experiments, for as soon as we formulate these skeptical strategies in language, or try to persuade others, we have smuggled in the social world. I believe this argument is incontrovertible. Even so, I think the best proof of our living intersubjectivity lies in our sensibilities, our knowledge by direct acquaintance. Don't think, look: all around us are these others organizing themselves as they go, interacting with us and with things, leaving or creating artifacts of their intentional powers.

Further, Merleau-Ponty shows that there is one kind of experience which is particularly illuminating of our relations with others, the experience of *language:*

> In the experience of dialogue, there is constituted between the other person and myself a common ground; my thought and his are interwoven in a single fabric. . . . We have here a dual being [*un être à deux*], where the other is no longer a mere bit of behavior in my . . . field, nor I in his; we are collaborators in a consummate reciprocity. In the present dialogue, I am freed from myself, for the other person's thoughts are certainly his. . . . And indeed, the objection which my interlocutor raises to what I say draws from me thoughts that I had no idea I possessed, so that at the same time that I lend him thoughts, he reciprocates by making me think too. (PP 354, PP-F 407)

The image here is quite powerful. In language, in dialogue, self and other *communicate,* that is, they "come together in one": conversation sweeps us into a common experience in which "subject" and "object" have no place, in which we are reciprocally drawn out of ourselves and our former thoughts toward the other. It is only by forgetting or refusing this experiential possibility and psychogenetic fact that our relationships collapse into subject-object duality, and it is certainly no accident that *Being and Nothingness* has little to say about language. Be that as it may, Merleau-Ponty reminds us that conversation, dialogue, language (through words or gestures) is a synergy of self and other— an interaction that exceeds the sum of its parts—in which one's self and ideas are transformed in relation with other living beings. There is no question that

Sartre is a target of these arguments. And there is no question that, for Merleau-Ponty, this is how we learn and psycho-socially develop—through these transformative interactions with others.

While Merleau-Ponty stresses that there is no dualism between self and others in living experience and conversation, he is also quite clear that there is no *monism* either—no fusion or "synthesis" into a simple unity. For although at times he uses the language of "unity," "relative indistinction," and "consummate reciprocity," this is more gestural than literal, and Merleau-Ponty typically qualifies this kind of language by underscoring the separation and distance that forever remains between self and others. For example, I perceive the grief or anger in another—in their face or gestures—and I "couple" with the other through our physiognomy. "But then, the behaviour of another, and even his words, are not that other.... For him [the grief or anger is] lived through, for me they are displayed" (PP 356). Paul suffers because he has lost his wife, but I suffer because Paul is grieved (PP 356), and there is no fusion of experience because we are in relation through our different bodies and perspectives. In a crucial sense, then, our experiences lived through our bodies remain *our own,* on the hither side of our behavior and yet *meant* by that behavior. In early and late writings alike, Merleau-Ponty takes great care to respect and express this subtle, non-reductive relation between one's qualitative experiences and one's manifest behavior. There is, he says later, a *distance* between the experiencing self and behavior which is not a transcendental chasm or a dualism, but precisely a separation (*écart*), such as between two lips.[16] This separation, this dehiscence, is why I am never *quite* at one with myself. It is why, despite all our corporeal and conversational reciprocity, there is irremediable distance between oneself and others. As Merleau-Ponty says in "The Philosopher and His Shadow": "This is what *animalia* and men are: absolutely present beings who have a wake of the negative. A perceiving body that I see is also a certain absence that is hollowed out and tactfully dealt with behind that body by its behavior. But absence is itself rooted in presence; it is through his body that the other person's soul is soul in my eyes" (SP 172).

We hereby encounter what Merleau-Ponty acknowledges as "the truth of solipsism" (PP 360): not that it is possible that I am the only actual mind among all these behaving beings, but rather that I am subtly separated from others. This separation is why a person can make mistakes in specific attributions that some entity is (or is not) an other. It is why one can retreat into oneself at the end of a long, exhausting day. It is why one can withdraw from others altogether after experiencing their cruelty. But again, one can only do so *against* the social world and thus one affirms its inestimable facticity.[17] For a natural being who is born *by parents,* for a being who behaves, for a being who says "I," there is no escape from sociality, and it is only philosophical machinations that trick us into doubting it. On the hither side of sense-data, mechanistic body-objects, and the objectifying gaze is our "living bond and communication" with other selves—humans and animals alike—through our coupling behavior, contact, caresses, greetings, and conversation. Those bonds can surely degrade and our communications may break down, but only as a modality of our living community with others. In the end, then, the episte-mological problem of other minds should not be viewed as "philosophy at its most ridiculous" but rather as an invitation to reinvigorate our sensibilities to-ward this inescapable sociality as the warp and woof of our living experience. As Merleau-Ponty puts it, and for reasons we now understand: "We are in-volved in the world and with others in an inextricable tangle" (PP 454).

3. The Ontological Problem of Alterity

In the last thirty years a new problem about otherness has emerged in philosophy. This problem is not the traditional one of knowing whether other minds exist, but rather the question about the precise nature of the ontological relation between self and otherness. Indeed, can I even have *relationships* with others? Or is rather the otherness of the other beyond all ontological relation, all inter-action? Do our efforts toward and language of "inter-relations" and "intersubjectivity" actually keep us from the shock of exposure to the radical alterity of the other? Are those efforts and that language subtle ways for the ego to minimize the shock and "reduce the other to the same"? Since the late 1970s, Jacques Derrida has claimed, time and again, that alterity is the primary ori-entation of his deconstruction: his intent is not to wage a skeptical war on the tradition, not to reduce the world to a text, but to uncover decisions and tra-ditional notions that efface radical alterity when we write or think. Thus, Der-rida says, his writings aim to keep us open to alterity (irreducible *différance*), and that "deconstruction is justice."[18] Now, whether his 1980s orientation to-ward alterity is a subtle change in Derrida's project or an emphasis of what was already present from the beginning (a question of some debate), it is clear that he is inspired in this direction by his former teacher, Emmanuel Levinas. Levinas is the thinker of "radical alterity," of "the other of the other," and Der-rida fully acknowledges his debt.[19] What then is this influential philosophy of alterity that Levinas has bequeathed to us? How does Levinas's account of the non-relation—the "ir-relation"—between self and other generate a philo-sophical problem to which Merleau-Ponty's thought may be relevant?

At the end of chapter 2, I briefly mentioned that Levinas's central philo-sophical project is to reveal the transcendence of the other and the ethical encumbrances that accompany it. His aims are to reveal how the other is experienced "beyond" totality, "before" systematic thought, action, or relations, and to show how the fundamental encounter with the other shatters what he calls the "ipseity of the 'I.'" Most philosophers who develop views on the self-other relation believe that their accounts open us to the other, but in fact, Levinas claims, they end up effacing the other's transcendence in the name of some totality. Levinas argues that this violence to the other is exemplified by Hegel's thought—in which the other is treated as an antithetical object through which the subject (the "I") synthesizes toward a higher possibility: "I" and "other" synthesized in the totality of the *Begriff* (Notion). But, he says, it is also deeply there in Heidegger, for whom particular beings, particular existents (which seems to include people), are typically passed over on the way to being. And Levinas implies that Merleau-Ponty is in a similar position: his phenomenology of reciprocal intersubjectivity gathers the other into a totality, a system of indifferent exchange, which ends up "reducing the other to the same."[20] As a result of all this, Levinas argues that we need a radically different way of understanding our relations with others: the other, in its infinite otherness, is experienced prior to such systematic relations. The other is never "present," never "here," never "given," but always transcending me, beyond any image or presentation. In a phrase, the other is "not-present" in "the face" through language—the language that asserts the other, that questions me, that appeals to me for bread.

Having said this much, the problem of alterity should be starting to emerge. For the great challenge after Levinas is to understand and evaluate his remarkable arguments that the fundamental relationship with the other is not a phenomenon, not empirically present to us. The other, he insists, is not present but "absolutely transcendent." My relationship to the other is not a totality, but infinity—a unique relation that reveals the limits of my self and its finite relations. How can we grasp the infinite? How can we understand a relationship the very character of which is to "not-be-in relation"? What does this view imply for Merleau-Ponty's promising account of intersubjective coupling and conversation? Is his account justly depicted by Levinas as a totalizing system that effaces alterity? While some contemporary writers appear to assume that Levinas is correct on these last questions, the truth is that the relationship between Levinas and Merleau-Ponty is extremely complex, and Levinas himself seems aware of this complexity. For while Levinas seems committed to sweeping Merleau-Ponty along in his critique of totality, he also seems hesitant to do so—hesitant to address him quite so freely or frequently as his other targets. Further, some of the criticisms that Levinas does develop (or imply) against Merleau-Ponty are peculiarly strained: some are illuminating to be sure, but others feel forced, ungenerous, even clearly mistaken.[21] Finally, some of Levinas's own positive terms and claims overlap with Merleau-Ponty and are perhaps inspired by his texts: for instance, the importance of language in our relations with others; Levinas's talk of the other as "the hither side" of presence; and his later emphasis on "substitution" in the flesh.

We see then that the relationship between these thinkers is complex and contestable, and therefore energizing as we attempt to understand our relations with others. Thus, in what follows I will endeavor to sort through and adjudicate some of the complexities. I will show some great advantages in Levinas's account, but also some difficulties that Merleau-Ponty's philosophy can ameliorate. The result will be an attempt to do justice to the best in each thinker: to begin rendering an account of alterity that remains firmly *elemental.* That is, an account that respects the irreducible otherness of others while remaining rooted in the elements of flesh, animality, and nature.[22]

It is important, I think, to begin by noting one final complexity: this is the fact that Levinas's two major works are themselves in tension on several important points. It is quite clear that Levinas partially intends *Otherwise than Being* to repair problems in the central themes of his earlier work, *Totality and Infinity*—themes such as the nature of sensibility, the univocity of expression, and the formation of the ego. So there is not just *one* "Levinas" with which we must contend. Thus I will start with *Totality and Infinity,* with an aspect of its argument that is particularly compelling: Levinas's deep insight that the other *interrupts* my living experience, my projective organizations of the world—his view that the other puts me and my ideas in *question.* We have already seen that for Merleau-Ponty the relation between self and other is about interacting or "coupling" through behavior. It is about distinct embodied selves coming together in syncretic overlapping, as in a conversation or a handshake. I have suggested that this is a promising, non-dualistic account of how we know and engage one another in the flesh. But, I hasten to add, it isn't *all* that happens at the fundamental level of those relations, for we are also, otherwise, challenged by others, thrown into question by them. To be sure, we can be arrested in our subjectivity, called into question by the other's face, behavior, or criticism. As Levinas says:

> Critique does not reduce the other to the same . . . but calls into question the exercise of the same. . . . We name this calling into question of my spontaneity by the presence of the Other ethics. The strangeness of the Other, his irreducibility to the I, to my thoughts and my possessions, is precisely accomplished as a calling into question of my spontaneity, as ethics.[23]

Indeed, there I was moving through the world, organizing it through my living body, projecting myself and my intention-directions, greeting others, thinking, opining in conversation, when suddenly, *wham:* the other forgoes "niceties" and suggests that I am mistaken. My spontaneity, my flowing self is arrested. My intellectual command is shattered—I am put in question. Or there I am on the way to work and a woman in the street appeals to me, holding up her hungry child. The woman is not seeking a handshake or dialogue. Rather, she is imploring me to give of myself to her. The moment puts me in question: "Why don't I give her more?" "Why did I try to look away?" "Am I really so insensitive and selfish?" On this score, Levinas is spot-on correct: the disruption of my stability and self-command is a fundamental way in which others are experienced, and the self takes shape through this experience and sets up egoistic defenses against it.

It is important to see here that Levinas is not talking about the Sartrean notion of "being objectified." On the contrary, he is clear that "being called into question" is not a process of objectification, but one of *subjectification:* of being thrown back into oneself, of being exposed as an ego who assumes too much in its joyous possession of the world. As Robert Bernasconi has argued on Levinas's behalf, this relation is not one of reciprocity in the sense of exchange; rather it is a one-way street and it heads toward me as a subject.[24] Having said that, it isn't at all clear that this shattering encounter is the primary or *only* fundamental relation. This strong, exclusive priority is not really established either by Levinas's arguments or by the findings in child-development research.[25] Nonetheless, "becoming subjectified" is at least one primary way the self encounters others—and Merleau-Ponty doesn't recognize it. Being called into question by the other: this basic experience illuminates several ethical dimensions of living experience. It begins to illuminate—at the heart of everyday life—the birth of responsibility, the inescapability of conscience, and our resistance to the ethical. These are aspects of our social life that Merleau-Ponty's account of intersubjectivity does not and perhaps cannot address.

Thus, I believe that Levinas's account of the "one-way" encounter with the other, marked by the breach of the same, is a great strength of *Totality and Infinity.* The interruption of the self by the other happens and it must be acknowledged as another way "other minds" are experienced and known. But there are also elements of Levinas's early book that I am confident Merleau-Ponty would have contested, some things in this text *he* would have "called into question." A first of these might be called the book's "problem of sensibility." As I already suggested (in chapter 2), in *Totality and Infinity* Levinas depicts the sensible, sensitive body as essentially consumptive and possessive.

For Levinas the eye, by nature, is "avid," hungry, totalizing.[26] The hand, in its "proper nature," is grasping, clutching. "Possession," Levinas says, "is . . . the destiny of the hand. The hand is the organ of grasping and taking, the first and blind grasping in the teeming mass: it relates to me, to my egoist ends, things drawn from the element."[27] Indeed, for Levinas, the body and its sensibility is a "regime" of sojourning enjoyment that "overcomes" the alterity of the Other.

However, at this point it should be clear that Merleau-Ponty's philosophy of the living body calls these explicitly Platonic allegations into doubt. The hand "takes," yes—but only in one of its modalities. For it is also the hand that caresses the child to sleep, that gestures, that surrenders to the textures of the world. And while the gaze that Sartre depicts is an objectifying one, we recall that for Merleau-Ponty vision is "more dispossession than possession" (PS 170). It is, he says in *Phenomenology of Perception*, "literally a form of communion." Consider the passage which accompanies this phrase:

> The relations of sentient to sensible are comparable with those of the sleeper to his slumber. . . . *I* am breathing deeply and slowly in order to summon sleep, and suddenly it is if my mouth were connected to some great lung outside myself which alternately calls forth and forces back my breath. . . . In the same way I give ear, or look . . . and suddenly the sensible takes possession of my ear or my gaze, and I surrender a part of my body, even my whole body, to this particular manner of vibrating and filling space known as blue or red. (PP 212)

Whatever else one wants to say about it, this is an account of sensibility that is not "totalizing consumption." It is an account that stresses sensibility as surrender, fascination, or communion with what is *not* me. Indeed, as we have already seen, for Merleau-Ponty sensibility is not possession but an *overture, opening, l'ouverture au monde;* it is our access to an over-spilling world, our greeting approach to other selves who are not present, but transcendent, who are "certain absences" traced out by their behavior (PS 170).

In sum, there is simply no room in *Totality and Infinity* for understanding sensibility as *communion,* and no understanding of communion that isn't *totality.* Instead, the logic of this text is a series of equivalences that Levinas seems content to affirm: *relation* equals *possession* equals *consumption* equals *the reduction of the Other to the Same.*[28] However, this basic premise is flawed: not only does it obscure the important differences between these terms, but it fails to engage Merleau-Ponty's extraordinary insight that sensibility is a relation that does not equal possession. This insight then brings enhanced understanding of the "reciprocity" between self and other. For Merleau-Ponty, the word does not denote an *exchange* that goes out and back with systematic equality and indifference. Instead, as we saw in the previous section, reciprocity and "coupling" is about *extending oneself* to another through the interactions of our behavior. It is about acknowledging the other and responding to this other as another self or person. I do not mean to suggest that Merleau-Ponty unpacks or even appreciates the ethical dimensions of this encounter—the sheer *responsibility* of it—for I don't believe that he does. But Levinas has a tendency to treat the language of reciprocity, inter-relation, and coupling as inescapably, essentially, totalizing systematics—as though these words *could only possibly mean* totality—and this is to ignore the transcendence Merleau-Ponty connotes with these concepts.

So there are these Platonic sediments in *Totality and Infinity,* this dubious view of sensibility and the body—a view with which Levinas will himself become uncomfortable. There is another problem relating to the body in his early book—what I think of as its "struggle with dualism." I want to be careful here because it is not uncommon to hear Levinas's thought rather quickly dismissed as "a retreat to dualism" and that is, I think, too unsubtle. *Totality and Infinity* contains important passages which strongly suggest that Levinas does not propose a dualistic relationship between the self and the body, for example: "Enjoyment accomplishes the . . . separation, which is not a cleavage made in the abstract, but the existence at home with itself of the autochthonous I. . . . [The soul] to be sure dwells in what is not itself, but it acquires its own identity by dwelling in the 'other' (and not logically, by opposition to the other)."[29] Elsewhere, Levinas stresses the relation of self to body as a "terrestrial" one: not a dichotomy, but a "separation." In passages such as these, Levinas evidently seems to be working toward a non-dualistic account of the difference between self and body, and by extension, between self and other. However, the problem or "struggle" is that Levinas says at least as much in his earlier work to drive this difference all the way to opposition and dichotomy. Thus, my concern here is not that Levinas's philosophy *is* dualistic, but that he substantially equivocates on the matter.

There is no question in this context of doing the close textual analysis required to expose this problem in all its details, but I hope to say enough to show that there is a problem. Part of the complexity is that this equivocation is closely intertwined with another one that mars some of Levinas's argument: his sliding use of negation, the "not" in his language, to mean both "interruption" and "opposition." To consider the first of these terms: Levinas uses negation to mean "interrupt" or "break up" or "breach," as in: "The psychic life . . . does *not* exhibit itself in history . . . it *interrupts* historical time."[30] I believe this is an important innovation. It is a radical and original way to redeploy negation and it has had tremendous influence on several strands of contemporary thought. However, Levinas also uses negation to *oppose* ontology, to place his ethics *outside* ontology, so far outside of ontology that ethics is *prior* to ontology. It is evident that using negation as "interruption" does not have the same meaning as "oppositional priority," even though Levinas frequently treats them the same or slides indiscriminately between them.

A similar problem—perhaps a permutation of the same problem—appears with the separation-relation between the self and the body, and the self and the other. On one hand, as suggested above, Levinas refers to the relation not as an opposition or a dichotomy, but as an "interruption" of enjoyment. Yet he also slides to formulations that cast the separation in strictly oppositional terms. Some of this dualism is implicit, such as when Levinas refers to the flesh of the face as a "plastic image," or to skin as a covering that dissimulates and deforms the other;[31] or when he argues (at some length) that the other cannot be murdered, suggesting that the other is so removed from his or her body that he or she is beyond violence. However, some of this dualism is utterly explicit—for example, when Levinas insists that ethics is opposed to sensibility and overcomes it; or when he says that the facing position, the moral summons, is "opposition par excellence."[32] In all this, then, we see a struggle, an equivocation, a temptation to dualism that writes its way rather deeply into the text and which, from Merleau-Ponty's perspective, must be challenged.

The third major problem of *Totality and Infinity* that I want to address is what I think of as its "problem of nature": Levinas's insistence that the ethical is *not* continuous with the natural world, that it is "outside" nature, that it *breaks* with nature. For Levinas, nature is the principle of mystification. It separates us from the infinite and has nothing to do with the ethical-theological relation that is delivered in the face through language. Indeed, Levinas defines language as the very power to break the continuity of nature and being.[33] One difficulty immediately arises: is such a definition of language really true? Is language really a "magical act" outside of nature? Doesn't contemporary work in cognitive development show us, on the contrary, that language is a natural phenomenon, that it is quite powerfully explained in terms of certain brain structures and capacities that have evolved in nature? In the early twenty-first century—in the wake of the cognitive revolution—can we plausibly deny this? But there is a second difficulty with nature in *Totality and Infinity*, and it rests in Levinas's claims about the specific modalities of language that demarcate the ethical: speaking, thematizing, stating, proposing, questioning. He insists: "Signification arises from the other stating or understanding the world, which precisely is thematized in his language."[34] What then is Levinas to say about animals? Nothing. Not a word. And for essential reasons: not only does his account of language as thematic spoken discourse preclude our being in ethical relations with animals, but Levinas repeatedly affirms that transcendence is only possible between humans, for example: "It is our relations with men . . . that give to theological concepts the sole signification they admit of," and "only man . . . could be absolutely foreign to me."[35] What seems evident then is that Levinas's ethics—his eschatology in *Totality and Infinity*—represents a dramatic break with nature, a break with animals, a break with our animal nature, and it becomes puzzling what sense Levinas could make of, say, "environmental ethics" or "the *ethical* treatment of animals."

I believe that this is an unsurpassable difficulty in his earlier work. Levinas has cast the ethical relationship through thematic language so specifically, so intellectually, and in such oppositional terms that it seems impossible to reconcile it with our natural life and natural history. As non-continuous with nature, as a radical break with the elemental, Levinas's notion of transcendence is, in an important sense, *supernatural*. However, one of the great strengths of Merleau-Ponty's account of carnal intersubjectivity is that we don't have to go so far: we get transcendence *within* nature, we get contact and interaction with the irreducibly other through our behavior—toward human and non-human animals alike. I have already shown that this is not a "reduction of other to the same," not a collapse into totality, for we have seen that this criticism is based on a flawed understanding of the sensible. Indeed, perhaps Levinas has misidentified the basic principle of ethics when he defines it as "thematizing language." Perhaps, more deeply, the ethical relation with the transcendent other is marked by embodied sentience and pain—as Levinas himself will later appreciate.

In all this we approach a question that frequently surfaces in contemporary discussions: "Is Levinas a transcendental philosopher?" The key term, "transcendental," of course derives from Kant who defined it in radical distinction to the "empirical," which to him meant something like empiricism. But perhaps two hundred years later—and after Darwin—we should give this frequent question about Levinas a new meaning: "Are Levinas's theories of the self and the other compatible and in continuity with the facts of evolution, with the evolutionary development of consciousness and language, with the organic animality we share with so many creatures around us?" Based exclusively on his views in *Totality and Infinity*—his break with nature, his driving alterity outside of animal nature, his critique of the elemental, his equivocal dualism—I would have to say "no."

However, a remarkable thing about Levinas is that his next major work, *Otherwise than Being*, ameliorates some of these difficulties. While his basic project and intention remain the same—to reveal the fundamentality and transcendence of the ethical relation—he develops new positions and reformulates some old ones. The results, I think, are more compelling in several respects and they move toward an account of alterity as an elemental relation. The two most important changes to observe in this context are that Levinas deepens his treatment of responsibility and substantially revises his understanding of sensibility, the flesh, and their role in the ethical relation. In fact, these two enhancements to responsibility and sensibility are intimately related. With regard to the first, Levinas is clearer in his later book that the encounter with the other is not just a "break up" of the self and being, but is also a *binding*.[36] Indeed, in *Otherwise than Being* the encounter with the other does not simply put me in question, but actually limits my free-play in the world and binds me to the other in responsibility. And it does so, he argues, not *outside* of sensibility, but now *through* it. For, he now says, it is in the flesh—not merely thematic language or "the said"—that the self and other are in "proximity." It is through their living bodies that selves experience "the painfulness of pain," "the malignity of illness," and "the adversity of fatigue."[37] Pain, fatigue, susceptibility: these are the lassitude of a corporeality that binds self to other, manifest in the inescapable diachrony of the living body that Levinas calls *ageing*:

> Temporalization as lapse, the loss of time, is neither the initiative of an ego, nor a movement toward . . . action. The loss of time is not the work of a subject. . . . Time passes. This synthesis which occurs *patiently* . . . is ageing. It breaks up under the weight of years and is irreversibly removed from the present. . . . Subjectivity in ageing is unique, irreplaceable, me and not another. . . . Temporality as ageing and death of the unique one signifies an obedience where there is no desertion.[38]

This passage is both beautiful and moving: the responsibility at the center of our lives, that is experienced "despite oneself," the binding of oneself to others, happens through what might be called our shared mortality. This sensible encounter, this "allegiance," Levinas argues, is less a "shock" than a *vulnerability*: an exposure of ourselves to the vulnerability of others, a wounding in the face of others' wounds. As Levinas now puts it: the response of responsibility for the neighbor resounds in our vulnerability.[39]

I must say that I find this notion utterly compelling. I am bound to others, responsible to them, through the lassitude of embodied life and the possibility of suffering. In our mortality, I am bound to them, bound to give of my bread to them. Through the flesh I am vulnerable to others' vulnerability. I am traumatized by my susceptibility to them—and we no doubt spend a great deal of psychic energy trying *not* to feel, trying to make ourselves "invulnerable." In all this I am reminded of a trip I made to Ethiopia, to trace back the path of my adopted daughter. We often talk about such trips in terms of "culture shock," but I think this misses the vulnerability that irrupts in such travels. The Ethiopian people I met and with whom I spoke were so dignified, so warm in the immediacy of their relations, so generous to give of their bread and coffee to me. But this is a country where polio rages unchecked, where the exigencies of daily life are met through great hardship and suffering, where medical care is shockingly scarce and prohibitively expensive, where people don't know, upon parting, if they will see their friends and family again. I was utterly overwhelmed. My senses came alive. Aware of the fragility of life, our mortal flesh, I saw the faces of the people around me—their beauty beyond aesthetics, the lines and wrinkles that testified to their daily struggles—and I was drawn out of myself toward these others, full of respect for them. It was the overture (*l'ouverture*) of approach, yes, but also the passion of a wound, and I leaked strange emotions that remain with me still: a sharper feeling for contingency, a keener sense of my binding to them, a greater generosity. To be sure, while Merleau-Ponty's philosophy powerfully explores the nature and virtue of *receptivity,* Levinas's revision of sensibility in *Otherwise than Being* promises more toward a phenomenology of *giving.*

Yet, this later work is also not without its difficulties. For while the above account of the ethical relation with alterity in terms of the lassitude and mortality of the flesh does not systematically exclude animals and need not be "outside" nature—still, oppositional dualism surges up. This is clear, for instance, when Levinas says that the animating psyche and the body "mark two Cartesian orders . . . which have no common space where they can touch."[40] Again in *Otherwise than Being,* the other is beyond the skin altogether, more nude than nudity, "without complexion."[41] Still—and again—erotic life is cast as "Luciferian."[42] The terms by which Levinas describes the other are still nearly suffocating in their negativity: the other is poverty, withdrawal, abyss; the other is experienced as immolation, abandonment, utter loss.

Here, once again, Merleau-Ponty's thought can inspire us differently: others are other in the flesh; others transcend us in their living carnality. The "in" here is not a reduction of the self or psyche to the body, but a "beyond" that is not allergic to the flesh and desire, that does not drive it to despair. The radically other, I would insist, is not "without complexion," but is lived in and through complexion. For instance, my daughter is here, *present, but beyond,* in her soft smooth skin, the freckle on her nose, the incessant bounce in her gait, and the smell of her neck. My son is here, *present, yet beyond,* in his flesh, in the slope of his posture, the ruffle of his hair, and the joy of his laughter. Indeed, corporeal style—so familiar to dancers, actors, athletes—is the trace of the other in their bodies, and there is no behavior at all if alterity is outside it. Further, there is no sufficient reason to cast transcendence exclusively in terms of loss, immolation, and negation, for it is also warmth, excitement, approach, and love. To be sure, while Levinas is insightful on the pain of our living relations, he is unable to appreciate or illuminate the soaring joy we find in them. And finally, in Merleau-Ponty you find an explicit language that is noticeably missing from both *Totality and Infinity* and *Otherwise than Being*: the language of community. As we have already seen, for Merleau-Ponty community is not about fusion or synthesis, not about totalizing systematics, but is rather a "coming together" of people who are irreducibly different through inter-animate behavior and conversation. While interruption of the self, being questioned, and vulnerability are fundamental aspects of our relations, so too indeed are the communities, the "living bonds," we find and forge as elemental beings.

So where then do we stand on the problem of alterity? No place secure, it would seem. For at this point it should be reasonably clear that neither Merleau-Ponty nor Levinas alone expresses the full nature and range of our relationships with others. Levinas, I think, teaches of the binding of these relationships, of the responsibility that flows toward others from our shared mortality, of the myriad ways our ipseity is called into question by the frank regard and appeal of others. He stresses the distance between self and other that cannot be consumed, and so illuminates the very nature of generosity and respect. Yet Merleau-Ponty reminds us of another binding: that the self and others are synergistically involved in living experience through interactive behavior. These intersubjective relations aren't the stuff of totality and they don't eliminate the differences between us. They are, instead, the very possibility of contact and community, the opening approach to transcendent others who live and breathe, suffer and perish in their bodies and not outside of them. Indeed, kindness and violence are actions performed upon others *in* the flesh and nowhere else.

But perhaps, in the end, someone will still object to that little preposition "in" and insist that if alterity is not *outside* the flesh of behavior and nature, then it is a "reduction of the other to the same." No doubt, this kind of argument has been tempting to some contemporary thinkers and is often present in Levinas's writings. However, by now it should be clear that this is really an abstract approach to alterity that trades on a conceptual dichotomy ("in/out"), when instead the task is to become alive, sensitive, and vulnerable to the multifaceted, transcendent relations we have with others in the flesh. What I have attempted to establish here is that this task must be pursued between Levinas and Merleau-Ponty, beyond them both and with, I would say, thinkers such as Alphonso Lingis and Luce Irigaray, as we seek to understand our alterity relations in ways that remain thoroughly elemental.

4. Final Words

In this chapter, then, I have argued that Merleau-Ponty's account of intersubjectivity offers relief from the longstanding epistemological problem of other minds. There is no going back to it: that philosophical problem is rooted in Cartesianism and ignores our embodied engagement with others, the social world, and language that is our legacy from birth. I have also argued that his account remains indispensable for contemporary efforts to understand the precise character of our alterity relations with others, including animals. Along the way of these arguments, I have hinted at some of the key innovations of Merleau-Ponty's late writings: his philosophically rich treatments of flesh, reversibility, and the irreducible difference (*écart*) at the heart of experience. In the next chapter my pleasant task is to elucidate these fascinating, important innovations and their implications for his ontology.

5 Later Developments: *Écart,* Reversibility, and the Flesh of the World

Here is the common tissue of which we are made. The wild Being. And the perception of this perception . . . is the inventory of this originating departure.
—MERLEAU-PONTY[1]

1. Merleau-Ponty's Transition

In the previous chapters I have sought to elucidate the central elements of Merleau-Ponty's ontology. We have seen the rationale for carrying out a phenomenology of perception. We have seen Merleau-Ponty's virtue of sensibility: the enhanced living and awareness that come from recognizing living perception as a synergistic opening onto the world. We have seen the fundamental place of living embodiment in his account of the self, as well as his important contributions toward understanding our elemental relationships with others. In sum, we have followed Merleau-Ponty's own plan in *Phenomenology of Perception* and have seen "the system 'self-others-things' as it comes into being" (PP 57). There are, of course, many other aspects to Merleau-Ponty's early ontology of living experience: for example, his treatments of time, lived space, and freedom. His work on these subjects is original and important, but not, I think, utterly essential for a primary purpose of this book: that is, uncovering his account of expressive cognition. What *is* essential to that end are the rather dramatic emendations Merleau-Ponty made to his ontology in his final writings. Indeed, in several of his working notes from the late 1950s, Merleau-Ponty writes of the need to "take up again, deepen, and rectify" his first two books.[2] This need, he says, is a result of having still retained vestiges of "the philosophy of consciousness" in the early work which keeps him from bringing his ontology to satisfactory explication. While I believe it is an error to take his comments as anything like a rejection of *Phenomenology of Perception*, there is no question that in the late 1950s, what turned out to be the final years of his life, Merleau-Ponty was inspired to a new way of thinking in which his philosophy is transformed in a remarkable way.[3]

With the recent publication of Merleau-Ponty's lectures on nature from 1956 to 1960, we can now discern that his research for them was an important source of this inspiration. Coinciding with the final years of these lectures, Merleau-Ponty composed a number of texts that manifest this transformation, in particular: "The Philosopher and His Shadow" (1958), *The Visible and the Invisible* (1959–1961), the "Introduction" to *Signs* (1960), and "Eye and Mind" (1960). In all this, as a kind of set, we see Merleau-Ponty working to "deepen and rectify" his ontology and to more fully integrate it with his account of expressive thinking and language. Nonetheless, many aspects of these late texts are consonant with his earlier works. For example, the late writings are also infused with a commitment to reveal living perceptual experience, embodied subjectivity, and our reciprocal relations with other selves. They too continue his practice of critically engaging a number of traditional ontologies that obscure our inherence in the world. However, Merleau-Ponty adds several new elements to the mix. Importantly, he develops some new master concepts for his ontology: "*écart*," "reversibility," and "the flesh." Further, he more fully works to articulate the complex relation of perceptual experience ("the Visible") to thought and ideality ("the Invisible"). And he now refers to his philosophical method as "interrogation," a method that is performed with a new voluptuous language, a new expressivity. In my conclusion to the book, after elaborating Merleau-Ponty's philosophy of expression, I will be able to say much more about his subtle, but decisive shift in method from phenomenology to expression. However, in this chapter my task is to elucidate his late, breakthrough concepts of *écart*, reversibility, and the flesh of the world. I will argue that, despite certain difficulties, these concepts remain quite compelling and productive for our contemporary attempts to understand and express our synergistic relationships with the transcendent world and with others.

2. *Écart* and Reversibility

Of all the late writings, Merleau-Ponty most fully develops and deploys his new ontological concepts in *The Visible and the Invisible*. My plan in the following sections is to work most closely with this text and draw on the other late writings as necessary. I should mention that this plan is not without difficulties, for what is published as *The Visible and the Invisible* is only the first third of a projected book that was interrupted by Merleau-Ponty's sudden death in May 1961.[4] Further, while the text is remarkably lucid, coherent, and well-organized, it was never edited by Merleau-Ponty for publication and contains some redundancies and obscurities. Finally, it must be said that despite its lucidity the book is flat-out challenging to read. This is true, I believe, because of the richness of Merleau-Ponty's new expressive language, but also because its argument is complex and subtle. As a result, I want to carefully articulate the main line of the book's argument as a necessary prelude to uncovering his new master concepts of *écart,* reversibility, and the flesh.

Merleau-Ponty begins *The Visible and the Invisible* by taking up a well-known statement from Saint Augustine: that we are all perfectly familiar with time until we try to explain it to others; then we are thrown into confusion and absurdity.[5] Merleau-Ponty says that what is true of time must also be said of perceptual experience. We are all deeply familiar with it; we are living it every day, and know it by direct acquaintance. This experience is, he says, a *perceptual faith:* not in the sense of a belief that is accepted without question, but rather as "an adherence beyond belief" (VI 28), a commitment to the world that is prior to propositional thought. The task Merleau-Ponty then sets before himself is to "interrogate" this "perceptual faith." This interrogation, he stresses, is not asking questions about perception and offering answers. On the contrary, it is, he says, an effort to take one's bearings amid the enigmatic constellations of the world.[6] It is an effort to "match this vision [of the world] with knowledge" in a way that does not deform them (VI 4). It is an effort that seeks to bring the things themselves "to expression from the depths of their silence" (VI 4). Merleau-Ponty hastens to add that his philosophical interrogation is not a reversion to radical skepticism, for that age-old gambit prejudges the answer: it starts (as we have seen in Descartes) by already deciding that perception is a form of consciousness that is metaphysically distinct from the real world. Far from that, Merleau-Ponty's interrogation seeks to ask and express what "we" and "seeing" and "world" are as lived through the perceptual faith (VI 4). For taken on its own terms, the perceptual faith is extremely difficult to discuss: it is a "closely woven fabric" that teems with paradox; it presents "figured enigmas" and "incompossible details" (VI 4). Given this complex character, we thus appreciate Merleau-Ponty's reference to Augustine's caution about time, for if this "fabric" of experience is untangled in order to explain it to others, "make sense" of it, "theorize" about it, or set up one's own philosophical agenda, then the skein of living experience is lost. Generally speaking then, Merleau-Ponty's project in *The Visible and the Invisible* is to find a way to articulate (to express) the nature and philosophical significance of this paradoxical fabric, this "wild being" (*l'être sauvage*), without deforming it in the process.

After these preliminaries, Merleau-Ponty begins by eliciting some of the strange enigmas that characterize our perceptual life. For one thing, he says, living perception is *mine* in an important sense of the word. Even without analytic knowledge of neurophysiology, one knows that perception takes shape through oneself, that one's living body is a vessel that perception cannot do without. Merleau-Ponty says:

> I see [the table] only if it is within [the] radius of action [of my eyes and my body]; above it is the dark mass of my forehead, beneath it the more indecisive contours of my cheeks . . . What is more, my movements and the movements of my eyes make the world vibrate . . . With each flutter of my eyelashes a curtain lowers and rises, though I do not think for an instant of imputing this eclipse to the things themselves. (VI 7)

Indeed, perception is something that *I* do through my living body; perceived things are organized by the contours and sensory possibilities of my body. Yet, for all that, living perception is still an encounter with what is *not me*. The things I perceive resist and displace my body; they can injure me. More, they elude my gaze, explorations, and willful judgments with their depths, solidity, and hidden sides. And the things surround me all around; they have distance, even when my eyes are closed or my attention is focused on something nearby. On the face of it then, living perception is this paradoxical experience of encountering the other-than-me *only through me*. This is deeply thought-provoking if we truly notice it. For if I envelop the things with my perceptual powers, this happens only by my being enveloped by them. (Incidentally, the grammar-check on my computer refuses to countenance the preceding sentence.) And indeed, we might notice how strange the "logic" of this double-envelopment is: it defies our usual dichotomies between activity and passivity, between subject and object. Of course, one's predicative thoughts can break this connected tissue apart by first conceiving one side ("my *subjective* perception") and then flipping over to the other side ("the *objective* things"), but in the flow of life we experience the double-envelopment without difficulty. Thus, we can see that the subjective-objective conceptual dichotomy, for one example, both draws upon the resources of the perceptual faith and also deforms it, for the dichotomy separates and juxtaposes what is in fact experienced as mutually involved.

Merleau-Ponty says that "this initial paradox cannot but produce others."[7] One of these other "paradoxes" is that one's own self has these two mutually informing aspects. For on one hand, one's living, embodied self is the seer who lights up worldly things with its sight and touch. At the same time, the seer is visible and tangible. Indeed, it is seer only insofar as it is seen; it is active and passive at once. Or again, it is beyond that classical dichotomy altogether, for it is activity in virtue of its passivity. To be sure, I touch the things of the world only by being a fleshy, bony mass. And I can touch myself as a fleshy mass, or see myself in the mirror as a thing, but only for a moment before my active powers resurge. Thus, the living self is thing and non-thing at once, and this weird fact undermines the traditional, Cartesian notion of the self as pure, transparent reflection. Instead of that abstract fiction, Merleau-Ponty says we are "a self by confusion, narcissism, through inherence of the see-er in the seen, the toucher in the touched, the feeler in the felt" (EM 124). He also shows that this strange inherence runs through our relations with others. For as we saw in chapter 4, the other's self is not reductively equivalent to his/her behaving body. Rather, Merleau-Ponty says, the selfness of the other is "a certain absence" in the flesh, a "hollow" that is "sketched out" behind their behavior (PS 172). This means the other is not utterly present in his/her flesh, but *beyond* it. Reductive behaviorism—as a reduction of the self to the present body—dissolves this subtle separation between self and body and thus violates what we know of it through experience. However, the converse error is to push this separation too far (as we sometimes see in Levinas), for if one is allergic to the flesh, one ends up turning transcendence into "the transcendental" and eradicating the possibility of a relationship between self and other. Instead of these deformations, Merleau-Ponty argues that living perception gives us something different, however weird it may be: that myself and others *overlap* through the world and the community of behavior, but still that other selves go *beyond* my behavior, gaze, and touch. "Somewhere behind those eyes, behind those gestures . . . coming from I know not [where], another private world shows through, through the fabric of my own" (VI 11).

Perceptual experience, then, is a very strange fabric indeed. It involves me and not me, self and other selves, seer and seen all at once. Even so, Merleau-Ponty argues that it would be a serious mistake to treat these paradoxical strands of the perceptual faith as "contradictions" or "problems," for then one might be tempted to strive for "solutions," "resolutions," or "syntheses." That would be to distort what we live, because these "enigmas," these "incompossibles," don't cause problems in the exercise of life; just as with time, we live them without difficulty. The problems only begin when we try to explain this familiar fabric to others or try capture it with our predicative concepts. For then we take experiences that are divergent yet co-given (me-and-not-me, self-and-body), and drive them into oppositions (subject/object, mind/matter, active/passive). In short, through a process of conceptual deformation we find ourselves not knowing what we live, waffling between "contradictories," and trying to resolve them through further conceptual machinations.[8]

So again, Merleau-Ponty's project in *The Visible and the Invisible* is to find a way to honor and express the enigmatic weave of "wild being" without following the path of those philosophies that have deformed it. The book's overall structure is a sort of deepening corkscrew. In chapter 1, "Reflection and Interrogation," Merleau-Ponty gives a first expression of the fabric of wild being. In chapters 2 and 3 (amid his critical discussions of traditional ontologies), he offers a second, more developed articulation of it. And in the rather famous, much-discussed chapter 4, "The Intertwining—The Chiasm," he gives a third, still more sublime rendering. At each level of articulation, Merleau-Ponty adds more to the mix and gradually introduces his evocative new concepts.

I want to discuss first the new concept: *écart*. Also referred to by Merleau-Ponty as "dehiscence" (*dehiscence*), "shift" (*bougé*), and "fundamental fission" (*fondamentale fission*), *écart* refers to a constitutive difference in the fabric of experience. For him, this constitutive difference is what opens, for example, the seer to the seen, but it is an opening that isn't so severe that the two aspects are divorced from one another. For Merleau-Ponty, this subtle difference, this "separation-in-relation" is what gets torn into opposition by the efforts to conceptualize experience through predication. I have previously been referring to *écart* (along with "reversibility" and "the flesh") as new concepts, even as "master concepts" of Merleau-Ponty's late ontology. However, I am now able to stress that *écart* isn't a concept at all in the usual sense; it is not used as the subject or object of a predicative statement. Rather, the term is an expressive device, we might say a "showing-concept," that Merleau-Ponty uses to gesture toward the subtle differentiation in experience that is not an opposition. As a strategically chosen, artful term—one that points toward a difference-separation that is no idea or object, substance or property—the word *écart* defies felicitous substitution and should probably remain untranslated. (I would say the same of Lao-Tsu's *Tao*, Heidegger's *Ereignis*, and Derrida's *différance*.) I should also mention that *écart* is already pre-figured in Merleau-Ponty's early writings. It is there, for instance, as the irreducible spread between figure and background in the perceptual *Gestalt*.[9] Be that as it may, *écart* becomes explicit in *The Visible and the Invisible* and Merleau-Ponty stresses that it makes possible the mutual envelopments of living experience.

Écart first receives explicit treatment in Merleau-Ponty's extended critique of Sartre, in chapter 2. It is well known that in *Being and Nothingness* Sartre offers an ontology of being and nothingness, of positivity and negativity. Sartre opens, following Hegel, by presenting consciousness (or the self) as nothing, as no *thing*. He says that no positive thing limits or defines it; the self is strictly identified as non-being, defined by the powers of evasion, refusal, and lack. On the other side of Sartre's ontology is being in its absolute plenitude: as the purely positive, the very being that nothingness lacks. What follows for Sartre, having started with these terms, is what Merleau-Ponty calls a philosophy of the "reciprocal alternative": consciousness is what is not, and being is nothing but what is. They are flip-sides of one and the same. It is in terms of this rigorous opposition that Sartre purports to speak about experience, to teach us, for example, about bad faith, the dialectic of interpersonal relations, and radical freedom. However, Merleau-Ponty argues that Sartre's "speaking about experience" can only be achieved by his equivocating on the original dichotomy.[10] This is because, strictly speaking, there can be no experience if we start with the "reciprocal alternation" of *Being and Nothingness*. Indeed, if being is truly *in-itself*, then it is completely silent in the identity of its plenitude. And if consciousness is truly nothing *for-itself*, then there is nothing to hold awareness or organize a perspective.[11] In short, Merleau-Ponty argues that Sartre's founding opposition makes perception impossible. But of course we do perceive, we do see, hear, touch, and smell the things of the world; we do see half-hidden things in perspective and profile. We do have vision as an initiation to the world that is other than ourselves. And, for Merleau-Ponty, *this entails that perceptual experience must involve a different kind of difference than opposition.* He writes to show that it involves a subtler difference, more of a separation, where the self is not divorced from the world, but rather is a part of the world that opens to it. As Merleau-Ponty puts it, "vision is a ubiquitous presence to the world itself . . . and at the same time irremediably distinct from what it sees, from which it is separated" (VI 76). Again, this separation-difference at the heart of living experience is what Merleau-Ponty calls *écart*.

In the above argument we see briefly how Sartre's dichotomy violates the perceptual faith in the name of an abstract, derivative ontological analysis. It deforms the opaque, carnal seers and hidden perspectives that are interwoven in experience by forcing them into absolute poles (being and nothingness). Merleau-Ponty says that, departing from the exigencies of the perceptual faith, Sartre's ontology sets up "a sort of Hyper-being" which is in fact mythical (VI 74). In this mythical ontology the separation-*écart* vanishes—the separation-*écart* that makes the interweaving possible in the first place. Indeed, the only difference that Sartre's ontology can countenance is the difference between being and nothingness, which is to say, the difference of opposition. But as Merleau-Ponty has shown, instead of that difference, we live something other in the perceptual faith: my flesh opens onto things and other creatures that are not me, but not opposed to me either. They are things that are not opposite, but separate from me. In fact, it is only possible to perceive them because they *are* separate from me—separate and different in space, composition, texture, function, density. If there were no difference, everything would blur into monochrome and perception as we know it would vanish. *Écart* then is elusive, easy to deform, and yet ontologically essential. It is, in a phrase, the separation-difference that makes perception possible. This separation-difference is no illusion, no fiction. Even though it is not an object, it is real and really there—as is, for example, the space between your eyes and this printed page. It is "there" as the generative possibility in every perception. At the same time, it is imperative to understand that *écart* is not a "transcendental" in Kant's sense, for it is not "external to," "outside," or "before" perceptual experience, but rather amid it, opening it up from within. We might then say that *écart* is the very working of openness in perceptual experience which creates the space or gap through which sensibility occurs. As Merleau-Ponty puts it: "My flesh and that of the world . . . involve clear zones, clearings, about which pivot the opaque zones" (VI 148), and it is, I think, in terms of *écart* as the space of these "open pivots" that Merleau-Ponty starts conceiving of living perception as our opening to the world (*l'ouverture au monde*).

However, there is another important aspect of *écart* for Merleau-Ponty, and this is his recognition that the difference-opening of self to world and others brings with it a specific kind of relation. To be sure, since the difference in experience is not so severe as to be opposition, there comes with it a certain kind of reflexivity. Merleau-Ponty says:

> When I find again the actual world such as it is, under my hands, under my eyes, up against my body, I find much more than an object: [I find] a Being of which my vision is a part, a visibility older than my operations or my acts. But this does not mean that there was a fusion or coinciding of me with it: on the contrary, this occurs because a sort of dehiscence opens my body in two, and because between my body looked at and my body looking, my body touched and my body touching, there is overlapping or encroachment, so that we must say that the things pass into us as well as we into the things. (VI 123)

At first glance the passage is overwhelming, but with closer reading the central idea here becomes clear: the *écart* that opens up in perception, between me and the things, between my vision and my body, between my self and other selves, brings with it a folding over of one onto the other. Indeed, in living perception I open onto things abidingly different from me, and yet we are not opposites. Thus, I see them "coiling back" around me; I am aware of my vision and my touching as taking shape from amid them.[12] This "folding over" is also true between oneself and others: we are so different in the flesh, in gender, race, and age, in cultural accoutrements and fashion, and yet our bodies apply themselves to the same tools. They fit themselves together in a handshake or an embrace. Further, I can *see you* seeing *me*. This type of folding-back relation is extremely difficult to think about, for it defies the categories of identity and opposition, the basic watchwords of classical thought and traditional logic. Instead, it is a relationship only through separation (*écart*), a "cohesion" of "extreme divergencies" (VI 84). It is, in a word, the very relation of *overlapping*—a folding back through difference.

In certain respects, "overlapping" may be the perfect word to express living perception. For it seems we find layers and levels of this weird reflexivity everywhere: things overlapping other things (the figure-background structure of perception), day-dreams overlapping reality, my living body overlapping things and others as they wrap themselves back around me. Alongside the various words we have already seen—"overlapping," "encroachment," "cohesion"—Merleau-Ponty also refers to this reflexive relation as "intertwining" and "chiasm."[13] In his early writings something very much like this relation was approached in the terms "symbiosis," "internal relation," and "reciprocity." But in the later chapters of *The Visible and the Invisible*, Merleau-Ponty brings these various expressions together under the master term "reversibility." *Reversibility* is his late artful term to point to the folding-back relation through divergence that runs throughout the fabric of experience. Merleau-Ponty's most well-known example of the reversibility relation is of one hand touching the other hand, which can in turn touch it back:

> There is a relation of my body to itself that makes it the *vinculum* of the self and things. When my right hand touches my left, I am aware of it as a "physical thing." But at the same moment, if I wish, an extraordinary event takes place: here is my left hand as well starting to perceive my right. . . . Thus I touch myself touching; my body accomplishes "a sort of reflection." In it, through it, there is not just the unidirectional relationship of the one who perceives to what he perceives. The relationship is reversible, the touched hand becomes the touching hand, and I am obliged to say . . . that the body is a "perceiving thing," a "subject-object." (PS 166, translation modified)

Indeed, for Merleau-Ponty, this reflexive, fluid relation of reversibility (or overlapping through difference) confounds our categories; it frustrates our customary dichotomies. Yet, just as with time, we live and know this weird reversibility perfectly well in the exercise of life.

Écart and reversibility: as Merleau-Ponty himself says, "such are the extravagant consequences to which we are lead when we take seriously, when we interrogate, vision" (VI 140, translation modified). We have seen that *écart* and reversibility are not properly understood as two distinct "things," but are rather different aspects of the same relation: the opening-divergence and the accompanying overlap. With these very subtle and difficult concepts in place, I am now in a position to evaluate a criticism of Merleau-Ponty's reversibility that has taken hold in contemporary scholarship: the claim that his view is a kind of *solipsism*. This type of suggestion has been put forth by Levinas, as we saw briefly in chapter 4, but also by Irigaray and Claude Lefort.[14] While each of these thinkers has different emphases for his/her criticism, the shared core of objection is that Merleau-Ponty's talk of reversibility sets up a relation of symmetrical exchange, in which, as Levinas says, "the terms are *indifferently* read from left to right and right to left."[15] If true, this would mean that Merleau-Ponty's reversibility relation fancies that it approaches the other, but really reduces the other and the different to the same, to the self. It would mean, in other words, that reversibility amounts to a kind of existential solipsism.

But is this criticism true? Does Merleau-Ponty's reversibility involve "symmetrical, indifferent exchange"? To begin answering this potentially devastating challenge, I observe that the criticism involves two different charges: (1) that Merleau-Ponty's account of reversibility involves "indifference," and (2) that it involves "symmetry." Now, given my earlier work in this chapter, I think the first of these two concerns is rather quickly dispatched. For I have already shown that reversibility doesn't stand alone: it is the reflexivity that folds around *écart*. And *écart* for Merleau-Ponty is not "indifference," but difference through and through. It is, he tells us, irreducible divergence, rift, separation, cleavage. Neither opposition nor identity, *écart* is the separation-difference that makes perception possible, my opening onto a world and others who are not me. Thus, I believe the charge (made particularly by Levinas and Irigaray) that Merleau-Ponty's reversibility involves the reduction or elimination of difference is, quite frankly, mistaken. These thinkers would appear to have not fully engaged and honored Merleau-Ponty's radical thought of *écart*.

How about the other component of the objection: the concern that reversibility is a relation of symmetrical exchange? I admit that answering this one is a little trickier. For while I have already argued (in chapter 4) that Merleau-Ponty's early talk of reciprocity is not about the commerce of exchange, it might appear different with his later emphasis on reversibility, because his late writings contain so many examples and models that trade upon symmetry. For example, two hands touching, two lips, two leaves of a book, two sides of a circle, two halves of an orange. However natural it may seem, though, I nonetheless believe it is an error to understand his reversibility *as defined by* symmetrical exchange—left to right and right to left. This is because Merleau-Ponty offers many other examples of the relationship that aren't symmetrical. Perhaps the best demonstration of this is his extended example of the reversibility between vision and touch. Merleau-Ponty says:

> We must habituate ourselves to think that every visible is cut out in the tangible, every tactile being in some manner promised to visibility, and that there is encroachment, infringement . . . between the tangible and the visible. . . . It

is a marvel too little noticed that . . . every displacement of my body . . . has its place in the same visible universe that I itemize and explore with [my hands], as conversely, every vision takes place somewhere in tactile space. There is double and crossed situation of the visible in the tangible and of the tangible in the visible; the two maps are complete, and yet they do not merge into one. The two parts are total parts and yet are not superposable. (VI 134)

In this passage Merleau-Ponty offers synaesthesia as an example of reversibility —an example in which the "parts" (seeing and touching, in this case) do not "fit" together (as with two hands), but there is still encroachment or overlap. In fact, Merleau-Ponty underscores at the end of this quote that the parts *cannot* be superimposed. This demonstrates, I think, that the heart of his reversibility is not symmetrical exchange, but again *overlapping*—overlapping through divergence. Thus, while Merleau-Ponty gives us several examples of reversible overlapping that involve symmetry (chosen, I suspect, for their rather evocative character), the crux of the relation isn't symmetry. To sum up, this second concern in the solipsism criticism mistakes a prominent feature of some of Merleau-Ponty's examples for the essential feature of the relation—a subtle error, but an error nonetheless.

In the end, then, I believe the objection that reversibility is a kind of solipsism does not hold up to a close reading of *The Visible and the Invisible,* nor really to its basic intentions. This is not to say there aren't problems with reversibility (I will discuss an important one in section 3, below), but I don't think solipsism is among them. Again, importantly: *écart* is difference, not the reduction of difference. It is the space or opening of a pivot through which self and world, self and others overlap in perceptual contact. And it is a difference beyond the traditional categories of identity and opposition. In this regard, Merleau-Ponty's work here anticipates the philosophical concern with difference that marks so much subsequent and contemporary continental thought.

Given the centrality of this concern to contemporary philosophy, I think it will be illuminating to explore the relationship of *écart* to another well-known and later philosophical difference—Jacques Derrida's *différance.* There is no question in this context of doing a full treatment of Derrida's *différance,* but I can say enough to yield certain insights about the relationship between the projects of these two preeminent French thinkers.

First, in his well-known essay of the same title ("Différance," 1968), Derrida tells us that *différance* is not a "thing," not an object, not an entity that can be pointed to, but is rather the difference-spacing between and around such things.[16] Nor is it really a concept, but rather a neologism designed to refer to that differential play at work in the world, language, and concepts.[17] In these respects, *différance* is extremely close to *écart,* a kinship that can be felt, for instance, when Derrida says: "*Différance* is the systematic play of differences . . . of the *spacing* by means of which elements are related to each other. This spacing is simultaneously active and passive . . . production of the intervals without which the 'full' terms would not . . . function."[18] Indeed, in this passage and others, one can substitute the term *écart* for *différance* and the claim would remain equally true. Now, Derrida underscores that his neologism articulates two modes of difference: the usual sense of things being not-identical in space and the temporal sense conveyed by the word "deferral." For him, the becoming-present to awareness or consciousness of any thing, word, or concept involves both the spatial differentiation from other things and the temporal difference of delay. Again, this is not at all unlike Merleau-Ponty's notion of perspectival perception with its multiple, differentiated spatial and temporal dimensions. The similarity here should not surprise us, I think, because both Merleau-Ponty and Derrida are deeply influenced by Heidegger's account of being and Husserl's theory of time-consciousness.

This is not, however, to suggest that *écart* and *différance* are strictly the same. For one thing, the two philosophers have irreducibly different styles. As I will show in detail starting in chapter 6, Merleau-Ponty comes to practice an expressionist philosophy. Rooted in the overflowing excess of experience, his task is to create new, illuminating ways of "singing the world," and his late language of *écart* and reversibility must be understood in light of that commitment. However, Derrida's deconstructive practice is *other*: it is what he has called a kind of "writing with two hands," an effort to respect the internal logic and content of a text or concept while also manifesting the *différance* (fissures) and aporias (paradoxes) that the content depends upon and represses.[19] We might think of this first line of difference as that between Merleau-Ponty's commitment to *lyricism* and Derrida's to *law* (the law of textuality or mark). The second aspect of their difference is the fact that the two thinkers work to articulate the "constitutive difference" from inverse domains. Derrida, starting from Saussure's linguistics, primarily identifies *différance* in the workings of language and textuality, and then extends those insights to experience and practices. Merleau-Ponty, on the other hand, starting from phenomenology, first reveals *écart* in experience and behavior and then gestures toward its involvement in language. These different starting points generate different areas of elaboration and, consequently, the thinkers confront distinct challenges that they then must work to deny. For Derrida, the objections are that his emphases on textuality and *différance* generate either "linguistic reductionism," radical skepticism, or both.[20] For Merleau-Ponty, it is assumed time and again that his phenomenology is subjectivistic, merely psychological, or Husserlian. (As we will see in chapter 6, this last assumption—that Merleau-Ponty's phenomenology grafts onto Husserl's—is one that Derrida himself makes in his earliest writings.)

All of the above sounds like "a lot of difference" between Merleau-Ponty and Derrida. Yes, true . . . but I also believe it is a serious, although common error to drive these thinkers apart into opposition. It is an error first of all because of their resonant, mutually elaborative similarities. One example, again, is the proximity of *écart* and *différance;* another is their career-long campaigns against ontologies that are rooted in either atomistic or binary concepts (including Husserl's phenomenology). And there is considerable contact between them, evident in Derrida's later writings, in their views of visibility and the flesh.[21] However, it is also an error because I believe that philosophy is well-served by practicing their different projects in tandem.

I am aware that this suggested coupling of ontology and deconstruction might seem absurd to many readers: "Hasn't Derrida, following Heidegger, rejected the very notion of ontology as 'onto-theology'? Hasn't deconstruction set as its one of its explicit tasks the de-structuring of any ontology?" However, I myself can see no reason to *abandon* ontology because of appropriate deconstructive vigilance against the sediments of binary, supernatural, and/or hierarchical metaphysics. On the contrary, as Todd May has argued in his defense of Gilles Deleuze's commitment to ontology, after Derrida (and Foucault) it is about doing ontology in the *right* way: by understanding ontology as *creative* (and not representational) and by honoring differentiation (instead of privileging unity).[22] I believe that Merleau-Ponty's ontology meets both of these standards even though most of it pre-dates the work of Deleuze, Derrida, and Foucault. In Merleau-Ponty's path-breaking work on *écart*—the constitutive difference (gap, spacing, rift, dehiscence) that makes possible the interwoven fabric of experience—he has met the second of those standards, as I will elaborate in section 3, below. And in the important development of his account of thinking, knowing, and language as fundamentally expressive (as we will start to see in chapter 6), he has met the first standard as well.

Put this way, I hope to have shown, against prevailing assumptions and prejudices, that ontology and deconstruction need not be viewed as opposite endeavors—"take your pick and the other is wrong." Rather, I see them as supplementary, yet fissioning ones: the rigorous, lyrical effort to articulate being ("singing the world"), and the rigorous, critical vigilance against the hidden sediments of traditional concepts and binaries in ontologies. How better to understand the proximity and distance of *écart* and *différance*? How better to appreciate Derrida's critical reminder (in *Memoirs of the Blind*) that the eyes not only see and caress the world, but also approach it through their *tears*?[23]

How better to understand that Derrida finds Merleau-Ponty's texts both "passionately exciting" and "also irritating or disappointing at times"?[24] How better to appreciate Derrida's perceptive observation that some of Merleau-Ponty's late expressive gestures (such as the "two hands touching") at once undermine and perpetuate traditional anthropocentric categories which obscure animal life?[25] In short, I believe that a recognition of these philosophies as "reversible" in Merleau-Ponty's precise sense, as "overlapping through their differences," will yield important new insights about our embodied life and experience in the world.

However, this is not the place to pursue this reframed conversation between Merleau-Ponty and Derrida—it would, I think, need a book of its own.[26] Even more, it couldn't proceed at all until we first understood Merleau-Ponty's extraordinary treatment of the flesh in *The Visible and the Invisible*—whose pages Derrida called "so strong, so alive, [and] which have contributed so much to open a pathway for the thinking of its time, and our time."[27] It is to Merleau-Ponty's third, late "master concept" that we now turn.

3. The Flesh of the World

Given the subtleties of *écart* and reversibility, as well as their singular importance in Merleau-Ponty's ontology, I have tried to present the meaning of these showing-concepts as directly as possible. In brief, *écart* is a difference-spacing-openness at the heart of perceptual experience which is not opposition. Reversibility is the overlapping perceptual relation that folds around *écart*—the "intertwining" or "cohesion" of what is radically different. However, in Merleau-Ponty's final writings these terms are presented in a less direct way. They are presented with an excess of metaphors, with a richer, sensual, and carnal language. Part of this voluptuousness in the late writings is the result of his now realized expressive method for philosophy (as I will discuss in the conclusion). But it also flows from Merleau-Ponty's deep sense that the sensual experiences of *écart* and reversibility are lived in *the flesh*. Indeed, talk of "flesh" pervades his final writings; clearly, he understands the flesh as a revolutionary innovation. For example, he says that flesh is "an ultimate notion" and further that "there is no name in traditional philosophy to designate it" (VI 139–140). But what precisely does he mean by this "ultimate notion"? What aspects of living experience do flesh express? I must say that the answers to these questions are not obvious, even as one closely studies *The Visible and the Invisible* and the other late texts. This term in particular has a habit of eluding the reader as the text unfolds, of always pointing to more than it seems to say. Thus, flesh is one of the most difficult conceptual dimensions of Merleau-

Ponty's thought and its centrality makes it all the more important for us to understand and employ in a rigorous way. In what follows, then, my aim is to clarify this concept and its ontological importance, even while later I will acknowledge a certain limitation in it.

Toward this goal, I have carried out a detailed textual analysis of Merleau-Ponty's uses of the word "flesh" in his late writings, and the summary results appear in the appendix. Given my arguments about the limits of analysis in chapter 1, I am well aware that this kind of approach is interpretative and necessarily incomplete. Even so, the results are revealing: they suggest that the source of the elusiveness in Merleau-Ponty's concept is that he uses the term "flesh" in substantially different ways. The analysis also can help us discern that this diversity of use is not merely vague, ambiguous, or equivocal, but rather reflective of the fact that Merleau-Ponty is deploying the term in a way that Gilles Deleuze and Félix Guattari can help us understand. That is, he is using it as an expressive, conceptual multiplicity.

To begin, the late writings reveal one clear sense of "flesh" as the obvious one: Merleau-Ponty uses the word to refer to the carnality and physicality of ourselves and our relations in the world. However different I am as a living being from inanimate things, we are still intimately related through our carnality. As Merleau-Ponty puts it in "Eye and Mind": "my body . . . is caught in the fabric of the world, and its cohesion is that of a thing. But because it moves itself and sees, it holds things in a circle around itself. Things are an annex or prolongation of itself; they are incrusted into its flesh, they are part of its full definition; the world is made of the same stuff as the body" (EM 125). My flesh and the things: we are "of the same stuff." We share thickness, worldly depth, weight, and surfaces; we come together in cool contact, firm resistance, and mutual influence. We are "counterparts" or "cohabitants" of the same world (PS 167). And what is true of the things is at least doubly so of our relations with other living creatures, "for they are not fictions with which I might people my desert . . . but my twins or the flesh of my flesh," caught up in the same fabric of experience (IS 15). This carnal ensemble of myself, other creatures, and sensible things is part of what Merleau-Ponty means when he speaks of "the flesh of the world": not the absurdity that everything is literally flesh and blood, but that despite all the irreducible differences, we all share kinds of corporeality. In this first sense of flesh as carnality, Merleau-Ponty uses the term as an intentional, strategic alternative to the age-old notion of "matter"—a notion that homogenizes everything it touches and eliminates every ounce of sensual contact. No doubt: "flesh" is sometimes used by Merleau-Ponty for its power to evoke the sensual carnality of living experience.

However, there are other senses of flesh at work, particularly in *The Visible and the Invisible.* In one passage Merleau-Ponty talks of flesh as a distance that brings with it proximity (135). A bit later he discusses it as an archetypal paradox, "because the body belongs to the order of things [just] as the world is . . . flesh" (137). Still elsewhere he refers to flesh as a "style of Being" (139). At this point a reader who didn't already appreciate Merleau-Ponty might be inclined to give up on "the flesh," suspecting that it means just about anything. This would be a mistake, I think, because closer study reveals that these three apparently different uses of flesh—as distance/proximity, as paradox, and as style—are simply different ways Merleau-Ponty refers to the second major sense of flesh: the sense of flesh as *reversibility.* For when Merleau-Ponty talks about a "distance" that is consonant with proximity, he is referring to *écart* and the proximity that folds around it is reversibility. Further, when he refers to the flesh as "paradox" he is gesturing toward the weird intertwining (reversibility) of things that are different but not opposite. Finally, it is quite clear from the texts that Merleau-Ponty understands this reflexivity through difference as the very "style of being." We can see these three superficially different uses fold together to mean reversibility, in one of Merleau-Ponty's most well-known passages on the flesh:

> There is vision, touch, when a certain visible, a certain tangible, turns back
> upon the whole of the visible, the whole of the tangible, of which it is a part,
> or when suddenly it finds itself *surrounded* by them, or when between it
> and them, and through their commerce, is formed a Visibility, a Tangible in
> itself . . . It is this Visibility, this generality of the Sensible in itself . . . that we
> have previously called flesh. (VI 139)

Flesh as carnality, flesh as reversibility: there is, however, a third sense of flesh in *The Visible and the Invisible* and this is as an *element of being.* Merleau-Ponty is moved to speak this way because, he says, the categories of traditional metaphysics cannot do justice to the carnal dynamic of flesh: "The flesh is not matter, in the sense of corpuscles of being which would add up . . . to form beings" (VI 139). Nor, he says, is flesh well understood through the categories of mind: idea, mental representation, predicative concept, psychic material. And we don't get to flesh through Aristotelian "substance" either, which is another abstract term that obliterates the carnal, yet differentiated character of living experience. Thus, Merleau-Ponty concludes: "The flesh is not matter, is not mind, is not substance. To designate it, we should need the old term 'element,' in the sense it was used to speak of water, air, earth, and fire, that is, in the sense of a *general thing,* midway between the spatio-temporal individual and the idea" (VI 139). I must say that I find this third sense of flesh to be quite provocative. Beyond fire, water, air, and earth, Merleau-Ponty is perhaps suggesting in this passage that flesh is the *fifth* element. We might think of it as the "element of experience," an element that is at play wherever there are creatures that perceive. In this third sense, flesh expresses a "*general thing*" or "principle" (such as earth, air, water, and fire): a general thing or principle that is as real as any of those elements, has countless, heterogeneous instantiations, and is presupposed in the life of anyone who offers an ontology. It is in this third, fecund sense of flesh that *The Visible and the Invisible* directs us toward an *elemental ontology.*

Flesh as carnality, as the reversibility relation, and as a basic element of being: in articulating these three primary, divergent senses of flesh in Merleau-Ponty's late writings, we see that this important concept is complex. But it is far from "empty-headed," vacuous, equivocal, or confused (each of which has been contended by passing critics). On the contrary, the concept is used rigorously in these three senses, and the sense at play in any given passage is almost always evident from the context. Indeed, the notion that flesh is "confused" results from a kind of overly general separation of the concept from its contexts. Nor is his concept self-contradictory. For these three senses are not inconsistent with one another and sometimes overlap in interesting ways. For example, the sheer carnality of experience (one sense of flesh) sometimes involves reversible folds (a second sense); elsewhere, reversibility as the style of being is an aspect of the "general element" of flesh. At the same time these three senses are not reducible one to the other and are importantly heterogeneous; thus they themselves involve a reversible intertwining through difference (*écart*).

We see then that Merleau-Ponty's flesh is not properly definable in terms of some feature or another; the senses of the concept are expressive gestures that may in some cases overlap and co-implicate, but are not unified. Nor do these senses exhaust or close the expressive possibilities of "flesh," as we see from Merleau-Ponty's occasional experiments with the term, primarily in the "Working Notes" (VI 165–275). (In this regard, see the appendix to the present volume: flesh as mother, flesh as horizon, etc.) It is because of these qualities that I think it is most fruitful to understand Merleau-Ponty's signature concept of flesh as a Deleuze-Guattarian multiplicity. As Deleuze and Guattari put it in *A Thousand Plateaus:*

> A multiplicity is defined not by its elements, nor by a center of unification or comprehension. It is defined by the number of dimensions it has. . . . Since its variations and dimensions are immanent to it, *it amounts to the same thing to say that each multiplicity is already composed of heterogeneous terms in symbiosis, and that a multiplicity is continually transforming itself into a string of other multiplicities, according to its thresholds and doors.*[28]

A "number of dimensions," "heterogeneous terms in symbiosis," immanent variations that cross thresholds and open doors: these are all aspects of the way flesh operates in *The Visible and the Invisible*. I suspect it is because flesh has this productive power as an expressive multiplicity that Merleau-Ponty thinks of it as "an ultimate notion." In flesh, he is trying to develop a complex concept that will honor rather than deform the proliferate, over-spilling life of what he now calls wild being (*l'être sauvage*). Moreover, flesh is a concept with the strategic power to emphasize what philosophies before him (and after him, truth to tell) have had great difficulty in thinking through: the fact that experience, thinking, language, the self and its relations with others, are inescapably carnal. It is quite easy, after all—an occupational hazard, as it were—for *thinkers* to get lost in intellectual images, models, and constructs, to literally lose sight of the flesh of the world.

However, having made this defense of Merleau-Ponty's concept of flesh— that it is best understood as an expressive multiplicity—I do believe there is something in the view that is troubled, and it has to do with the reversibility aspect of the flesh. Specifically, it is the question of whether *reversibility is the primary sense* of the flesh. Now, to be careful here, when one merely counts the textual references in *The Visible and the Invisible*, Merleau-Ponty uses the sense of flesh as carnality more than the others, as we can see in the appendix. Nonetheless, one gets an overwhelming sense from the text that Merleau-Ponty understands the folding over or overlapping through *écart* as the fundamental sense of flesh. For an obvious example of this prestige, in the final words of the manuscript he calls reversibility "the ultimate truth" of the flesh (VI 155). But is this hegemony of sense acceptable? Instead of centralizing this one meaning, perhaps the three senses of flesh are equally profound. And perhaps there are still other senses to flesh beyond these, other tissues in wild being? (I am thinking, for example, of what Deleuze might call the virtuality of flesh in its genetic inheritance.) Lest the reader think I am undoing my previous arguments, let me be clear: my concern is not with the carnal or elemental aspects of flesh, nor am I challenging the *fact* of reversible, overlapping relations in experience. My concern is with the privilege Merleau-Ponty gives reversibility for describing our experiential relations.

In this line of questioning, I am inspired by Deleuze and his work with Guattari, and by others who have extended his ideas in critical relation to Merleau-Ponty.[29] In general, I think it is especially productive to bring Merleau-Ponty into close conversation and fission not only with Derrida, but also Deleuze (and they in turn with each other). For again, Merleau-Ponty and Deleuze are remarkably kindred spirits: they are both working at the forward edge of their times to re-conceive difference outside of opposition. Nonetheless, in *Differ-*

ence and Repetition,[30] Deleuze attempts to think difference even more radically than that, for he argues that in the traditions of philosophy, difference has always been understood through the categories of identity, as subordinate to identity, as "the negative of the same."[31] For example, Deleuze shows how Aristotle's "greatest difference" of contrariety only makes sense in terms of identity at some other level of the system—in, for example, a thing's matter or its genus. Further, Deleuze shows how Hegel's "negative" is always in the service of synthetic identifications, however infinite the process. And Deleuze argues that the result of this traditional subordination is that we have never really understood difference in its proliferate positivity.

Having said that, I do not believe that Merleau-Ponty performs this kind of subordination. That is, I do not believe that he cashes out difference (*écart*) through the categories of identity—an assessment of Merleau-Ponty with which Deleuze seems to agree.[32] Indeed, as I argued earlier (when rejecting the charge of solipsism), the reversibility that folds around *écart* is not a relationship of identity, nor is it essentially symmetrical. It is rather, as Merleau-Ponty explicitly says, an overlapping through "extreme divergence," an "overlapping and fission" (VI 142). But there is a different problem, for as Deleuze goes on to articulate his sense and logic of difference, it quickly becomes clear that his difference disrupts the privilege that Merleau-Ponty gives to reversibility.

To uncover this I need to briefly discuss the difference that Deleuze is trying to recognize. Usually we think of difference in terms of something being distinguished from something else (such as a figure from its background), but, he says, there is another fundamental differential relation:

> Imagine something that distinguishes itself—and yet that from which it distinguishes itself does not distinguish itself from it. Lightning, for example, distinguishes itself from the black sky, but must also trail behind it. . . . It is as if the ground rose to the surface, without ceasing to be ground. There is cruelty, even monstrosity, on both sides of this struggle . . . In truth, all the forms are dissolved when they are reflected in this rising ground.[33]

What Deleuze is directing us to is a differential relation where the "background" bleeds through or disrupts the figure even while the distinction is operating. Lightning is a great example, for it involves the electrical flashes (figure) and black sky (background) as distinct, but the sky breaches the flashes and unsettles any set, stable form. "Raise the ground and dissolve the form": this is the very principle of Deleuze's difference. Already we can see the Deleuzian challenge to Merleau-Ponty, for if Deleuze is correct, then it would seem that experience offers us other differentiated relations than *Gestalt* structures. It would also seem to break through Merleau-Ponty's later emphasis upon folding reflexivities. As Deleuze puts it: "difference ceases to be *reflexive* and re-covers [its own concept and its own reality] only to the extent that it desig-nates catastrophes: either breaks of continuity in the series of resemblances or impassable fissures between the analogical structures."[34] "Catastrophes," "im-passable fissures in analogy," "monstrous ruptures of form": I am persuaded by Deleuze that these are all things or relations we experience in the flesh beyond reversibility.

In this context, it is not necessary or possible to evaluate Deleuze's sugges-tion that difference is only properly conceived "to the extent" that it is "cata-strophic," nor his larger claims that all other forms of difference are deforma-tions of his catastrophic sense. For my criticism of Merleau-Ponty, all that is required is that such ruptures of *Gestalt* structure or reversible overlapping are things we really do experience. Deleuze, again, gives us the example of light-ning, but perhaps all ergonomic relations fit the bill: consider the non-serial processing of computers, or the firing of neurons in the brain as revealed by new imaging technology. These relations do not seem properly conceived in terms of figure-background structures or the folding over and back of things; in fact they seem to disrupt or explode such forms. I think we can find such dis-ruptions not merely in natural phenomena, but also in familiar, relatively mun-dane experiences: intoxication, exhaustion, illness, profound ennui, or a fit of rage. About such experiences, we say things such as "I couldn't see straight." In them, *Gestalt* structure gets discombobulated; background breaks up through the figure but without blurring into utter non-distinction. However, it isn't just negative cases or "limit experiences" that defy the relation of overlapping, re-versible contact. Consider bursts of joy, or slack-jawed astonishment in watch-ing an expert magician. Consider also the experience of profound desire or the differentiating dissolution of orgasm. In all these experiences, it seems that "the ground is raised and the form is shattered." These are rich, salient experi-ences, ones we frequently have and sometimes intentionally pursue—perhaps to have a refreshing vacation from our customary forms of life and percep-tion. However that may be, my point again is not that *Gestalt* structure and the overlapping through divergence do not occur. Rather it is that when Merleau-Ponty privileges reversibility, he misses these other weird relations and differ-ences that have a frequent place in the life of the flesh—ruptures of form, non-reflexive fissures. Indeed, it seems that, despite his extraordinary sensitivity, Merleau-Ponty's emphasis on reversibility yields a certain homogenization in his account of experience.

Having made this argument, I hope it is also clear that I don't believe the correct response is to abandon "the flesh." As I argued earlier in this section: Merleau-Ponty's concept of flesh is not *defined* by reversibility, but is best read as a conceptual multiplicity that bears and deploys other senses as well. These senses of the flesh, along with reversibility, are far too provocative and strategically useful to leave behind; they express crucial aspects of living experience that most philosophers before and after Merleau-Ponty have not been able to appreciate. No, I believe the best response to what I think of as "the hegemony of reversibility" in Merleau-Ponty, is not to abandon the flesh as an operative philosophical concept. We should rather, in Deleuze-Guattarian fashion, multiply the senses of flesh even further: work to show our own flesh and the flesh of the world as a more radically heterogeneous cohesion of different senses, corporeal operations, and carnal densities—sometimes fissured, non-continuous, and not overlapping. Would this new work be a violation of Merleau-Ponty's project? I don't think so, for already in the late writings flesh is presented as a sort of multiplicity in Deleuze's sense. Already Merleau-Ponty is aspiring to express "wild being." So perhaps being is a little wilder than he thought—an even weirder collocation of forms, fissures, overlappings, and dissolutions . . . I would like to suggest, at the end of this section, that this doesn't contradict Merleau-Ponty's final writings, but rather takes up and radicalizes their promise.

4. On the Way to Expression

Over the course of these five chapters I have primarily worked to elucidate Merleau-Ponty's phenomenology of living experience—his carnal, elemental ontology. I have done this by illuminating his views and arguments as offered in his texts, but also by elaborating and evaluating key elements of this ontology in relation to host of contemporary ideas and criticisms. In the course of these chapters, my goal has been to carry the reader from Merleau-Ponty's early ontology as a symbiosis of worldly things, embodied subjectivity, and other selves, to his later reformulations of this synergy in terms of *écart*, reversibility, and the flesh of the world. While Merleau-Ponty's language has changed between these two phases (as has his philosophical method to some extent, as I will argue in the conclusion), I believe I have shown that one key aspect of his project has not changed: early and late, Merleau-Ponty is seeking to reawaken our sensibilities to the nature and dynamics of living experience. In this way, my first five chapters have illuminated what Merleau-Ponty calls *The Visible*. However Merleau-Ponty also speaks at considerable length about *The Invisible*. To what does this refer? Putting it all together from diverse texts, Merleau-Ponty's answer to this question becomes clear: the invisible is the domain of ideas, language, and knowledge—all given birth through the process of expression. *The Invisible:* ideas, language, knowledge, surging up amid the visible, and yet transforming the visible and ourselves along the way. What is this process of expression for him? How does it work? How is it different from the dominant western tradition that treats knowledge and language as representation? How does it provide—beyond Platonism, beyond Cartesianism, beyond empiricism—a new paradigm for understanding the relationship between thought and experience? I am now, finally, in a position to begin answering these questions, to begin showing how Merleau-Ponty's account of expressive cognition gives rise to a new understanding of "the life of the mind" and with it, a whole new possibility for philosophy to start "singing the world."

6 Expression and the Origin of Geometry

We touch here the most difficult point, that is, the bond between the flesh and the idea . . .

—Merleau-Ponty[1]

[M]athematical objects are by their very nature dependent on human thought. They have properties only insofar as these can be discerned in them by thought. . . . Faith in transcendental existence . . . must be rejected as a means of mathematical proof.

—Arend Heyting[2]

1. The Promise of Expression

My primary task in the preceding chapters was to articulate the main elements of Merleau-Ponty's phenomenology of living experience. Even though it is difficult to "know precisely what we see," Merleau-Ponty attempts to show that living experience emerges through the symbiotic intertwining of one's own pulsing body, the overflowing, transcendent world of things, and the living bodies of others. Further, he reminds us that experience is sensual, affective, inter-dynamic, and inescapably carnal. Indeed, against intellectual systems and models that suppress, deform, or denigrate these basic truths, Merleau-Ponty's phenomenology "says to show" what we actually experience in life. Not mechanistic objects constituting an abstract Newtonian universe, but flesh, organic life, and a natural world. Not clusters of sense-data, but sensually rich things and artifacts: trees and mountains, chairs and buildings. Not solipsism, but complex relations and carnal contact with other creatures. Moreover, we have seen that this phenomenology is not a naïve return to some pre-philosophical immersion in merely private experience. On the contrary: in revealing the derivative character of abstract concepts and models, Merleau-Ponty's phenomenology uncovers reality as we live and share it with others, and endows it with a philosophical status (PP vii). Indeed, for him (as for Heidegger), phenomenology is ontology.

In chapter 1, I also argued that Merleau-Ponty's project is not rendered obsolete by the astonishing explanatory powers of science. This is because phenomenology speaks for and about qualitative life—an aspect of lived reality that can never be replaced or exhausted by analytic explanation. Thus, we have seen why so many thinkers continue to be excited by Merleau-Ponty's thought: it awakens our sensibilities to the living world, enriching the relationships we have there, and in doing so it yields powerful resolutions to a number of traditional metaphysical problems (the mind-body problem, the problem of other minds, dualism, idealism, and so on). In these achievements, despite certain difficulties that I have discussed, Merleau-Ponty offers a phenomenological ontology that keeps us connected with the earth and that is consistent with our everyday experiences and natural history.

But there is more, because Merleau-Ponty's philosophy also seeks to uncover the life of the mind. That is to say, his writings also offer an extremely promising account of thought, language, and knowledge as occurring through a process called *expression.* I indicated in the introduction that this aspect of his work has received comparatively little attention, even among continental philosophers—an oversight that I think has been deeply problematic. For Merleau-Ponty's philosophy of expression is explicitly offered as an alternative to the dominant western view of these cognitive processes (thinking, language, and knowing) as fundamentally representational. Given the depths and prestige of this tradition, there is a lot at stake in understanding Merleau-Ponty's account of the expressive life of the mind. In this chapter, chapter 7, and the conclusion, my overarching project is to articulate this important yet neglected aspect of Merleau-Ponty's philosophy, to explore its consequences, and establish its plausibility. I believe that his account of expression offers a promising new paradigm for understanding our cognitive life within a naturalistic framework, a paradigm that overcomes the well-worn problems of reductive empiricism and dualistic transcendentalism. Further, in studying Merleau-Ponty's expressive theories of thinking, language, and knowledge, we will be able to more fully understand the side of his ontology that he calls "the invisible," and its specific relationship to "the visible." What will emerge, then, by the end of this book is a detailed picture of Merleau-Ponty's understanding of what he calls "the most difficult point": the relationship between "the flesh and the idea," between "eye and mind," between "the visible and the invisible"—one that escapes and overturns the profound grip of Plato's "divided line."

Given this overarching plan, my first step is to carefully show what Merleau-Ponty has in mind when he talks about the process of expression. To do this, I will focus on what I take to be his clearest example of the process: that of performing a mathematical proof. This example will allow me to specify the primary features of his account of expressive cognition and then explore some of its powerful implications, for one example, in the philosophy of mathematics. These insights, in turn, will give us the resources to uncover a subtle, but irreducible difference between Merleau-Ponty's and Husserl's phenomenologies—a difference that has been overlooked and obscured by subsequent thinkers, and which has supported the general neglect of what we might call Merleau-Ponty's epistemology of expression.

2. The Process of Expression

The emergence of expression as a pivotal concept in Merleau-Ponty's philosophy has a complicated lineage. It is reasonably clear that after completing *Phenomenology of Perception* in 1945, Merleau-Ponty became fascinated and energized by the notion. We can determine this from the fact that expression plays a key role in several important essays from the late 1940s and in *Humanism and Terror* (his early book on politics, 1947).[3] Further, in "The Unpublished Text" (1951)—his statement of application to the Collège de France—Merleau-Ponty explicitly states that expression is the key to his theory of knowledge and truth.[4] That same year, he began writing *The Prose of the World,* a book focusing on expression and language. He subsequently offered lectures at the Collège de France that had expression as a theme, and in his final writings Merleau-Ponty explicitly refers to his philosophical method as expression (a point to which I will return in the conclusion). In stressing this thematic focus after 1945, I do not mean to suggest that expression is absent from *Phenomenology of Perception.* On the contrary, my view is that Merleau-Ponty gradually, haltingly, develops the concept over the course the book, and by the end brings it to fruition. For example, early in the text Merleau-Ponty discusses the process of expression several times without naming it (PP 30, 87–89, 112, 129–130). He also talks about the living body in the world as "expressive," a capacity that neurological patients such as Schneider lack (PP 98–115). And a bit further on, he offers a somewhat flawed chapter on "The Body as Expression, and Speech" (more on this in chapter 7). Nonetheless, I think the concept all comes together in the late chapter, "The *Cogito*"; here, Merleau-Ponty gives us his clearest, most concentrated discussion of the process of expression. Understanding the content of this discussion is thus pivotal for understanding his account of the life of the mind. I think it is also especially important because Merleau-Ponty pursues expression here in order to undermine the last, seemingly unassailable bastion of Cartesian and transcendental philosophy: the apparent fact of the *cogito*.

Merleau-Ponty begins "The *Cogito*" chapter by posing a problem for himself. So far in *Phenomenology of Perception* he has argued that philosophy must replace Descartes's idealistic, dualistic, and abstract picture of subjectivity with the recognition that the self is fundamentally embodied and situated in the intersubjective, transcendent world. Yet, he says, how are we to account for the apparent fact that every experience seems to presuppose one's thinking self? How are we to explain the deep sense that one's thinking self must already be directed toward something in order to see it? As Merleau-Ponty recognizes (PP 371), these are questions that Descartes would press upon him, were he alive, and they are closely related to the problem of knowledge posed for Socrates in the *Meno*: "How will you set about looking for that thing the nature of which is totally unknown to you? . . . And if by chance you should stumble upon it, how will you know that it is indeed that thing since you are in ignorance of it?"[5] Indeed, as Socrates and Plato reply (with Descartes, Leibniz, Kant, and Husserl in their wake), there *must* be a knowledge—a presence of the self to itself— that precedes and constitutes our experience.[6] In this recognition—that one's thinking self is already there prior to any experience—Merleau-Ponty says we arrive at what seems to be the obvious truth of the *cogito,* a truth that can be apparently confirmed by the simplest moment of self-reflection. "Whenever I look, thinking is *already there*": this is the basic insight that points all those thinkers to a transcendental sphere of self-knowledge that is both presupposed and then forgotten by any form of realism.

Having posed this tough challenge for his own experiential realism, Merleau-Ponty begins to respond by setting appearances aside and asking whether we actually do find a pure, unmediated presence-to-self. When do we get an unmediated knowledge of self that does not pass through the circuit of the world? Not, he argues (PP 374–377), through a radical skepticism that seeks to expunge the world. For as I argued in the prelude and chapter 1, Cartesian doubt can only purport to find a non-worldly self by presupposing the very world it seeks to discredit; it can only reduce worldly and social experiences to a screen of ideas by presupposing them. Nor, Merleau-Ponty continues, do we find a pure, transcendental self-presence in our emotions. For not only can we discover that our emotions were mistaken (as in "I really believed I loved her!"), but our emotions are mediated, sometimes surprisingly so, by our actions in the world and by the affective resonances in particular situations (PP 377–383). Then Merleau-Ponty wonders: how about mathematics? Don't we have access to pure thought in this domain? After all, transcendental philosophers such as Plato, Kant, and Husserl have typically made their most compelling arguments for transcendental cognition by appealing to mathematical truth. How else, they reason, are we to explain the apparent necessity, certainty, and universality of such truths? Time and again, their arguments suggest that no philosophy committed to the fundamentality of worldly experience can adequately account for mathematics. In the subsequent pages of "The *Cogito*" chapter, Merleau-Ponty sets out to answer this foundational argument of transcendental philosophy by showing that, on the contrary, one can account for the force and origin of mathematics without requiring transcendental subjects, categories, or objects.[7]

Merleau-Ponty begins his argument by examining the process of mathematical proof. He invites us to consider, for example, a proof for the theorem that a line drawn through the apex of a triangle results in three angles equal to the angles in the triangle (PP 383–384). He says we can prove this theorem by drawing "on paper or in our imagination" first a triangle, then an extension of one of the sides, and then a line through the vortex that is parallel to the extended line. His verbal description of this proof can be schematized as follows:

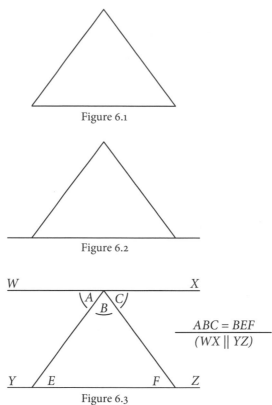

Figure 6.1

Figure 6.2

Figure 6.3

The final image, Merleau-Ponty says, contains lines and angles organized in such a way that we see the truth of the theorem and regard it as proven.

But *how* do we "see" and "regard" it as proven? Merleau-Ponty's answer goes directly to heart of what we need to understand, because he argues that the activity of the geometer is fundamentally expressive. That is, he argues that arriving at the conclusion of a proof (or at critical steps along the way) is an act of expression. Here is how he describes it:

> I commit the first structure [figure 6.1] to a second one, the "parallel and se-cant" structure [figure 6.2]. How is that possible? It is because my perception of the triangle was not, so to speak, fixed and dead, for the drawing of the tri-angle on the paper was merely its outer covering; it was traversed by lines of force, and everywhere in it new directions not traced out yet possible came to light. In so far as the triangle was implicated in my hold on the world, it was bursting with indefinite possibilities of which the construction actually drawn [figure 6.3] was merely one. The construction possesses a demonstrative value because I cause it to emerge from the dynamic formula of the triangle. It ex-presses my power to make apparent the sensible symbols of a certain hold on things. (PP 386)

Merleau-Ponty unpacks this very dense description of the expressive pro-cess in his subsequent passages. The first thing I want to emphasize is a later, explicit claim that he makes: that "causing the conclusion to emerge" is *not* a deductive process of restating what is already given in the initial figure of the triangle (again, figure 6.1). Rather, he says, the conclusion "goes beyond" or "transgresses" that initial figure. This happens not because the initial triangle is "fixed and dead," that is to say, *meaningless,* but on the contrary, because the triangle is "traversed by lines of force," shot through with "indefinite" meaning possibilities and sense-directions. Indeed, it is because the geometer encoun-ters the initial triangle as a *Gestalt*—as an open, incomplete, and sense-laden situation—that he or she must try to discover one particular line of mean-ing that can be pursued toward the conclusion. Merleau-Ponty thus says that reaching the conclusion of a proof, or some breakthrough step along the way, both "transcends and transfigures" the initial situation (PP 388). It doesn't merely restate what is already given, but rather demands "crystallizing insight" through which some meaning-possibility suddenly "reorganizes" and "syn-chronizes" what was before a *con*-fusion of meaning, a problem to be solved. All this is for Merleau-Ponty to argue that the process of mathematical proof (and by extension any act of expression) is fundamentally *creative* (PP 391).

Again, I would stress Merleau-Ponty's view that "transfiguring," "reorganiz-ing," or "creative" insight is required not because the initial figure is utterly im-poverished ("fixed and dead"), but rather because it is so open and sugges-tive. As a *Gestalt,* it overflows with meaning-possibilities and "lines of force": the process of proof is about "tapping into" one of those possibilities that will get you to the result. As mathematicians know, there are typically several ways to solve any given problem, although of course many avenues of approach are excluded or won't work. To be sure, what makes the process of mathematical proof (and by extension any act of expression) so frustrating at times are not the complexities of a mechanical operation, but rather the overwhelming, open possibilities of the *blank page*. I also observe that this encounter is what makes the process of proof (and expression) so exciting: it feels good—pleasurable and relieving—to come up with a particular line of insight that overcomes the *con*-fusion of possibilities, the overwhelming openness of the initial situation. This pleasurable overcoming is, no doubt, why we talk about these creative insights as "breakthroughs, "inspirations," or "aha moments." This is why we feel as though "a light bulb is going on." As many of my friends and colleagues in mathematics tell me, experiencing this pleasure is one of the main reasons that they pursue mathematics.

Besides its creative dimension, a second thing to see is Merleau-Ponty's view that the process of mathematical proof presupposes an embodied subject. As he puts it: "The subject of geometry is a motor subject" (PP 387). Merleau-Ponty means by this, first of all, that the living body provides stable vectors of organization that inform the process of proof at every step: vectors such as "up," "down," "left," "right," "in," "through," "intersect," and "extend" derive their meaning and orientation from embodied operations.[8] There can be no geometrical proof without tacitly assuming the meaning these terms get from living embodied experience, or without working on pictorial or imagined triangles that tacitly retain these vectors. In a closely related chapter from *The Prose of the World,* "The Algorithm and the Mystery of Language," Merleau-Ponty argues that algebraic proof equally presupposes the corporeal vectors of temporality such as "next," "succession," and "progression."[9] But in the claim that "the subject of geometry is a motor subject," Merleau-Ponty also means that the body in its perspectival relations with things in the world opens up the *con*-fusion of spatial meaning-possibilities that the geometer seeks to creatively overcome. To be sure, it is because I am *not* a transcendental subject, but rather an incarnate being who is open to an overflowing, transcendent world with half-hidden sides and multiple meanings, that I find myself having to "make sense" of it through expression. As Merleau-Ponty puts it: "Our body, to the extent that it moves itself about, to the extent that it is inseparable from a view of the world . . . is the condition of possibility, not only of the geometrical synthesis, but of all expressive operations" (PP 388).

Thus, for Merleau-Ponty, mathematical proof as an act of expression is fundamentally embodied and essentially creative. At first glance, this combination may seem paradoxical. It brings together what has traditionally been driven apart: creative thinking, usually thought to be transcendental, and the body, which would usually be the domain of empiricism. However, this is precisely Merleau-Ponty's revolutionary insight: the process of expression is the crux of a new understanding of the relationship between the mind and the body, between the visible and the invisible. It is a central part of his new ontology that is neither dualistic nor reductionistic. In the following pages and in chapter 7, I will try to elaborate this new understanding in great detail and show how it undermines the age-old dichotomy between the empirical and the transcendental. For now, it might suffice to point out that both transcendental philosophy and classical empiricism have been predicated on a shared, but mistaken premise: the premise that the body and its worldly relations are essentially impoverished—atomistic, mechanistic, and merely reflexive in function. Instead of that, following Merleau-Ponty, we have seen that the living body plies itself to a rich, overflowing world in which there is always more than can be grasped in any perception (chapter 2). We have seen that this open relation generates a two-fold dynamic between the impersonal-biological layer of one's body and one's personal-intentional projects (chapter 3). We have also seen also that, in the ebb and flow between these two layers, the living body is able to acquire or incorporate new forms or habits such as dancing or riding a bike. Recalling all this, we can begin to see that the creative transformation of some initial figure, as in the geometric proof, is the cognitive manifestation of an ability that is already working in behavior itself. Indeed, instead of some transcendental mystery divorced from the body, it seems that creative, transfiguring insight is one of our carnal powers.

The third, equally important thing to see about Merleau-Ponty's account of mathematical proof as an act of expression is that it has what he calls "demonstrative value." This is to say that although such expressions are genuinely creative, they have the force of necessity. For Merleau-Ponty, there are two interrelated sources for this necessity. In the first place, he observes that the additional lines in a developing geometric proof are not successively random images; the process is distinctly unlike a child's drawing in which each new line completely alters what was there before ("it's a house—no, it's a boat—no, it's a man") (PP 384).[10] Conversely, Merleau-Ponty stresses that in a proof, the initial triangle *perseveres* throughout the additional stages of development: those stages, and the conclusion itself, don't erase or obscure the initial figure, but rather illuminate it along one possible line of development. The geometer then is yielding new insight about *that* initial figure, demonstrating something new about *it* that all others should find there. As Merleau-Ponty puts it, the process involves a "recognition that traverses the length of the series of cognitive events, grounds its value, and posits it as . . . repeatable in principle for any consciousness placed in the same cognitive situation" (PW 120). The second aspect of this necessity can be gleaned from Merleau-Ponty's observation that the new insight "transcends" and "transfigures" the initial figure. It synchronizes what was before "bursting with indefinite possibilities." It gives relief from the *con*-fusion of meaning. Thus, while in fact the geometer, in the throes of the creative process, might well have proceeded down other "lines of force," some particular solution, once achieved, brings a retrospective feeling of necessity. This feeling is not unlike what one experiences with a great mystery novel: along the way everyone seems a likely suspect, but after the dénouement it feels as though it couldn't have been any other way. "Of course! It had to be the butler! I thought so all along!"

With this insight in place we see that Merleau-Ponty's view of mathematical proof as embodied, creative expression accounts for the force and necessity of mathematical theorems. And it does so without reverting to transcendental subjectivity or making mathematical truths mere reflections of transcendental (or Platonic) objects. Mathematical truths, he argues, are best understood as expressions: that is, powerful, meaning-bestowing transformations of worldly experience that nonetheless belong to the world. Or to put it another way, they are embodied-cognitive acts of transcendence in and amid the world, not transcendental operations outside it. Hence, Merleau-Ponty insists that such truths are historically and geographically located; they are "cultural acquisitions" (PP 390). To be sure, they might never have come to be expressed. Imagine, for instance, if Cantor had died as a child, or if Descartes had been killed as a soldier. And they could in fact disappear if the tradition, milieu, and artifacts that sustain them were utterly destroyed. Who knows what was lost when the library at Alexandria burned? But once created, once articulated, they have necessity in their demonstrative value and organizing power: they synchronize what was before a *con*-fusion, they make sing what was before a babble. While it is true that future expressive transformations may leave these expressive breakthroughs behind, it is not clear to us how they could ever be revoked. As Merleau-Ponty puts it, once a mathematical theorem has made its first appearance, "subsequent 'appearances,' if successful, add nothing and if unsuccessful subtract nothing, [and it] remains an inexhaustible possession among us" (PP 390).

In this section we have seen Merleau-Ponty's answer to the traditional argument that mathematics attests to a pure, thinking *cogito* that contains truths which are independent and prior to worldly experience. He argues, instead, that when we remember to look at the actual *process* of mathematics rather than being mesmerized by its results, we see that mathematical proof and the truth that emerges therein involve a worldly, creative act of expression. Through this important, admittedly complex argument about mathematics we also have been thrust into Merleau-Ponty's larger theory of expression. For while he acknowledges that there are differences between the modalities of expressive thought and practice—between, for instance, mathematics, language, art, and science—he also maintains that all acts of expression share the features I have discussed above. Again: (1) they are rooted in the living body and its relations to the world, (2) they involve intellectual-imaginative insight that transcends and transforms some open, initial data into a new, powerful form, and (3) they bear a powerful sense of necessity. In short, expression is an embodied, creative way of arriving at truths and communicating with others; it is a way of knowing that is consonant with our lives as natural beings in the world.

With all this in place, we are now able to understand one of Merleau-Ponty's most important passages on the subject of expression:

> It seems to me that knowledge and the communication with others that it presupposes not only are original formations with respect to the perceptual life but also [that] they preserve and continue our perceptual life even while transforming it. Knowledge and communication sublimate rather than suppress our incarnation, and the characteristic operation of the mind is in the movement by which we recapture our corporeal existence and use it to symbolize instead of merely to coexist. (UT 7)

Notice: Merleau-Ponty says here (and repeats in other texts) that knowledge and language *sublimate* experience. When they are expressive, knowledge and language take up certain formations and give rise to powerful, new articulations, even while carrying along the initial form. With this in mind, we can see that an act of expression is dramatically different from one of representation (re-presentation). For at its core, expression is not about imitation (*mimēsis*), correspondence, or isomorphism—these are the basic watchwords of representation theories of thought, language, and knowledge. Rather, expression is about the creative transformation of some previous data or experience so that it yields new knowledge or radiates a powerful, new sense without the original data disappearing or being covered up. This is, rather precisely, what *sublimation* means. In my view, this account of expression rooted in embodied, perceptual life, amounts to a new paradigm for understanding the natural life of the mind—a shift that is rather Copernican in its scope and possibilities. In the next section I will go some way toward supporting this claim by showing how it offers relief from a set of entrenched philosophical difficulties, all the while eschewing transcendental, supernatural underpinnings on the one hand and reductive materialism on the other.

3. Exploring Some Implications

In the previous section I articulated Merleau-Ponty's view of the key features of the expression by considering his claims about the expressive nature of mathematical proof. I am aware that there is a lot to digest. For one thing, we are so accustomed to using the notion of "expression" in a loose, free-flowing way, perhaps associating it exclusively with art, that it might seem strange to think of mathematical proof as an exemplar. Or from another perspective, it may be jarring at first to think of mathematics as essentially creative and embodied. In what follows I hope to be able to alleviate some of these puzzles by showing some compelling implications of Merleau-Ponty's view, and in doing so, to further clarify its meaning. A first thing I want to establish is that his account of the process of proof as an expressive act addresses one of the cardinal concerns in twentieth-century philosophy of mathematics. That is, the search for a non-Platonic foundation for mathematical thought.[11] It is also the case that Merleau-Ponty's account is markedly different from the most prominent non-Platonic theories and, I believe, has particular advantages over them. In this context, there is no question of treating this topic in detail, much less exhaustively. However, by briefly considering the three predominant non-Platonic theories of mathematical truth—the analytic view, formalism, and intuitionism—I hope to begin illustrating the originality and promise of Merleau-Ponty's expressive account of mathematics. I should also add that I believe the following claims and arguments on Merleau-Ponty's behalf could be extended by analogy to ground and explain the necessity of logical axioms and theorems, such as the law of non-contradiction, though I will not pursue that application here.

Historically, the most influential explanation of mathematical statements is the early modern view that such statements are *analytic.* Inaugurated by Leibniz in his work on logical necessity and underscored by Hume in the first *Enquiry,* this thesis was embraced in the early twentieth century by both empiricists (Ayer, Russell, Carnap) and logicists (such as Frege, Russell, and Wittgenstein in the *Tractatus*) who attempted to ground mathematics by reducing it to logic. This analytic theory has been attractive to philosophers because in claiming that mathematical theorems cannot be denied without contradiction, that is, that they are true by definition, it accounts for their apparent necessity without having to posit transcendental Platonic objects. However, the view demands that anything we could ever show about triangles and real numbers is already contained in them, and this is directly what Merleau-Ponty has argued against. Far from being a re-articulation of what is already known, the process of mathematical proof—as an act of expression—involves the "miraculous" human ability to "go beyond" what is given, to transgress the *con*-fusion posed by the initial figure and make sense of it through a crystallizing insight. To repeat what I just argued, mathematical proof is a creative or "spontaneous" endeavor, not a mechanistic one. As Merleau-Ponty directly puts the point in "The *Cogito*" chapter: "The necessity of the proof is not an analytic necessity: the construction that enables the conclusion to be reached is not . . . contained in the essence of the triangle, but merely possible when that essence serves as a starting point. There is no definition of a triangle that includes in advance the properties subsequently to be demonstrated" (PP 385).[12]

Merleau-Ponty's criticism here of the analytic account of mathematics also indicates a second difficulty for the view: the analytic view assumes that the basic nature of a mathematical concept (such as "triangle" or "number") is constituted by its formal definition. However, on Merleau-Ponty's account a triangle, for example, cannot be reduced to its formal definition, since "no logical definition of the triangle could equal in fecundity the vision of the figure" (PP 385). As we have already seen, a triangle is not initially present to someone as a machine that automatically cranks out theorems, but rather as a *Gestalt*. That is, as an open and incomplete formation, one bursting with indefinite meaning-possibilities and many possible lines of development. Again, this is why the process of proof is fraught with difficulty and even failure. This means that mathematics begins with one's *living interaction* with a triangle, on paper or in one's imagination, and not with the formal definition of "triangularity." Thus, Merleau-Ponty says, the triangle's basic nature is properly understood as *concrete* and *informal,* consisting of a "style" or "a certain modality of my hold on the world" (PP 386).

This second criticism of the analytic theory of mathematics also implies a critique of the alternate theory known as formalism. Formalism, first articulated by David Hilbert and developed into its full, strict form by Haskell B. Curry, is the view that a mathematical system contains statements about the manipulation of certain uninterpreted symbols.[13] Given this, formalists argue that these symbols need not refer to anything outside of themselves, such as Platonic transcendental objects—the symbols are just "marks on a page." This means that such a system can be understood as grounded by nothing other than its internal formal consistency. Historically, the great strength of the formalist view, and part of its impetus, was its promise to ground mathematics while avoiding the intractable problems that emerged for the efforts by logicists to ground mathematics by reducing it to logic. However, we have just seen Merleau-Ponty's arguments that formal thought is secondary to expression, in the sense that the process of moving from the initial form to the conclusion can be formalized only after it has first been expressed. Thus, Merleau-Ponty explicitly concludes that formalization is always retrospective, always abstract or second-order. Of course there is no question that formalization brings order and clarity to our thought, and a sort of rigor, but it is not itself the creative operation that gives rise to mathematical truths. In short, the formalist mistakes an upshot of mathematical activity, that is, our ability to formalize the results, for its foundation. In so doing, the creative, embodied process of expression that gives rise to the results drops out of sight.

Perhaps the most illuminating theory to compare with Merleau-Ponty's expressionist theory of mathematics is intuitionism. Prefigured by Kant, developed into a theory by Brouwer and later by Heyting, and taken up somewhat idiosyncratically by Michael Dummett, intuitionism is the view that mathematical statements are synthetic, self-evident representations of the pure intuitions of space and time.[14] On this account, the character of these pure intuitions determines the kind of mathematical proofs that can be actually constructed, and thus also, the mathematical theorems we can assert. Since, intuitionists say, the formal statements of mathematical theorems are constructed in keeping with these internal intuitions, it is essential not to mistake the linguistic form of the proof (or theorem) for the internal process of constructing the proof. Indeed, intuitionists argue that it is because we allow mathematical talk to go beyond what can actually be constructed that leads to the Platonic notion that mathematical objects exist independently of and prior to those constructions. Thus, intuitionists happily insist upon restricting mathematics to the study of actually constructible mathematical theorems, entities, and systems— with all the limiting consequences such an axiom implies for the procedure and contents of formal mathematics. For instance, intuitionistic mathematics is famously *finitistic,* that is, it rejects all talk of actually existing infinite sequences since such a sequence cannot be actually constructed.

Having laid this out, a first thing to be said is that there are certain resonances between Merleau-Ponty's theory and intuitionism: both accounts maintain that mathematical truths are the upshot of a human operation, that this operation is located in history and culture, and that it precedes all formalization. As Heyting's epigram to this chapter indicates, both accounts embrace the notion that mathematics is dependent on human thought, and that the transcendental existence of mathematical objects must be rejected. Further, given Merleau-Ponty's use of the term "intuition" in certain passages of the "The *Cogito*" chapter, it might appear that his theory of mathematics is intuitionistic. However, the difference between the accounts is in fact profound because they each understand the "human operation" that is involved in incommensurable ways. For the intuitionist, following Kant, mathematical construction is about *re-presenting* internal, self-evident, a priori intuitions about space and time, and so unfolds along the deductive lines of necessity. But for Merleau-Ponty mathematical proof happens amid an array of proliferate possibilities and takes shape through genuinely creative, transgressive insights— insights that, once formalized, retrospectively disguise the open character of the work and the multiple lines of possible development. One crucial point to make about this distinction between "necessary representation" and "creative expression" is that Merleau-Ponty is able to account for a genuine multiplicity of results and formal systems. For instance, far from having to treat non-Euclidean geometry as a threat to the whole system of self-evident intuitions and law-abiding representations (à la Kant), Merleau-Ponty's account grasps such geometry—or any non-intuitionistically justifiable system—as an expression of space or "triangle" along some radically different "line of possibility." Indeed, Merleau-Ponty's theory has the impressive power to embrace the multiplicity of formal systems rather than having to de-legitimize them. Considerably more could be said here, for instance, about how Merleau-Ponty's account avoids the intuitionists' commitment to mathematical finitism. For example, infinity and trans-finite cardinals can be understood as expressive possibilities of number. But I think we have seen enough to say that the difference between *in*tuition and *ex*pression is *all* the difference.

In certain respects then, Merleau-Ponty's philosophy of mathematics, understood as an example of the embodied, thinking process of expression, promises what some thinkers have considered a sort of "holy grail" in this field. That is, it offers a non-Platonic theory of mathematics that recognizes the fundamentality of the process of construction (or proof), while also permitting transfinite operations. I must say, for Merleau-Ponty to offer a theory that combines these features is sufficient to consider his theory of expression a major contribution to contemporary philosophy. But there are other compelling features of this theory of expression as well. For one thing, after centuries of perceived oppositions, his view establishes a rapprochement between science, mathematics, and art. There is, Merleau-Ponty argues (PP 390–392), no one of these activities that can claim privilege as the one, pure source of truth; they are all expressive. That is to say, they are all ways of taking up the world and transforming it ("sublimating it") into new, knowledge-bearing formations. There are, of course, salient differences between each of these endeavors. For example, he argues that with science (and mathematics to some extent), one is expressive in relation to nature, whereas with the arts one begins with previous cultural constructions, that is, other artworks or movements within a field (PP 391, PW 124). Further, one can see that these are activities pursued toward different objectives. Nonetheless, recognizing that they all involve the same expressive process starts to dissolve the deeply entrenched dichotomy between the sciences and the arts, and it does justice to certain aspects of these domains that otherwise go unacknowledged. For instance, this recognition accounts for the genuine creativity involved in mathematics and science: the process of expression is the hidden source, for example, of one's hypotheses or of ingenious set-ups to insure experimental control. But this rapprochement also helps us appreciate the felt necessity that art, literature, and poetry can have: it was in fact possible for the Mona Lisa to have had some other facial expression, but for us now "it wouldn't be the Mona Lisa" if it did. Art, science, mathematics . . . indeed, as fundamentally expressive activities, they are all modalities of knowing; they are all different ways of "singing the world" (PP 187).

Expression: for Merleau-Ponty, again, this term refers to a "characteristic operation of the mind" (UT 7) whereby some overwhelming initial form, figure, datum, or image, is creatively transformed and reorganized in a way that radiates new meaning or insight, and which brings a strong feeling of necessity. This operation—the cognitive analogue of the living body's ability to acquire habits or incorporate some new practice—is central to the processes of knowledge and communicating with others. It is how, Merleau-Ponty says, truths are "discovered"; in fact, they are *acquired* through the patient, sometimes frustrating, sometimes delirious labor of expression. Again, the reason such a reorganizing, crystallizing operation is required for knowledge is not because our experience of the world is impoverished, but rather because it is so full of half-hidden forms and figures, overflowing in meaning and possible perspectives.

In what follows, I will have a great deal more to say to assist our understanding of this complex but important view. We will see, for example, how it allows Merleau-Ponty to offer an exceptionally promising philosophy of language, and how it leads him to a more radical understanding of his own philosophical method. But one thing to be underscored here is that his epistemology of expression keeps the modalities of knowledge and truth squarely rooted in history and culture. Science, mathematics, knowledge, and art do not happen by tapping into some transcendental sphere that is free from "the push and shove of being." Nor are they necessitated by some Hegelian *telos.* The work of expressing the world is contingent through and through. It is contingent upon the people who labor through the trauma of expression to transfigure what has been given to them, contingent upon their ability and commitment to being creative, when so much around them is mimetic. And it is contingent upon previous cultural acquisitions, upon the material and political conditions amid which such people are thinking. Indeed, there is no internal principle or force or "world spirit" that necessitates, for instance, Frege's *Begriff-schrift*, Cantor's proof for transfinite cardinals, or Manet's early impressionistic use of color. Having said that, however, once these expressive acquisitions take hold, there seems no way to have avoided them; their transformative fecundity makes them inescapable and a whole new tradition is born. In short, the process of expression presents us with the extraordinary combination of cognitive acts that are in fact utterly contingent, but which bear the aura of eternity.

Merleau-Ponty argues that it is in terms of this enigmatic combination in expression—radical contingencies which seem eternal—that we can finally understand the Cartesian *cogito*. For as we have seen against the transcendental tradition, tackling its own best case of mathematics, there is no pure, self-present thought independent of and prior to worldly experience. What there is, instead, is either thought in the process of expression ("thought in the making"), or a later thought which rests content with the results or acquisitions of that process. It only *seems* as though the finished thought comes first. It only *seems* as though a unitary, self-contained entity called the *cogito* comes first. In fact, what really comes first are the disparate acts of an embodied being who is thrown into a world: a being surrounded by rich possibilities and sense-directions who acts both through impersonal, biological forces and the most personal of intentions. This embodied being, we have just seen, also has the cognitive wherewithal to pause and gather (some of) those disparate aspects into a coherent image, to *express itself* as a unitary being called "a self," to say with great truth and force that "*I* exist."[15] But to pass from this result to the notion that the unitary, coherent, self actually *precedes* embodied life is to be in the grip of a "transcendental illusion." This specific transcendental illusion—I call it "the *cogito* illusion"—is not one that Kant identifies in the first *Critique*, but rather one that Kant himself commits when he posits the transcendental subject. However tempting it may be—and transcendental illusions always are—it is simply not true that the ability to reflect upon and collect myself points to a pre-existing transcendental *cogito*. It is not true that my thinking guarantees my existence. On the contrary, Merleau-Ponty argues that the necessity and certainty of my thoughts stem from my existence in the world and the embodied acts of expression that give voice to them. As he rather poignantly says:

> [S]elf-possession, coincidence with the self, does not serve to define thought:
> it is, on the contrary, an outcome of expression and always an illusion, in so
> far as the clarity of what is acquired rests upon the fundamentally obscure
> operation which has enabled us to immortalize within ourselves a moment of
> fleeting life. We are invited to discern beneath thinking that basks in its acqui-

sitions, and offers merely a brief resting-place in the unending process of expression, another thought which is struggling to establish itself. (PP 389)[16]

Later in "The *Cogito*" chapter, Merleau-Ponty argues that the ground of this transcendental illusion is time. Not time as a "form of sensibility" in a transcendental subject (Kant), but rather natural time as it is lived through my ageing body, as it exceeds my consciousness. It is, he says, because natural time is constantly dispersing, seeping into the past, that thought has to "struggle to establish itself." It is also because thought is able to overcome that lassitude, to collect itself in a creative, transformational moment that one feels as though the achievement leaves time behind. As Merleau-Ponty says, "What is called the non-temporal in thought is what, having thus carried forward [*repris*] the past and engaged the future, is presumptively of all time, but is therefore nothing transcendent to time" (PP 392, PP-F 450). Later, and in other scattered passages in *Phenomenology of Perception,* Merleau-Ponty refers to the relationship between natural time and the illusion of eternity, between the actual contingency of expression and its retrospective sense of necessity, by using the Husserlian language of *Fundierung.*[17] Whatever one calls it—*Fundierung* or "active transcendence" (PP 376)—Merleau-Ponty is clear that these presumptions of eternity and necessity which adhere to expression "after the fact" play a substantial part in one's losing sight of the expressive process itself.

Merleau-Ponty also underscores how we forget the process of expressing the world because we culturally come to be "obsessed with objective thought." Indeed, the ill-defined yet utterly pervasive demand for "objectivity" in our institutions and pedagogies obscures the creative, transformational thinking required to have knowledge of the world and our own ideas. This demand also perpetuates the false idol of a complete and final knowledge, an epistemic Eden freed from the trauma of expression. Dream though we will, all it takes is the experience of the blank page, an unsolved crime, an undiagnosed illness, the lack of a hypothesis, or a particularly resistant theorem to *wake us up* and remind us that such an idol is an unrealizable fantasy for beings who are born.

In all this, we have begun to see that Merleau-Ponty's account of expressive cognition offers a substantial new paradigm for a post-supernatural age. That is to say, for an age that really takes the fact of human evolution and natural history seriously. For recognizing the process of expression, Merleau-Ponty is able to utterly eliminate the need for transcendental metaphysics. He is able to account for the force, necessity, and seeming priority of certain cognitive acquisitions (mathematics, the *cogito*), while showing them as the work of embodied beings in a natural world. At the same time, Merleau-Ponty's view exposes why the reductive analytics of contemporary physicalism is also unsatisfying. For in its efforts to understand thought and meaning in terms of analyzed parts, and the parts of the parts (which is certainly acceptable for a certain mode of discourse and understanding), reductive materialism fails to systematically understand the embodied mind's extraordinary power to take up and transform the world through expression. Without recognizing this process, and without acknowledging the rigorous philosophical method (phenomenology) that reveals it as an equally important order of discourse, there will always be a lurking feeling that God is required, always a sense that explanatory science is deadening because it flattens the dynamic, qualitative life out of things. In recent years there has been a surge of writings by physicalists to insist that analytic explanations aren't cynical, but rather give rise to wonder about the complex workings of nature.[18] Setting aside the dogmatism that sometimes mars this discourse, I read and enjoy these books. Nonetheless, I am convinced that these writings will not succeed until they celebrate the creative power of the mind to expressively transform the *con*-fusion of possibilities that the natural world provides. Again, no God is required—merely sensitivity to the transcending powers at work in the least moment of reflection. As Merleau-Ponty puts this exact point:

> [T]he positing of God contributes nothing to the elucidation of our life. We experience, not a genuine eternity and a participation in the One, but concrete acts of taking up and carrying forward by which, through time's accidents, we are linked in relationships with ourselves and others. In short, we experience a *participation in the world,* and "being-in-truth" is indistinguishable from being-in-the-world. (PP 394–395)

4. Expression, Husserlian Phenomenology, Deconstruction

In the preceding sections I have sought to elucidate Merleau-Ponty's account of expression as a specific capacity of the embodied mind. Responding to the open, overflowing possibilities of perceptual life, expressions are ideas or insights that reorganize and creatively elaborate aspects of it without obscuring or covering it; thus they bring knowledge and a sense of necessity. I have also attempted to establish the contemporary promise of this account by showing how it refutes founding principles of transcendental-supernatural philosophy and also embraces the transcendent processes of knowing and thinking while keeping them rooted in the natural world. In this way, Merleau-Ponty's philosophy of expression offers a new epistemological paradigm for a post-Darwinian age—one that leaves behind the lurking dualism of transcendental philosophy and the reductive analytics of traditional empiricism. But again, it might be wondered: if Merleau-Ponty's account of expressive cognition is so promising, why have philosophers missed it? Why is it that, nearly fifty years after he developed his view, the arguments of this chapter are necessary? I would begin to reply by saying that our "missing" expression shouldn't surprise us because it is natural to overlook expressive cognition. This is just part of how it works: after the trauma of expression and the reorganizing clarity this expression brings, we reside in the results and lose sight of the creative, embodied, contingent process itself. In short, "missing" the expressive struggle to give birth to knowledge and truth is an aspect of the process. However, the oversight by scholars has also been fuelled by genuine difficulties in Merleau-Ponty's writings. For example, consider how much work a reader has to do to make out his account of expression: not only does it involve understanding his phenomenology of living experience, but the account is poorly articulated until very late in *Phenomenology of Perception*. Indeed, one has to go a long way with Merleau-Ponty in order to get to his philosophy of expression. A third reason that this important part of Merleau-Ponty's thought has been largely overlooked has to do with a particular contingency of recent philosophical history: the widespread, but flawed assimilation of his philosophical project to Husserl's phenomenology.

It must be said at the outset that this historical assimilation was inadvertently perpetuated by Merleau-Ponty himself. Early on, he embraces the language of Husserl's phenomenology, and when he offers his own critical reinterpretation of its terms, he softens the blow by suggesting places and passages where Husserl might seem to agree with him. Further, in some texts and passages, right up until the final writings, Merleau-Ponty can be correctly criticized for overly generous, even fallacious readings of Husserl's project.[19] Nonetheless, I believe Merleau-Ponty's philosophy of expression is an important site of his rift with Husserlian phenomenology; and the failure to appreciate this difference—the tendency for philosophers to criticize their projects as one—has also contributed to the problem. Of course, the relationship between Merleau-Ponty and Husserl is a large, complex issue that could be explored in great detail, but I believe we can quickly get to the crux of the difference between the thinkers by considering Husserl's late essay, "The Origin of Geometry."[20] This essay is particularly appropriate here because it presents Husserl's view of the very issue we have just studied in Merleau-Ponty—the nature and ground of mathematical proof. It also exemplifies Husserl's late efforts, no doubt inspired by Heidegger's *Being and Time,* to articulate his phenomenology in a way that is not merely "static," but "genetic."[21] That is, in a way that respects the historicity of ideas and accounts for their birth and development in the world.

Saying only that, it might seem that Husserl and Merleau-Ponty *are* engaged in the same project, a notion exacerbated by the fact that Husserl also speaks of mathematical truth as "expression," and "creative activity."[22] However, it is at this relatively superficial level that the similarities end, for almost immediately it becomes clear that Husserl is driven by a transcendental intention. As Husserl says:

> The question of the origin of geometry . . . shall not be considered here as the philological-historical question. . . . Rather than this . . . we inquire into that sense in which it appeared in history for the first time—*in which it had to appear,* even though we know nothing of the first creators and are not even asking after them. Starting from what we know, from our geometry . . . [this] is an inquiry back into the submerged original beginnings of geometry as *they necessarily must have been* in their "primally establishing" function.[23]

We see in this passage a classic Kantian gesture. Bracketing language, history, and the worldly particularities of mathematical creators, Husserl's so-called "regressive inquiry" is after those necessary "conditions of possibility" that gave rise to geometry as we know it. What is different from Kant is Husserl's genetic recognition that these transcendental origins of geometry irrupt within history and give rise to a whole historical tradition of geometry. As a result, for Husserl the driving question becomes one of how what is *inside* the "conscious space" of the geometer can have a life *outside* in history and culture—how the initially "subjective" ideas of geometry can become "objective" and thus found a tradition.[24]

Already we can discern irreducible differences from Merleau-Ponty. For Merleau-Ponty, geometrical ideas, the process of proof, are not "inside" trying to get "outside"; they are already outside, already "objective" in Husserl's sense. That is, they are the insights and acts of embodied beings who are bound up with and conditioned by the world, history, and the traditions of mathematics. Those conditions—embodiment, history, world, tradition—cannot legitimately be "bracketed" in order to uncover the pure "primal" sense of geometrical ideas, for the simple reason that those conditions inextricably inform their sense from the start. Further, Husserl's view that there *has to be* an origin to which we can trace back assumes that mathematical ideas unfold through deductive necessity (the analytic view of mathematics), while Merleau-Ponty holds that the necessity involved is the retrospective sense that comes *after* acts of expression and then disguises their contingent character. In short, Husserl is in the grip of the transcendental illusion we described in section 3—the illusion through which we posit prior necessity (in Husserl's case, tacitly tied to a transcendental subject) when there is in fact only contingency.[25] Thus, for

Merleau-Ponty, there can be no "regressive inquiry" to an ahistorical, transcendental origin of *the* geometrical tradition. On the contrary, there are many traditions or paradigms of geometry, rooted in the values, projects, and embodied life of the cultures that have given rise to them. Again, who knows what mathematical traditions were lost when the Alexandrian library burned? And who knows what mind-bending paradigms are yet to come? What we do know, however, is that our common Euclidean tradition is not an utter vagary; it forcefully explicates things, figures, and ideas along certain lines of possibility, and therefore maintains a kind of objectivity, even though other traditions currently exist and are yet to come. Euclidean geometry is not a link in one unbroken chain, but rather, as Merleau-Ponty puts it, a system that was "operative for a certain period in the history of the human mind": it "signifies that for a time, men were able to take a homogeneous three-dimensional space as the 'ground' of their thoughts" (PP 393–394).

With these insights in place, we are thus able to see how irreducibly different the two philosophers are when it comes to "expression." This is because Husserl's use and sense of "expression" in mathematics and thinking is all about "reactivating" and "recollecting" the primal meanings through a process of resisting (or bracketing) the "passivity" and "equivocation" of the world, history, and culture. This basic definition of "expression" can be found in all of Husserl's writings, from the early *Logical Investigations* to this very late essay, "The Origin of Geometry." However, this concept of expression has nothing in common with Merleau-Ponty's use of expression to refer to historical, contingent creative acts that take up and transform the world and our ideas in powerful, new ways.

At this point someone might object that Husserl also talks about creativity, that at the very end of his transcendental regression he finds "the complete freedom to transform . . . the life-world" as the first origin of geometry.[26] Doesn't this bring our two thinkers back together? The answer is: only if you ignore that Husserl and Merleau-Ponty are referring to irreducibly different things with their notions of creativity. For Husserl, "creativity" specifically refers to his famed method of "free variation": the method whereby one uses the imagination ("thought and phantasy") to run through and vary all the conceivable possible properties of an object until you find the ones that simply cannot be varied for that object. For then, Husserl says, "there arises, with apodictic self-evidence, an essentially general set of elements going through all the variants . . . Thereby we have removed every bond to the factually valid historical world."[27] However, in this chapter we have seen Merleau-Ponty's view that the creativity in expression is not about *eliminating* possibilities to find a necessary property (Husserl's view), but rather about imaginatively *produc-*

ing a whole new possibility that solves a problem. It is not about finding, in a Platonic fashion, the necessary property or *eidos* that defines some object, but rather about illuminating some open, ambiguous *Gestalt* along one line of possibility among many. Indeed, creativity at the origin of geometry for Husserl is about using imagination to discover imagination's absolute limit, not about celebrating its power to produce a multiplicity of whole new fecund forms.[28]

In sum, there is no rapprochement or assimilation between Merleau-Ponty and Husserl on the origin of geometry and the nature of expression. This is just one of the misunderstandings that have taken hold amid the extraordinary complexities of their texts and the contingencies of philosophical history. One important episode in this contingent history can be seen by briefly considering Jacques Derrida's early, influential essay, "Speech and Phenomena: Introduction to the Problem of Signs in Husserl's Phenomenology."[29] This text, and Derrida's still earlier *Edmund Husserl's Origin of Geometry: An Introduction,* are brilliant, even devastating deconstructive arguments against Husserl's philosophy. The problem is that Derrida's arguments apparently intend (and have been taken) to criticize Merleau-Ponty's project as well. One reason scholars have assumed this is because Derrida's arguments in "Speech and Phenomena" center squarely on Husserl's notion of *expression*: if one fails to appreciate the differences between Merleau-Ponty's philosophy of expression and Husserl's transcendental regression it would seems that Merleau-Ponty's thought is equally compromised. But another reason for this assumption is that early in his career, Derrida seems happy to make this equation: he suggests time and again that his deconstructive argument bears against "all phenomenology," and "phenomenology itself." Consider, for instance, the following passage: "[Our] whole analysis will thus advance in the separation between *de facto* and *de jure,* existence and essence, reality and intentional function . . . we would be tempted to say that this separation . . . defines *the very space of phenomenology.*"[30] Elsewhere in the text, Derrida claims that "the whole of phenomenology has followed" Husserl's "essential distinction" between expression and the empirical.[31] In light of what we have seen in this chapter, this is a stunning claim—stunning in its uncustomary lack of caution and in its falseness. I could continue to list examples of this totalizing gesture in "Speech and Phenomena," places where Derrida implies that his argument bears upon Merleau-Ponty.[32] But the point to be made is that Derrida's early text, for all its power and historical influence, fails to understand and has contributed to a general obfuscation of the distinctly non-Husserlian, anti-transcendental character of Merleau-Ponty's philosophy of expression.

However, the assimilation of Merleau-Ponty to Husserl at the origin of geometry has also had another consequence: it has kept many contemporary philosophers from seeing that Merleau-Ponty's philosophy of expression offers an extremely promising and productive account of human knowledge for a postmodern, post-Darwinian age. Again, for Merleau-Ponty, knowledge—in mathematics, science, logic, philosophy, and art—is not a re-presentation of what has come before, but a creative transformation or "sublimation" of the given field into new, powerful, fecund forms. And, to extend my observations from last chapter about the "differentiated proximities" between Merleau-Ponty and Derrida, this productive epistemology is something rather different from what Derrida envisions. For in a number of his early works, Derrida both implies and explicitly claims that knowledge, self-knowledge, and philosophy itself come down to a dilemma between transcendental thought ("the metaphysics of presence") and his own deconstructive epistemology.[33] While Derrida himself abandons this binary gesture by the late 1970s, I must say that Merleau-Ponty's philosophy of expression provides an excellent example of why the dilemma is false. This is because expression is yet another way to understand and practice knowledge beyond the frame and limits of "onto-theology."

Having made this argument, I want to underscore that I am not de-legitimizing deconstruction. I have already argued (in chapter 5) that it is an indispensable method for uncovering constitutive aporetic structures and hidden vestiges of onto-theology. And Merleau-Ponty's account of the transcendental illusion that haunts our knowledge and truth-claims forcefully reminds us why we need to be critically vigilant about such claims—a vigilance that has probably had no greater advocate and practitioner than Derrida. Nonetheless, I am arguing that knowledge and philosophy itself does not *have to be* the project of unsettling univocal thought by "writing with two hands" under the sign of the *law* (of the text or the mark). It can also be *other*: expressing the world, singing the world in a plurality of ways, and with a multiplicity of voices. Here is a "place"—a region of concepts—in which Merleau-Ponty's philosophy of expression is profoundly consonant with Deleuze's ontology of immanence: an ontology in which Deleuze centalizes "expression" as the operation through which univocal being perpetually unfolds, multiplies, produces, and differentiates itself.[34]

Perhaps, however, someone will object that Merleau-Ponty's philosophy nonetheless betrays what Derrida (and Deleuze too) might call "a nostalgia for origins"—something exposed in Merleau-Ponty's talk of expression as "originating" thought and in his language of "acquired" thought as "secondary." Or perhaps, this nostalgia is exposed in Merleau-Ponty's continued use of "bracketing" to return our attention to living perception. I do not dispute this: I have already argued, in chapter 1, that Merleau-Ponty's ontology *is* open to this critique in his early talk of living perception as "primary" to scientific explanation or as "more fundamental" than scientific discourse. I have argued that this way of understanding phenomenology is flawed, that phenomenology is one important mode or level of discourse about the world, but not more "fundamental" than all others. However, I am also confident that Merleau-Ponty's gradual recognition and developing articulation of expressive cognition permits him to start conceiving his philosophical method in ways that unsettle and challenge his own early Husserlian talk of the "primary." Not yet, I think, in *Phenomenology of Perception*—the idea of expression is still formulating; it is really only worked out in the third to the last chapter ("The *Cogito*"). But already by 1951, in *The Prose of the World,* Merleau-Ponty explicitly states that the phenomenon of expression requires a radical revision of the whole notion of "primacy." For on one hand, he says, "secondary" or "ready-made" thoughts are the upshots of expressive activity—expressions that have settled into clichés or habit. However, he also argues in this text that new, expressive thinking and speaking always emerge amid secondary or sedimented thoughts, meanings, or language without being reducible to them. In short, Merleau-Ponty comes to grasp the relation between expressive and sedimented thought and language as mutually informing, symbiotic, yet non-reductive. As he says in *The Prose of the World:* "We must therefore say about [sedimented] language in relation to meaning [that is, expression] what Simone de Beauvoir says of the body in relation to mind: it is neither primary nor secondary. . . . There is no subordination . . . between them. What we have to say is only the *excess* of what we live over what has already been said" (PW 111–112, emphasis added).

Merleau-Ponty comes to see, then, that expressive thought and language is not derived in any deductive or causal sense from sedimented "givens." But neither is it more "primary" than or foundational to them. The relationship, he comes to say, is something different: marked not by empiricist or phenomenological reduction, but rather by *excess, creativity,* and *freedom:* "We are not reducing mathematical evidence to perceptual evidence. We are certainly not denying . . . the originality of the order of knowledge vis-à-vis the perceptual order. We are trying only to loose[n] the intentional web that ties them to one another, to rediscover the paths of sublimation which preserves and transforms the perceived world into the spoken word" (PW 186). In the conclusion, I will say more about this important but elusive relationship, for what is at stake in it is Merleau-Ponty's final view of the non-reductive "reversibility" between thought and perception, "the visible and the invisible." However, for now, it may have been noticed that a new term has crept into the discussion: that of *language.* Indeed, for Merleau-Ponty, expression, thinking, and language are closely intertwined aspects of "the invisible"; rarely does he discuss one aspect of this triad without also interweaving the others into the discussion. In this chapter, I have intentionally avoided the complexities of language in order to promote understanding of Merleau-Ponty's specific account of expressive thought. With this understanding in place we can now turn our attention to his expressive theory of language and the way in which it resolves certain intractable problems that have plagued contemporary thought about language.

7 Behold "The Speaking Word": The Expressive Life of Language

These considerations enable us to restore to the act of speaking its true physiognomy.
—MERLEAU-PONTY[1]

Without language, thought is a vague, uncharted nebula. There are no preexisting ideas, and nothing is distinct before the appearance of language.
—FERDINAND DE SAUSSURE[2]

1. An Introduction to Merleau-Ponty's Philosophy of Language

So far in this book we have seen central elements of Merleau-Ponty's perceptual ontology: his phenomenology of living perception as our synergistic opening to the transcendent world (*l'ouverture au monde*), his important accounts of embodied subjectivity and intersubjectivity, and his later rearticulations of these phenomena in terms of flesh, *écart,* and reversibility. In the previous chapter we turned our attention from these ontological themes—what Merleau-Ponty calls "the visible"—toward "the invisible," that is, toward his account of the life of the mind as the expressive transformation of already acquired ideas (or perceptions) into powerful new forms. At the heart of this account of expressive cognition is a distinction between (1) expressive, creative, spontaneous thinking, and (2) already acquired, sedimented thinking. Further, Merleau-Ponty argues that these two types of thinking are in a strange, elusive relationship. For on one hand, expressive thinking is the source (*Ursprung*) of our conceptual acquisitions and sedimented thoughts; expression is the process by which new breakthrough thoughts are acquired. Nonetheless, the organizing, clarifying, relieving power of the breakthrough obscures the originating process, and the derivative acquisition appears always to have been true. This is a strange dynamic, Merleau-Ponty suggests, but such is the life of the mind: acquired results obscure the expressive process, that is, the *re-presentation* disguises the expressive *coming-to-presentation* of our ideas. As we saw in chapter 6, in *Phenomenology of Perception* Merleau-Ponty refers to this complex dynamic (in which representation displaces and supplants expression) as the *Fundierung* relation; and he calls this relation an "ultimate" fact of our cognitive life (PP 394). I myself would prefer a less obscure name than *Fundierung,* perhaps "the expression relation." Whatever we call it, we saw that this weird dynamic is the source of transcendental illusions about mathematical objects and the self—illusions which, once dispelled, return those ideas to their place within culture, history, and nature.

Expression: again, this is Merleau-Ponty's master term for a creative, productive cognitive power—a power that is rooted in the excess of embodied perceptual life. For him, expression is absolutely central for mathematics, science, and art. While these truth-seeking domains are distinct in many respects, they all proceed and historically unfold through expression. Merleau-Ponty also holds that this power is central to language, and that any theory of language which overlooks its expressive life will be dramatically inadequate. It is often said among philosophers that the twentieth century is the time of "the linguistic turn," the time in philosophical history when language passes from being largely unremarkable to being treated as a preeminent concern. It is also well-known that important claims and arguments to this effect have been offered by thinkers such as Wittgenstein, Heidegger, Quine, Derrida, and Rorty. As this chapter unfolds it will become clear that Merleau-Ponty's philosophy of language dovetails with the work of these thinkers in many respects. However, I also believe that Merleau-Ponty's view, which uncovers and emphasizes language's expressive character, offers singular and indispensable insights for understanding language. For one thing, his expressive theory of language explains the complex continuity between language and our natural life in a most compelling way. That is, it shows how language, for all its transcendent character, is still an outgrowth of our living embodiment and perception. But also, in uncovering the expressive life of language (what he calls "the speaking word") beneath and beyond its representational function, Merleau-Ponty is able to offer a clear, compelling account of the intimate, internal relationship between language and thought. Finally, I believe that his account shows a way to leave behind, once and for all, the two main, deeply problematic theories of language that still shape much contemporary thinking about it: representationalism and structuralism.

The task, then, in this final chapter is to make good on these claims: to begin to establish Merleau-Ponty's expressive theory of language as a major contribution to the field, one that offers extraordinary resources for perhaps fulfilling the promise of "the linguistic turn" in philosophy. Having said that, I must also acknowledge that there is no easy access to Merleau-Ponty's theory of language—a fact that begins to explain why his work in this domain has gone largely unrecognized. For as we have seen—as the organization of this book itself exemplifies—one first has to gain understanding of Merleau-Ponty's ontology before one can grasp his expressive theory of thought and language. That is to say, one has to get to "the invisible" by way of "the visible." Further complicating the matter is the fact that Merleau-Ponty's thinking about language is a "work-in-progress" during his entire career: it takes shape piecemeal throughout several writings. For example, he makes a first, partial attempt in the early chapter on language in *Phenomenology of Perception*, but he hasn't yet crystallized his sense of the expressive process that is so central to his theory. As I argued in chapter 6, this had to wait until "The *Cogito*" chapter with its rich example of mathematical proof. However, even if we piece together his treatment of language in *Phenomenology of Perception*, Merleau-Ponty still doesn't have a complete theory—not until 1947, when he reads the breakthrough work of Ferdinand de Saussure.

Merleau-Ponty's encounter with structuralist linguistics is utterly transformative and inspiring to him—in the resources it offers to complete his theory of language, but also in his clear sense of its limits. Looking at Merleau-Ponty's career as a whole, we might say that his encounter with Saussure provides something of a tailwind: it gives rise to several lecture courses and essays on language in the late 1940s and early 1950s,[3] and to *The Prose of the World* in 1951, an important but unfinished manuscript on language and expression. It also seems clear that Saussure's notion of "diacritical" difference is the direct inspiration for *écart* in *The Visible and the Invisible*. In the pages that follow I will elucidate Merleau-Ponty's expressive theory of language as a whole by piecing together elements and arguments from writings over the course of his career. In fact, I believe there is no other way to adequately understand his theory of language. Nonetheless, I am convinced that a coherent and compelling theory of language emerges in the end. To establish this, over the course of the chapter I will elucidate and evaluate his theory in relation and contradistinction to two major theories of language: the predominant, traditional view of language as representation (section 2), and Saussure's structuralism (section 3).

2. Beyond Language as Representation

It might seem strange that "the linguistic turn" in philosophy had to wait until the twentieth century, but it is true that before then, concentrated philosophical discussions on the nature of language are relatively scarce. For example, there is barely a mention of language in all of Descartes; it is, for him, as though there is nothing to be said. Similar claims could be made about thinkers such as Spinoza, Leibniz, Berkeley, Hume, Kant, Hegel, Marx, and Kierkegaard (even Nietzsche to some extent): theory of language remains at the margins of their philosophies and does not become thematic. We might well wonder how this could be. I would answer that it is because all these philosophers take the nature of language to be self-evident. More precisely, they accept as self-evident the classical theory that defines language as *representation,* as the means to re-present our ideas, thoughts, or concepts. I use the word "classical" for this theory because it literally is: the theory's earliest articulation is found in Plato's *Cratylus,* in which he argues that names and words, in their letters and syllables, must *imitate* the conceptual forms (*eide*) of things.[4] However, its more well-known articulation appears in Aristotle, *On Interpretation:* "Spoken words are the symbols of mental experience and written words are the symbols of spoken words. Just as all men have not the same speech sounds, so all men have not the same speech sounds, but the mental experiences, which these directly symbolize, are the same for all."[5] What we have in this passage (following on from Plato and taken up later by Augustine in the *Confessions*), is a quite particular theory about the relations at work in our conceptual-linguistic life. That is, we have ideas or concepts about the things of the world around us, and then we use language, written or spoken, to represent those ideas to others. Language is a device for representing our ideas.

This representational theory of language is reinforced and extended in the modern philosophical era. Surprisingly, this is not done by Descartes, for whom the theory was a natural fit, but rather by that great Cartesian-empiricist, John Locke, who expresses it in unequivocal terms in book 3 of the *Essay.*[6] What Locke adds, first, is a stronger claim about the origin of language and its utilitarian function: humans devised language primarily to communicate our "internal Ideas" and thus to increase our "Sociability" with others. More importantly, Locke offers an explicit and very influential theory of linguistic *meaning:* "The use then of Words, is to be sensible Marks of *Ideas;* and the *Ideas* they stand for, are their proper and immediate Signification."[7] Again, the meaning of a word just is the idea it represents, or the idea I intend it to represent; thus the meaning of the word "cat," for instance, is nothing other than the idea I have in mind when I say it. At first glance this "idea" or "psychological" theory of linguistic meaning may seem strange, but it is in fact quite familiar. It is the theory that is presupposed every time one says "I didn't *mean* to hurt your feelings," or "I didn't *intend* it that way." At the very dawn of the "linguistic turn," in the late nineteenth and early twentieth centuries, work by Frege and Wittgenstein attempted to jettison the psychological theory of meaning for accounts that were cashed out in terms of the object itself (Frege's reference), or the structural isomorphism between a sentence and a complex fact (Wittgenstein's view in the *Tractatus*). But these modifications to the theory of meaning didn't essentially change the larger theory of language: the fundamental nature of language remains representational; language is a means of representing, if not our ideas and concepts, then the things of the world.

There is no question that this type of language theory has seemed utterly compelling to philosophers and to our common sense as well. Apparently, Aristotle's and Locke's articulations of the theory are so incisive that they go virtually unchallenged for centuries and centuries; and this theory has the great virtue of meshing with our everyday intuitions about how language works. After all, what other purpose could language have if not to represent our ideas to others? The problem is that this representational theory of language—whichever account of meaning one adopts—generates such extraordinary difficulties that it cannot be possibly be correct.

For one thing, the theory generates the much-discussed "problem of reference." The problem of reference is a problem with two distinct sides; it is a sword that cuts with two edges. One "edge" is the ontological challenge: given that language is defined as representing our ideas or things, how exactly does this work? What precisely does "represent" here *mean*? Plato, for instance, says words "imitate" the conceptual forms. Aristotle says language "symbolizes" mental experience. Locke says it "signifies" our ideas. Yes, but what do *those* words mean? Philosophers have found it notoriously difficult to specify these terms without begging the question. They have found it difficult to satisfactorily explain how it is possible for spoken or written words to "match up with" or "hook onto" our ideas or the world itself. Yet this unspecified relation is nothing less than the definitional heart of the theory.

The second "edge" of the problem of reference is no less vexed. It is what is sometimes called the epistemological problem of decidability, or, more simply, "the problem of communication." To understand this, recall that the representation theory maintains we use language to communicate our ideas to others. Yet the details of the theory would seem to make genuine communication impossible or at least unknowable. This is because the theory (in most versions) maintains that the meanings of my words are inside my head, in my ideas or my intentions; the words themselves refer to these private, internal meanings. How then are we supposed to know that we understand each other when we speak? For instance, modifying Quine's famous argument, assume I use the word "rabbit" to convey to you my mental idea of "rabbit."[8] Nothing in the theory entails or even makes conceivable that you, upon hearing the word, thereby have or know *my* idea. Even if you tell me that you understand what I mean, that doesn't mean you actually do, for you might have the idea "rabbit-parts" in your head instead. Nothing in the representation theory precludes this misunderstanding; nothing precludes the constant, perpetual lack of communication between people. In *Philosophical Investigations,* Wittgenstein argues (against his earlier view in the *Tractatus*) that this "under-determination of reference" is equally troublesome for versions of representationalism which hold that our words mean and refer to worldly things themselves. For on this type of account, one's words mean by pointing to the object. However, as Wittgenstein argues time and again, an ostensive definition—even the physical act of pointing—"can be variously interpreted in *every* case."[9]

Now, for Merleau-Ponty, the epistemological problem of reference would be enough to reject the representation theory of language. He is preeminently concerned, in all his writings on the subject, that an adequate theory of language must be able to explain how communication and understanding between people is in fact possible. However, Merleau-Ponty also rejects the representation theory because it has implications that flat-out contradict our living experiences of language. First, the theory can't explain how our *words themselves bear meaning*.[10] Indeed, on this theory, all meaning resides in my idea, my intention, or the object being referred to; the word itself is an empty shell passing my meaning along, or alternatively, it is a "pointer" toward the object-meaning. But our actual experiences with language reveal something quite different. For one obvious example: racist language and symbols (such as the Confederate flag) still *mean* bigotry and oppression to people, even if the user doesn't have that idea or intention in mind. Thus, it seems that to some extent meaning is borne by words, phrases, signs, and sentences themselves.

Merleau-Ponty's second concern is that the representation theory structurally insists that thoughts, ideas, and concepts are ontologically prior to language, and this is clearly not always, or even typically, the case. He says:

> [I]f talking were primarily a matter of meeting the object through a . . . representation, we could not understand why thought tends towards expression as towards its completion, why the most familiar things appear indeterminate as long as we have not recalled its name, why the thinking subject himself is in a kind of ignorance of his thoughts so long as he has not . . . spoken or written them, as is shown by the example of so many writers who begin a book without knowing exactly what they are going to say. (PP 177)

As writers, teachers, and public speakers well know—indeed as we all know from our everyday conversations—we are often surprised by the new thoughts to which our written and spoken language lead us. We very often speak and write to *discover* what we think, not merely to report what we already know.

This important insight leads us to the heart of Merleau-Ponty's alternative theory of language: the distinction he draws between already acquired or sedimented language and expressive language. To be sure, if one only acknowledges already acquired language, then it *would* seem that language is merely a representation of already formed ideas—merely a record to pass on those ideas.[11] However, Merleau-Ponty argues this forgets that there is, *and has to be,* a whole process that gives rise to our linguistic acquisitions: the process of "originating" language, or expression. Already we are on familiar terrain: as we saw in chapter 6, just as the powerful results of mathematical thinking obscure the creative, contingent, expressive process that gives rise to them, so too this sort of obfuscation characterizes our linguistic life. That is, the deep familiarity of already acquired words, terms, sentences, and phrases leads us to forget the expressive life of language. We forget how we first learned those familiar words, how we learn language in the first place, and how we continually create new words and meanings. Recall in the case of geometrical proof that one starts expressing from the over-spilling fecundity of the triangle, the *con*-fusion of meaning-possibilities that this simple *Gestalt* opens up. In the case of language, being expressive starts from the overwhelming babble of the world, or those moments when words fail us. With language, being expressive requires that one creatively reconfigure the words, phrases, and perhaps even syllables that are already at one's disposal so that they are infused with new articulating sense and power. Alternatively, in some cases (we will soon see), it involves being actively open to some strange new sense being offered by another person. In either case, Merleau-Ponty says: "This power of [linguistic] expression . . . does not merely leave for the reader and writer himself a kind of reminder, it brings the meaning into existence as a thing at the very heart of the text . . . it [establishes] it in the writer or the reader as a new sense organ, opening a new field or a new dimension to our experience" (PP 182).

Once we start looking beyond the most familiar, habituated uses of language ("the cat is on the mat," "tree," "how are you?"), it becomes quite easy to recognize this expressive level of language. For instance, I remember as a kid in the 1960s when I first heard the word "groovy." This word was weird, but oddly compelling. It expressed something I previously had no word for, and before I knew it "groovy" had become part of my everyday lexicon. It became part of everyone else's also: before long the word had become a widespread cultural acquisition. This same dynamic—a new, surging expression that eventually becomes sedimented in our language—can be seen throughout our popular lingo and slang: after "groovy," things were "cool," then "hip," and then "phat"; a few years ago we were "up on" things, then we were "down with" them, and now they are "sick." But we can also see the transformational, originating life of language in the way infants learn it: one day something dramatically new happens—the child's desire and development gears into the surrounding linguistic field—and, for instance, the word "Ma" is born. In *The Prose of the World,* Merleau-Ponty calls this creative, productive side of language *the speaking word* (*le langage parlant*): it is the side of language "which creates itself through its expressive acts" (PW 10, PW-F 17).[12] And he distinguishes the speaking word from *the spoken word* (*le langage parlé*), that is, "language after the fact, or language as an institution" (PW 10), which results from previous expressive acts, but which also supplies the linguistic field with materials for future, new expressions. For Merleau-Ponty, drawing this important distinction between "the speaking word" and "the already spoken word" allows a promising way for us to move our understanding of language beyond the impasses and difficulties of the representation theory.

For one thing, acknowledging the expressive life of language allows us to put representational language in its proper place. It isn't, for Merleau-Ponty, that we don't use language to represent ideas or objects. Certainly we can and often do use language in this way, for example, when we say things such as, "The tree is brown," or "There is Joe." Here the ideas and words have already been acquired; the expressive work has already been done and the words do merely point to objects or recollect finished ideas. But to make just *this* the nature and definition of language is to mistake a derivative and partial modality of language for all of language itself.[13] As we have seen several times in this book, this reification is a familiar error in representational accounts of thought and perception: they mistake a second-order result for the primary process. However, we can also understand that it is a motivated error, for as Merleau-Ponty has also shown, our cognitive life is marked by this strange dynamic where the comfort-giving, organizing power of certain results obscures the difficult, open work of expressing them—the "*Fundierung* relation." Further, this reifying dynamic helps us understand why the representation theory of language has seemed so compelling to the philosophical tradition and our common-sense intuitions, even though it is deeply flawed. Indeed, our thoughts, ideas, and concepts appear complete and prior to our linguistic experiences by way of the transcendental illusion at the heart of our cognitive life. It is the same transcendental illusion that gives rise, for example, to the Cartesian *cogito* as a pure thinking mind divorced from the body and the Platonic notion of number and shape as transcendental objects. Thus, it is no coincidence that the early framers of the representation theory of language (Plato, Aristotle, Augustine, Locke) are ultimately dualists about the relation between the mind and body, nor that they all adhere to a transcendental theology.[14] These are all illusory manifestations of the same dynamic that obscures our fully natural, embodied, and expressive life of the mind.

Be that as it may, recognizing this transcendental illusion, what I call the *cogito* illusion, allows Merleau-Ponty to articulate a rather powerful picture of the intimate relation of *language* and *thought*—one that meshes with rather than violates our living experiences of them. For again, it is only at the completely sedimented level of cognitive life that thought appears to be complete and prior to language.[15] For example, right now I can think or imagine a "tree," and then go on to say, "There is a tree." But to move from this exercise to the view that thought just *is* complete and prior to speaking and writing is to forget the originating level of cognitive life, the expressive modality in which we need to write and speak to figure out what we think. This expressive "figuring out" is what journaling and note-taking are all about; it is why we so often verbally "brainstorm" or "process" with others. Giving birth to new ideas, meanings, and words amid the clamor of old notions and clichés is difficult, uncertain work indeed. Part of the difficulty is that to become alive, originating thought needs language or its ephemeral ideas and meanings will evaporate.[16] At the same time, expressive thought supplies the new, creative sense that language etches out. It is worth emphasizing that Merleau-Ponty's view isn't that thought *just is* language, but rather that prior to becoming acquired, thought and language, idea and word are reciprocally intertwined. They are separate, nascent idioms that mutually elaborate one another. That is to say, they are "reversible" in Merleau-Ponty's precise sense of that word from *The Visible and the Invisible*. This is why he says that expressive, productive language "does not translate ready-made thought, but accomplishes it" (PP 178), and that such language is nothing less than "the presence of . . . thought in the phenomenal world" (PP 182).

For Merleau-Ponty then, at the expressive level, idea and word are not divorced from one another, nor are they hierarchically ordered. On the contrary, they belong together as reversible aspects of the same birthing process. With this major insight, Merleau-Ponty begins to solve the epistemological problem of communication. For his view entails that we are rather directly *at* someone's thoughts and meanings in their words. Those thoughts and meanings are there, borne by the words and sentences themselves; there is no ontological barrier between them. Again, the notion that there is such a barrier is the result of mistaking secondary representational function for primary expressive process—the *cogito* illusion. At the same time, however, the accessibility to someone's thoughts and meanings through his/her words doesn't mean for Merleau-Ponty that we are in some perfect fusion with that person. For then the problem of communication is reversed: we pass from never understanding others to never *mis*-understanding them. Contrary to both of these options, what living experience reveals, what our everyday mistakes and occasional successes reveal, is that understanding and taking up the thought-worlds of others through their language is every bit as possible as it is difficult. And importantly, Merleau-Ponty argues that the labor of understanding and communicating with others is itself another manifestation of the expressive process.

Merleau-Ponty elaborates the expressive nature of communication in *The Prose of the World* in a memorable passage about how one understands while reading. I need to quote at some length:

> Once I have read *the* book, it acquires a unique and palpable existence quite apart from the words on the page. . . . I feel . . . as though I have written the book from start to finish. But that is an afterthought. In reality, one must read it first and then . . . it "catches" like a fire. In the same way, I start to read a book idly, giving it hardly any thought; and suddenly, a few words move me, the fire catches, my thoughts are ablaze . . . and the fire feeds off everything I have ever read. I have given my knowledge of the language; I have brought along what I already know about the meaning of the words, the phrases, and the syntax. I have also contributed my whole experience of others and everyday events. . . . But the book would not interest me so much if it told me about things I already know. It makes use of everything I have contributed in order to carry me beyond it. (PW 11)

What we see here in the case of reading are several of the same elements we saw with expressive thinking: one brings his or her own perceptions and already acquired ideas to the fecundity of the blank page or, in this case, the page written by someone else. In this open space, prepared for by self and other, a new expressive connection is born, "catching like a fire." Merleau-Ponty continues the above passage with an example:

> Before I read Stendhal, I know what a rogue is. Thus I can say what he means when he says that Rossi the revenue man is a rogue. . . . I have access to Stendhal's world through the commonplace words he uses. But in his hands, these words are given a new twist. The cross references multiply. More and more arrows point in the direction of a thought I have never encountered before and perhaps would never have met without Stendhal. . . . I get closer and closer to him, until in the end I read his words with the very same intention that he gave to them. (PW 12)

We all have had such experiences while reading great novels. We find ourselves drawn into the extraordinary thought-worlds of Tolkien, Stendhal, Austen, or Lovecraft. I begin reading with my own acquired ideas, meanings, and lexicon, but if I read well and attentively, the author's words and sentences subtly twist those senses and ideas, provoking me to think and imagine what I had never dreamed before. Soon "the fire is lit": I am consumed and transformed by Middle-earth (or Parma, Devonshire, or Arkham), and I cannot imagine a time when it wasn't a part of my thought-world. This same expressive dynamic in reading can also be seen in our conversations with others. We come together with different backgrounds and experiences, but in that worldly space where ideas, meanings, and words are passed back and forth, we may become changed, informed, enriched. That is to say, what we commonly call understanding and communication happens. It is important to remember Merleau-Ponty's view that there is nothing at all necessary in this. Just as with mathematical proof, the process of genuine communication with others is contingent through and through. For we could go on speaking to one another in platitudes and clichés forever: "How are you?" "Fine." "I'm fine too." Without our fresh, creative energy, our commitment to saying and hearing something new, no *conversation* will occur. To be sure, it is no accident that people so often end up arguing when they are tired. Further, Merleau-Ponty is careful to immediately qualify one of his above claims: even at the end of an excellent conversation I never have the *exact* intention and thought as you.[17] He insists that there is no perfect fusion of minds, and misunderstanding is always a horizon of understanding. However, this fact also entails the converse, something we know from the workings of everyday life: the possibility of actually understanding one another is always a horizon of misunderstanding. In short, one of the great strengths of Merleau-Ponty's expression theory of language is its ability to explain the experiential fact of understanding (and misunderstanding) one another.

In this section we have seen several ways in which Merleau-Ponty's expressive theory trumps the traditional representation theory of language. For one, it offers a picture of the intertwined, "reversible" relationship between thought and language that coheres with our living experiences of them. It also offers relief from the epistemological problem of communication—something that the representational theory cannot do in principle. A further strength of his expression theory is that it can address the problem of "the first word." That is to say, it has the resources to explain, in principle, how written and spoken language could come to manifest in the natural world. Indeed, if we take naturalism and evolution seriously—if we are to avoid making language into some new transcendental idol—then we are obligated to have a theory that can theoretically explain how language, in all its diverse glory, comes to be from a world of what Merleau-Ponty calls "primordial silence." After all, facts are facts: there was a time on this planet, not all that long ago in evolutionary terms, when there was no language. So how did we get from there to here? How, in principle, could the first word come to pass? For a moment, consider some of the more famous claims and views about language that have surfaced during the era of "the linguistic turn." We have heard that language is the house of being (Heidegger). It has been said that language is a structure (Saussure), or that it is the play of *différance* (Derrida). We have been told that language is the limit of the world, or a toolbox, or a game (Wittgenstein). We have been told that language is the revelation of the Other (Levinas). These are all thinkers with whom Merleau-Ponty's thought is in very close proximity. But which of them explains the first word? For Merleau-Ponty, if we are to prevent language from becoming some new transcendental sublime, we need to have a theory of language that at least dovetails with natural history rather than ignores it.

The beginning of Merleau-Ponty's answer to this problem of "the first word" is a simple truth about language that seems to be avoided by the above thinkers: whatever else it may involve, language is a *form of behavior.* It is performed by and through living bodies—creatures who have lungs, who pass air through their larynxes and past their tongues, who write, sign, and gesture with their hands. Again, these are not the machine-bodies and mechanistic behaviors of the Cartesian-empiricist tradition, but rather organic bodies who open up an array of *possible* actions, an intentional arc, in their holistic orientation toward the world (chapter 3). As we saw earlier, the living body's experiences in a virtual field generates an interwoven dynamic between biological-impersonal life and personal life—a dynamic in which the living body has the power to take up and acquire dramatically new behaviors and habits such as dancing and bike riding. And we have seen in this chapter that our cognitive and linguistic acts of expression also have this productive power. This means that language and thought is an extension or "sublimation" of our carnal life, not some God-given domain supernaturally appended to the body. Simply put, for Merleau-Ponty the expressive life of the mind is rooted in the transformational powers of the living body; it is the same transcending dynamic raised to a second power. Thus we are able to see his response to the problem of "the first word." For just as at some point in evolutionary history certain organisms developed the cognitive wherewithal to learn and incorporate new behaviors, so too was there a point when some of those organisms developed sufficient cognitive wherewithal to gesture significantly toward others, to express themselves with their body gestures, verbal sounds, or physical marks. The "first word" then is no more a mystery for Merleau-Ponty than the "new words" or new behaviors to which we give birth on any given day: they are all the upshot of a natural power—a naturally selected power—to take up, transform, and make real a possible sense that emerges for cognitive-embodied beings in the overflowing world.[18]

However, beyond the natural-material-carnal side of language, we also know that there is a social-cultural side. Merleau-Ponty certainly acknowledges the social-cultural side of language in the language chapter of *Phenomenology of Perception,* but I don't believe he does very well at articulating how it functions. A further problem in *Phenomenology of Perception* is that his theory of linguistic meaning is extremely unclear. The reader can tell from his arguments there that the meaning of a word or sentence isn't merely one's ideas or intentions, nor is it the referred-to object in the world. Indeed, Merleau-Ponty straightforwardly holds that words themselves bear meaning. But the question remains: precisely *how*? In my view, his early work contains considerable ambiguity on this subject. In some places in the text Merleau-Ponty will suggest, in consonance with the later Wittgenstein, that the meaning of a word is its "use." In another place he will say that meaning is "given" by the word. In still another passage, meaning is only "delineated" by language. It seems clear then that at this point in Merleau-Ponty's thinking about language he hasn't yet figured out his theory of linguistic meaning.

I believe it is these two early areas of struggle—that is, the social-cultural dimension of language and the theory of linguistic meaning—that make Merleau-Ponty's encounter with Saussure in the late 1940s so energizing for him. This is because Saussure's structuralist theory of language addresses these areas with tremendous originality and great promise. Our next step in the project of understanding Merleau-Ponty's expressive theory of language, then, is to elucidate some central elements of Saussure's theory so that we can measure the remarkable extent to which Merleau-Ponty's philosophy of language is enriched by Saussure's thinking, and yet is deeply critical of his structuralism.

3. Beyond Language as Structure

In 1906–1911, Ferdinand de Saussure delivered his now famous lectures at the University of Geneva that have come to us as the *Course in General Linguistics.* This slim volume—constructed by his students from course notes, memories, and rough-draft outlines by Saussure—is arguably the birth of modern linguistics. It is certainly a leading force in twentieth-century French thought: it informs and inspires the whole structuralist movement in the human sciences and literary theory, as well as the poststructuralist correctives offered by Derrida, Foucault, Lacan, and others. At the heart of Saussure's extraordinary influence is his new way of cutting things up. That is, he offers a methodological breakthrough that not only lends itself to diverse applications, but which seems both natural and promising with regard to language. No doubt, this is how it also appeared to Merleau-Ponty when he finally read Saussure in the late 1940s.[19]

Saussure's text begins by attributing the lack of scientific rigor and results in all previous language studies, such as comparative philology, to the failure to draw a foundational distinction between language (*la langue*) and speech (*la parole*). *Speech,* for Saussure, refers to concrete speech acts performed by individuals: they are highly contingent, heterogeneous, and executed through willful acts. However, he argues that there is another side of the phenomenon that had hitherto been completely overlooked: *language* as a non-concrete, social structure. Language (*la langue*) is the universal, holistic system that underlies and informs any individual speech act (*la parole*) or any particular idiolect (*la langage*). We can thus understand language by analogy to the rule-bound game or system of football, which is distinct from and yet structuring of particular teams, plays, or players (who come and go all the time). For Saussure, by rigorously studying and analyzing this non-concrete system of language (*la langue*) as it functions at a particular time (synchronically), as opposed to over time (diachronically), we can create an actual, universal science of language—a science that he proposes to call *linguistics.*

And so language, not speech, is the "well-defined object" of linguistic science; it is a homogeneous system or structure operating behind "the heterogeneous mass of speech facts."[20] More specifically, Saussure insists that language is a system of *signs.* He says: "Language, unlike speaking, is something that we can study separately. . . . It is a system of signs in which the only essential thing is the union of meanings and sound-images, and in which both parts of the sign are psychological."[21] What we see in this quote is the heart of Saussure's influential theory of the sign: the sign is a two-fold phenomenon comprised of a sound-image, the *signifier,* and a meaning, the *signified*—elements that "are intimately united, and each recalls the other."[22] For example, the signifier "tree" bears with it the *meaning* "🌲," but also, awareness of that signified carries along the *sound* "tree." This basic insight leads Saussure to explicitly reject the representation theory of language on several grounds, one of which—in consonance with Merleau-Ponty—is that it "assumes that ready-made ideas exist before words."[23] Furthermore, Saussure insists that both elements of the sign are "psychological" (non-material), because they are separable from their material instantiations. For instance, he says, sound-images are not material because we can talk to ourselves without moving our lips, and most often our meanings have no material correlate.[24] What we see then in Saussure's work is that the system of signs, the linguistic structure, becomes un-tethered from the carnal-material world. It isn't for Saussure that the "physical" world isn't involved at all, but rather that it functions as a "material substrate," the analysis of which, he says, properly belongs to physiology and physics, but not linguistics. In this way, Saussure's structuralism avoids the traditional problem of reference because our words don't have to "hook onto" objects: language is not "about" the world at all. For him, signs are about themselves and other signs within the holistic, non-material structure of language.

We will soon see Merleau-Ponty's response to this bracketing or "reduction" of materiality, but for now, with the above elements in place, I can show two other well-known themes in Saussure that are relevant to this discussion. The first is the so-called "arbitrariness of the sign." That is, Saussure's claim that the relationship between a signifier and its signified is wholly conventional. For example, he says the meaning "sister" is not *naturally* linked to the sound-image *soeur* ("sister" in his native French), but could be (and factually is) linked with other sequences in different languages.[25] In truth, this thesis of arbitrariness (or purely conventional linkage) between a word-sound and its meaning is a very old, traditional claim: Aristotle and Locke, among others, both explicitly argue for it. (It is worth noting, in passing, that in the language chapter of *Phenomenology of Perception*, Merleau-Ponty argues against this traditional view as depending upon an uncritically accepted dichotomy between nature and culture.[26]) Much more novel, and more important for us in this chapter, is Saussure's second theme: his differential or diacritical theory of linguistic meaning. This is perhaps Saussure's most enduring insight, his claim that a signified has meaning through its differences with other related signs in the holistic language structure. As Saussure puts it:

> If words stood for pre-existing concepts, they would all have exact equivalents in meaning from one language to the next; but this is not true. French uses *louer* . . . indifferently to mean both "pay for" and "receive payment for," whereas German uses two words. . . . Instead of pre-existing ideas then, we find in all the foregoing examples *values* emanating from the system. When they are said to correspond to concepts, it is understood that the concepts are purely differential and defined not by their positive content but negatively by their relations with the other terms of the system. Their most precise characteristic is in being what the others are not.[27]

At first glance, this diacritical theory of meaning is elusive, and no doubt this is part of the reason for its neglect among many Anglo-American philosophers of language. However it is important to remember that Saussure had already rejected, as would Merleau-Ponty, the only traditional alternative: the representational account of language with its theory of meaning as either preexisting ideas or as reference to objects in the world. Saussure indicates that the idea theory of meaning is predicated on an abstract, illusory dualism, and (against the referential theory of meaning) he argues that the vast majority of meaningful signs do not even seem to pick out material objects. (Consider, for example, the words "in," "philosophy," or "running.") So how then does linguistic meaning work? Again, Saussure's central insight is that a signifier's meaning is determined by its differential relationship to other signs in the system. He offers the example of how the English word "sheep" and the French word "*mouton*" do not have the same meaning-value, precisely because English also has the different term, "mutton," to qualify the sense of "sheep."[28] To grasp the idea here, we might think of the pieces in chess: each piece (knight, rook, bishop, and so on) has its value in the game—its meaning and power—precisely in its differences from the other pieces and the board. For example, the meaning of the "knight" is "move two squares, then over one," but this meaning-value emerges and has weight in contrast with the other elements of the game. It is just so, Saussure argues, with linguistic meaning: the word "friend" bears meaning by being distinct from the meaning of other terms for personal relations in the language system, such as "spouse," "child," "partner," "relative," and "lover." And similarly, each of those words bears meaning by its differential relation with the others. The classic structuralist image then is to understand *la langue* (the non-material language structure amid which we find ourselves thinking and speaking) as a *net*: any particular knot of meaning in the vast fabric can only exist because there are other knots around it. Saussure puts it succinctly: "Language is a system of interdependent terms in which the value of each term results solely from the simultaneous presence of the others."[29]

In the above passages I have articulated some of the central elements of Saussure's structuralist approach to language: (1) his founding distinction between the holistic social structure and individual speech acts, (2) his "psychological" theory of the sign, and (3) his differential theory of linguistic meaning. Admittedly, this has been done briefly, but we have seen enough to make out the main lines of Merleau-Ponty's response to Saussure—a complex response that has Merleau-Ponty both heralding Saussure's structuralism as a major breakthrough (PW 23), and yet making claims that subtly devastate some of its most basic premises. I should note, as we saw in chapter 6, that this is the same relationship Merleau-Ponty enacts with Husserl. That is, we see claims of loving praise, clear lines of influence and inspiration, and yet trenchant critique of certain foundational assumptions. My aim in the remainder of this chapter is to give further clarity, content, and force to Merleau-Ponty's expressive theory of language by elucidating the central elements on both sides of his response to Saussure.

I will begin by clarifying the lines of inspiration. First of all, Saussure's account of language (*la langue*) as a non-material, yet real and effective social structure is a major breakthrough for Merleau-Ponty. He embraces this as a perfect way to understand the "invisible" life of already acquired language, *the spoken word*: it is a non-material, yet real and effective social structure. Already in *Phenomenology of Perception,* he used the image of an orator "reaching back" to find a word, suggesting that words "are behind me, like things behind my back, or like the city's horizon round my house" (PP 180). But Saussure's account of *la langue* gives substantial content to the image, for Saussure argues that a person quite literally finds himself or herself amid the language system, thinking and speaking *according to it*—"channeling it," we might say. To use Merleau-Ponty's preferred term, culturally sedimented language is a *field,* not unlike the perceptual field. It surrounds us and goes beyond us; we intellectually "reach out" into it as we try to "find the words." We draw upon it, just as we breathe air. To be sure, this social-cultural field of sedimented language is not "visible"; rather, it belongs to "the invisible." Be that as it may, the social field of sedimented language informs our thoughts, words, and actions no less than nature does. It is, we might say, the "background" against which new expressive breakthroughs are formed. Further, while Saussure studiously avoids the question, there is no problem for Merleau-Ponty about the ontological status of this "invisible" social-cultural field of constituted language: it is no more a mystery than are ideas, thinking, or perception itself. They are all emergent, synergistic phenomena that come about through biological beings with bodies and brains that have evolved in certain ways. And in the case of the linguistic field in particular, it emerges through the *social life* of those beings. Indeed, Merleau-Ponty's encounter with Saussure allows him to deepen and expand his understanding of the social dimension of language beyond the carnal-material one.

The other aspect of Saussure's thought that inspires Merleau-Ponty, and preeminently so, is his differential theory of meaning. As indicated at the outset of the chapter, this theory is so influential upon Merleau-Ponty that it resurfaces in one of the most central aspects of his late writings: his thematic concern with difference, dehiscence, and *écart.* Clearly, Saussure's diacritical theory of meaning is a major breakthrough for Merleau-Ponty's work on language as well, and it is not difficult to understand why. First, he already held some of Saussure's premises: in *Phenomenology of Perception* he had thoroughly rejected the representational theory with its dualistic ontology of preexisting thought; and he had explicitly claimed that an adequate theory of language must explain how words *themselves* have meaning. This kind of account is what Saussure's diacritical theory of meaning offers: words themselves bear meaning through their differential relation to other words in the linguistic system. No transcendental ideas or purely material references are required. In sum, Saussure's theory of meaning is greeted as a rigorous account of what

Merleau-Ponty knows is required, but which *Phenomenology of Perception* could not deliver. Hence, time and again, in all the later writings on language, we see Merleau-Ponty enthusiastically embrace Saussure's diacritical account of meaning and then weld it to his own expressive theory of language. For just one example of this enthusiasm, consider the opening passage of "Indirect Language and the Voices of Silence":

> What we have learned from Saussure is that, taken singly, signs do no signify anything, and that each one of them does not so much express a meaning as mark a divergence [*écart*] of meaning between itself and other signs. Since the same can be said for all other signs, we may conclude that . . . the terms of language [*la langue*] are engendered only by the differences that appear among them.[30]

It seems clear then that Saussure is a major, transitional influence upon Merleau-Ponty's philosophy of language and upon his late thinking of *écart*. Nonetheless, along with the praise and the direct influence, Merleau-Ponty's writings offer several lines of criticism which I believe are quite compelling for our contemporary efforts to understand language and the nature of non-material, yet real social structures. Now, Merleau-Ponty's *explicit* criticisms of Saussure, just as with Husserl, tend to be underdeveloped. For example, in *The Prose of the World,* Merleau-Ponty says he "wonders" whether Saussure has "realized to what extent [his] own findings remove us from positivism," and a bit later he suggests that Saussure's view of language structure is too divorced from historical contingencies and transition (PW 39). Further, in several places Merleau-Ponty argues against some of Saussure's key distinctions, for example, the rigid distinction between synchronic language (at a moment) and diachronic language (over time),[31] and also the foundational dichotomy between *la langue* and *la parole*.[32] In these explicit comments it is not difficult to discern Merleau-Ponty's rather profound line of criticism: that Saussure's desire to isolate his domain from historical contingency in order to legitimate the "objectivity" of his "science" has led him to tear apart phenomena that are in fact interwoven. As Merleau-Ponty puts it in *Consciousness and the Acquisition of Language:*

> [For Saussure] speech [*la parole*] is what one says; language [*la langue*] is the treasure out of which the subject draws in order to speak; it is a system of possibilities. But how can one arrive at this French "in itself"? In reality, each time that I speak, I allude to my language as a totality. It is [thus] difficult for me to delimit the frontiers of speech and language. The distinction cannot maintain itself.[33]

In my view, this is an extremely strong objection. One doesn't have to read very far in Saussure to recognize that these dichotomies for the sake of "science" violate important features of the phenomena, for example, the important extent to which *la langue* is itself historically and culturally contingent. However, I think Merleau-Ponty's *implicit* criticisms of Saussure are devastating. These implicit criticisms flow from what we have seen to be central elements in Merleau-Ponty's philosophy, elements to which he always remained committed.

To understand the first of these criticisms, we need to recall that Saussure's structuralist theory of language avoids the ontological problem of reference: since words do not essentially represent pre-formed ideas, nor refer to material objects, the traditional question of the precise nature of how language can be "about" or "represent" non-linguistic elements just dissolves. Indeed, language is a structure that takes shape and *means* through the internal, differential relations within the linguistic system itself. Thus, Saussure would say, the traditional ontological problem of reference is an artifact of a dualistic commitment that is inherent in the representation theory of language: the notion that linguistic elements are "about" non-linguistic elements. This dissolution of the ontological problem of reference is an aspect of Saussure's thought with which Merleau-Ponty would likely agree. However, for Merleau-Ponty, this cannot be the end of the issue. For what then is the precise relationship between language (*la langue*) and the world? How are they inter-related? These are questions that Saussure never really addresses. Time and again, for him, "matter" is reduced to and excluded as a kind of substrate—the province of physiologists and physicists. Time and again, the system of language is depicted as exclusively "psychological" and distinguished from the "material." Time and again, Saussure argues that the "materiality" of a sign is irrelevant to its meaning, or the system as a whole. In the end then, it seems that "matter" essentially drops out of Saussure's structuralist theory. It isn't for him that such stuff doesn't exist, but rather that it has no substantial or meaningful role to play within the workings of the structure itself. In effect, the structure overwrites or effaces the material world.

In this aspect of Saussure's thought it is not hard to see the roots of the problems about materiality that have plagued some leading poststructuralist thinkers. It is not hard, for instance, to see Saussure's "reduction of materiality" as the hidden predecessor of Derrida's early, problematic claim that "there is nothing outside the text." It is not hard to see it operating as a hidden influence in Foucault's strong social constructionism, with its suggestion that the body is a "blank slate" which is "totally imprinted" and "defined" by social structures and powers. However, at this late point in our study of Merleau-Ponty, we should deeply suspicious of views that efface materiality or reduce it to a substrate. For again, what we are really talking about here, with "matter," is nothing less than living embodiment and the natural world.

Further, when it comes to understanding language, this "check" upon the structuralist "reduction of materiality" is doubly important. For, as we saw in the previous section, language is a form of behavior. That is, language is performed, not by chunks of Cartesian matter, but rather by living creatures who open up and organize a meaning-laden perceptual field, who in the course of natural history developed the brain tissue and cognitive wherewithal to create and express new meaning beyond sedimented structures. Indeed, with Merleau-Ponty's philosophy of living corporeality, language is not divorced from, but rooted in the natural world. For him, below the abstract level of representation, language is a marvelous conjunction of a social-cultural structure sustained by carnal life, but a structure which can be transformed and transcended by embodied acts of expression. In a phrase, carnal life and nonmaterial linguistic structures are in a relationship of *reversibility*. They are an intertwining of the visible and the invisible. I must say that this is what having a *living* body in your philosophy of language does for you. And it is no small achievement, for it amounts to a promising new way of conceiving language that leaves the structuralist (and the occasional poststructuralist) reduction of the flesh behind.

These last comments—about Merleau-Ponty's alternative picture of the reversible relationship between the carnal world and language—point us toward his second major, implied criticism of structuralism. This is that Saussure's theory of language, just as the representation theory before it, has completely overlooked the *speaking word*—the expressive life of language. Indeed: where in Saussure is the recognition that individual, creative acts of expression can transcend and transform the *system*? In fact, this possibility has been precluded by Saussure's inaugural premises. Recall that he begins with the distinction between language as a universal, stable system (*la langue*) and historically contingent speech acts by individuals (*la parole*). The result is a foundational separation that looks like this:

Language Structure (La langue)	*Speech Acts (La parole)*
ahistorical	*historical*
universal	*particular*
fixed	*contingent*
homogeneous	*heterogeneous*
(admits of scientific	*("a confused mass of . . .*
study and classification)	*unrelated things"* [34]*)*

It is clear that Saussure understands this distinction as a methodological breakthrough because it isolates *la langue* as the "well-defined object," which thereby legitimates his claim for linguistics as a proper science. However, this foundational distinction generates a problem that almost immediately begins to vex Saussure: since all contingency, agency, and individual activity belong to *la parole* and thus have been systematically excluded from the language structure, how can the language system itself change? Saussure agonizes over this question, acknowledging that "mutability is so inescapable that it even holds true for artificial languages," but also that he hasn't said enough to explain how change is possible.[35] In the end, Saussure's response to the problem of linguistic change is to multiply the distinctions: before long he maps the synchronic-diachronic division onto the foundational distinction, and then calls for two different linguistic studies—one on each side of the divide. But since he also claims that the fundamental principle of change is the passage of time, *which is, by definition, only the diachronic side,* it is not at all clear that he has solved the problem.

Merleau-Ponty would say that it is not clear Saussure *can* solve this problem, because if one starts from a distinction that methodologically divides history, culture, contingency, and individual linguistic acts from the linguistic system, then it is impossible, in principle, to understand how they are interwoven. As I argued in chapter 3, this is like trying to put the mind and body back together once they have been cleft in two. Thus, from Merleau-Ponty's perspective, Saussure's structuralist theory of language proceeds from the exact *wrong* distinction. Instead of beginning with Saussure's dichotomy between *la langue* and *la parole*, Merleau-Ponty would say that we must understand language as an interwoven duality between constituted language and expressive language. That is, a movement between the culturally and historically sedimented field of the already spoken word, and the expressive acts which transcend and transform it. The result is a relation that looks like this:

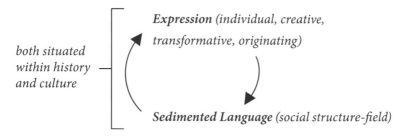

both situated within history and culture —

Expression (individual, creative, transformative, originating)

Sedimented Language (social structure-field)

In my view, the consequences of Merleau-Ponty's substitution—his alternate model of language—are substantial and revolutionary. For one thing, it makes the operating force of linguistic change not just any act of speech or writing, but rather the expressive ones. Further, it places the creative, contingent, expressive acts of individuals amid the field of already acquired language. This means that change and transformation burst up from within the "system" and flow back into it. Thus, on Merleau-Ponty's account, language itself—as an interwoven dynamic between the culturally sedimented system and expression—is far more morphological than Saussure is able to see. Indeed, his account insists upon what we in fact see in the world: an extraordinary, proliferate multiplicity of linguistic forms, not only between different languages but within any given one. Further, this bubbling, shifting morphology is not merely at the level of semantic contents, as in Saussure, but in syntax as well. The upshot of this, for Merleau-Ponty, is that language (just as perception) is ceaselessly excessive, unanalyzable: "one cannot reduce to a system the modes of expression of even *one* language" (PW 27). This result doesn't help much if one hungers for an "objective science" of language, but it certainly does seem to fit with the wild, prolific contingency we see in our own language and in those around the world.

In the end, then, I believe it is perfectly correct to say that Merleau-Ponty's expression theory of language is a "poststructuralist" one. Not in the sense that it supersedes structuralism—Merleau-Ponty is too indebted to Saussure for that. I believe we have to wait for Deleuze and Guattari to see such an account.[36] But Merleau-Ponty's account is poststructuralist in the sense that both Derrida and Lyotard have advocated for understanding the term: it is a theory that "interrupts" the structure from within, that reminds us of the contingent forces that disrupt all efforts to totalize and purify the structure.[37] In the last thirty years we have seen several such poststructuralist philosophies of language, from Derrida's "grammatology" to Foucault's "discourse." However, what one uniquely gets from Merleau-Ponty, beyond the limits of representationalism and structuralism, is a theory of language that embraces the living body and its expressive life.[38] We get a theory that respects the worldly multiplicity of linguistic forms. We get one that richly explains the possibility of communicating with one another and the fact of "the first word." In short, I believe that Merleau-Ponty's expressive theory of language, with its commitment to embodied naturalism and radical linguistic change, is an extraordinary contribution to twentieth-century thought about language—one with which we must reckon in our most contemporary discussions.

Conclusion: The Visible and the Invisible

This new reversibility and the emergence of the flesh as expression are the point of insertion of speaking and thinking in the world of silence.
—MERLEAU-PONTY[1]

With all our correct representations we would get nowhere . . . unless the uncon-cealment of beings had already . . . placed us in that cleared realm in which every being stands for us and from which it withdraws.
—MARTIN HEIDEGGER[2]

From the very outset, this book was designed and written to carefully lead the reader through central areas of Merleau-Ponty's philosophy, and to examine his views in relation to the work of contemporary thinkers and criticisms. We have seen, for example, the rationale and continuing need for a phenomenology of perceptual life, even in the age of the "cognitive revolution." Phenomenology is a method for uncovering and studying the features of reality as it is lived; it is an indispensable order of discourse that cannot be exhausted or replaced by analytic explanations, no matter how powerful those may be. We have also seen Merleau-Ponty's unprecedented, patient, and occasionally flawed labors to uncover the features of perceptual experience, living embodiment, and intersubjective relations with others. In *Phenomenology of Perception,* he refers to this triad as the "symbiotic" system "self-others-things"; in the final writings he simply calls it "the visible." And in chapters 6 and 7, I have sought to articulate an elusive, yet central aspect of his philosophy: his account of thinking, language, and knowing ("the invisible") as expressive processes that are rooted in our perceptual life and yet go beyond that life. Indeed, for Merleau-Ponty, our expressive cognitions are rooted in living experience, transformative of it, and yet not reducible to it. They are natural processes that "sublimate" and "signify" our incarnate life without covering it. They are *transcending* processes of ideality that are not transcendental. At this late stage in the book, I hope that all these ideas and arguments are reasonably clear and that the reader finds them as provocative and promising as I do for enriched life experiences and ongoing philosophical thought.

However, in these final pages, there are two last promissory notes I must try to fulfill. To start work on the first of these, it may be remembered that I have claimed that Merleau-Ponty's account of expressive cognition offers a revolutionary paradigm for understanding the life of the mind. A paradigm, I said, that gives us a powerful alternative to the ancient model of Plato's "divided line." I believe finding such an alternative would be a rather extraordinary thing, because Plato's hierarchical, dualistic model of the visible and the intelligible has remained quietly determinative of most western philosophical theories of ideality and its relationship to the world. We recall Plato's image from *Republic*:[3]

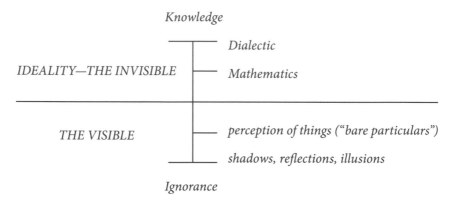

One striking thing about Plato's model of "the visible and the invisible" is that it denigrates and deforms the processes of visibility. Casting perceptual life as constituted by "images" and "bare particulars" (never mind treating the body as a "prison of the soul"), Plato has to search beyond this "feast of illusions" for truths that correspond to a transcendental reality, that correspond to transcendental being and not becoming. Of course this ontology, this ontotheology, is explicitly taken up by Descartes when he denigrates the senses and underwrites all of his knowledge by the "divine guarantee." But Plato's divided line is more subtly invested in Aristotle's substance metaphysics. This is because Aristotle's depiction of reality as a collection of objects and their properties, that is, substances and their predicates, subjects and objects, is the direct descendent of Plato's image of the visible as "bare particularity." To be sure, Aristotle seeks to correct Plato's view by building generality into the collection of substances, but this doesn't change the ontology: "correct" thought and language, "truth" itself, become defined in terms of the mimetic correspondence between ideal formations and discrete, real objects. The Age of Representation (and Reflection) is born.

Yet over the course of this book I have attempted to demonstrate how derivative and abstract is this idea of "real objects." It is an artifact of intellectually cutting into the tissue of visibility and dividing into separate parts what is rather lived as interwoven, as an intertwining of difference. Indeed, far from a collection of discrete objects (with discrete predicates), Merleau-Ponty gives us a dramatically different understanding of the visible:

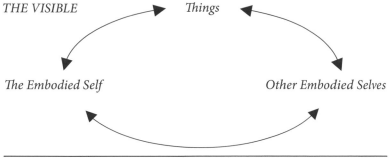

THE VISIBLE

Things

The Embodied Self

Other Embodied Selves

The World

All along, we have seen that a crucial feature of this view is that the "parts"—the embodied self, worldly things, and other selves—are symbiotically, synergistically involved. We have seen that perceptual experience as we know and live it takes shape as a carnal interweaving of these parts. We have also uncovered Merleau-Ponty's view that there is another movement involved in our living experience: the movement whereby thought and language are able to creatively transcend some sedimented situation toward a powerful new organization or acquisition, the movement of expression:

THE INVISIBLE

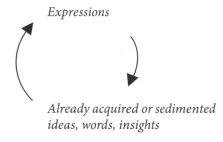

Expressions

Already acquired or sedimented ideas, words, insights

About this movement of thought and language, this "new reversibility," this "second meaning of vision," Merleau-Ponty says: "it is a relationship with oneself and the world as well as a relationship with the other; hence it is established in the three dimensions at the same time. And it must be brought to appear directly in the infrastructure of vision" (VI 144–145). Thus, I am finally able to bring this "infrastructure" together; I am able to provide a model of Merleau-Ponty's ontology of the visible and the invisible:

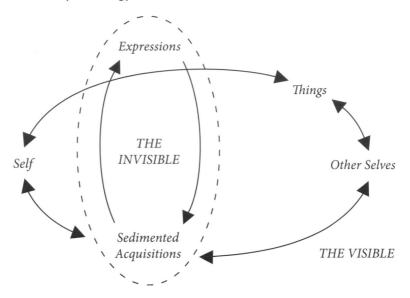

There are a number of things to be stressed about this final picture of Merleau-Ponty's ontology. First, the movement of ideality ("the invisible") does not trump or over-ride the movement of visibility. There is no Platonic hierarchy or division between thought (and language) and our carnal relations with the world. Creative new ideas, words, meanings, paradigms, theories, and thought-acquisitions surge up amid the world as ways of ideally organizing the world. But also, the artifacts of those acquisitions (writings, artworks, images, texts, spoken words) literally, actually become part of "the visible" and may go on to inspire further transcending articulations. There is thus, for Merleau-Ponty, a movement to Becoming, a "history of being" (Heidegger would say), but it is not one that unfolds through the conceptual necessity of a Hegelian *telos*. Rather, it unfolds—when it does at all—through contingent, creative, culturally and historically informed acts of transcending amid an overflowing world, acts which themselves leave sediments in and thus transform that world. This interfolded account of ideality and visibility reminds us that there is no Platonic dualism or opposition between these spheres of life. They are, instead, "the obverse and the reverse of one another" (VI 152). That is to say, there is an irreducible difference, but not an ontological gulf between the expressive movement of thought and the carnal movement of vision. For Merleau-Ponty, they are themselves to be understood—as are vision and touch, self and worldly things, self and others—as a reversible intertwining or "overlapping" through extreme divergence (*écart*).

I will be the first to admit that Merleau-Ponty's new, revolutionary picture of the visible and the invisible is rather difficult to think. Plato's old, traditional, hierarchical model of the divided line is much tidier and easier to conceive. Part of the difficulty of course is that, in the western world at least, we are rather deeply inclined and trained to divide, then oppose and hierarchize what is merely divergent. I believe that it requires a new flexibility of mind—and "the virtue of sensibility"—not to deform these double movements at the heart of life. And I hope that the present volume might serve as a propaedeutic for that flexible, fluid, expressive thinking.

Another difficulty is our apparent temptation to reduce these double complexities to one or the other. In fact, these two difficulties, oppositional division and unifying reduction, are two sides of the same coin: they are both ways of failing to honor the differentiated interweaving between "eye" and "mind." But over the course of this book I believe we have been able to see that there are *two* modes of reductionist thinking. One of them might be called "analytic reduction"—which involves the distillation of a complex whole into analyzed parts. I have said more than enough in these pages to demonstrate how fiercely Merleau-Ponty criticizes this mode of reduction. However, for twentieth-century continental philosophers (and certainly for Merleau-Ponty), another mode of reduction has been acutely tempting: a practice of thought that *grounds* one region of life or experience in another. No doubt these philosophers are influenced by Husserl's practice of a "phenomenological reduction" of the "natural attitude" in order to isolate and reveal the fundamental features and structures of "possible experience and experiential cognition."[4] Indeed, I believe that wherever we see a claim for the "more *fundamental*" we are encountering this second form of reductive thinking. This is because "grounding" one domain in another, conceiving one domain as more "fundamental" than another, entails that the grounded or founded domain effectively loses its heterogeneity and its ability to constitutively influence the other. Weirdly enough, this second mode of reduction absorbs a certain domain while excluding it from consideration.

One might be tempted to simply label this second mode of reduction "phenomenology," since we see the strategy of grounding X in Y not only throughout Husserl's texts, but frequently in Heidegger's way of talking about being as ground (*Grund*). And again, it is often there in Merleau-Ponty's early writings as well, for example, when he reduces scientific thought (an "abstract sign-language") to living experience (the underlying "countryside") (PP ix). The problem with equating this second form of reduction with phenomenology is that we can find this reductive practice of thought enacted throughout the entire history of western ontology. It is there, for example, in Plato: "the divided line" is precisely this kind of reduction of visible reality to the idea (*eidos*). It is acutely there in Aristotle, who sees substance as fundamental, in Descartes's *cogito*, Kant's transcendental, Marx's "economy," Nietzsche's will to power, and Freud's libido or "primary process." This grounding-reductive impulse can also be found in post-phenomenological thought, such as Foucault's account of *le vivant* as "unreason" *prior* to reason, and Deleuze's notion of "life" as a *pre-phenomenological* self. Apparently, the grounding reduction is a most tempting way to think.

However, in the course of this book we have also seen that Merleau-Ponty gradually becomes a thinker of *expression,* of the cognitive-linguistic operation that takes up and transfigures sedimented acquisitions amid the overflowing field of visibility. Indeed, for Merleau-Ponty, a resulting proof about the triangle is explicitly not a derivative of the initial figure (chapter 6). And the fresh, new insight—"the speaking word"—is a creative upsurge, not a reduction to the already "spoken word" (chapter 7). In Merleau-Ponty's more developed view, there is no absorption of the result in an "origin" or "foundation." Rather, he is striving to articulate a distinctly different (and differential) relationship between the visible and the invisible, between "the flesh and the idea." It is a relationship that is marked by irruptive creativity, sublimation, and excess. As we have seen, the breakthrough idea, concept, model, or word illuminates and organizes the sedimented data or field in powerful ways, but does not reduce to it; and the expressive result goes on to become part of the sedimented field, which may itself give rise to further expressive acts. In short, this relationship isn't one of "foundational grounding," but one of inter-dynamic transformation, a non-reductive interweaving of different spheres. Although it is rather difficult to think (just as Augustine says of time), Merleau-Ponty's non-reductive account of expression has the great virtue of apparently honoring what we experience and know by direct acquaintance in the flow of life.

In short, I believe that Merleau-Ponty's gradually developing philosophy of expression is the very path by which he leaves the reductive habits and concepts of (Husserlian) phenomenology behind. This conclusion underscores the fact that over the course of his career, Merleau-Ponty's philosophical method itself is transformed from phenomenology (revealing a fundament) to expression ("singing the world"). As Merleau-Ponty explicitly puts it in *The Visible and the Invisible:*

> The philosopher therefore suspends the brute vision [*le vision brute*] only in
> order to make it pass into the order of the expressed. . . . [Philosophy] accord-

ingly would not lose sight of the brute thing and the brute perception and would not finally efface them. . . . On the contrary, it would set itself the task of thinking about them. . . . with a perhaps difficult effort that uses the significations of words to express, beyond themselves, our mute contact with the things, when they are not yet things said. . . . It must use words not according to their pre-established signification, but *in order to state* this prelogical bond. (VI 36, 38)

It is important to notice that this "difficult effort" to express living experience isn't about covering it over with a veil of ideas or significations, nor is it about mimetically representing them. Instead, Merleau-Ponty's new expressive vision for philosophy is an uncertain, contingent effort to find new words (beyond their "pre-established signification") that open up a powerful, illuminating way to articulate the silent, mute "concordance of the world" (VI 39).

In this new philosophical practice, beyond representation, beyond analytic or grounding reductions—this effort to illuminate the world by creatively expressing it—there is nothing final and nothing triumphal. As we have already seen with the example of a geometrical proof, there are multiple ways of achieving the desired result; and there are an untold number of things we can expressively reveal about its initial figure (the triangle). As Merleau-Ponty says, "Expressing what *exists* is an endless task" (CD 66). But again, this does not mean that the effort is pointless, for felicitous expressions make the initial configuration come alive in new, powerful, culturally productive ways. Whether it is a triangle, already spoken words, or the world itself, the contingent labor of expressing them genuinely adds to our understanding of what we live and transforms *how* we live. And our expressions become part of our ongoing, but highly conditional efforts to find and create meaning in an overflowing, overwhelming, intersubjective world.

I must also say, in conclusion, that Merleau-Ponty's expressive method for "singing the world" has guided my own efforts in writing this book. That is, I have sought to organize and illuminate Merleau-Ponty's writings in a powerful, fecund way, beyond the impulses of mimetic representation or reduction. I acknowledge and embrace the fact that there are and will be other ways to let his philosophy come to light and life. Nonetheless, I hope that this book has found one productive and transformative way to express Merleau-Ponty's remarkable philosophy . . . and with it, the weird, heterogeneous relationship between carnal, intersubjective life and creative ideality—between the visible and the invisible.

Appendix: The Multiple Meanings of Flesh in Merleau-Ponty's Late Writings

For abbreviations of Merleau-Ponty's titles, consult the table at the front of the volume.

Summary of Findings from *The Visible and the Invisible* (March 1959–May 1961)

Three primary senses of "flesh":

1. Flesh as *carnality*. It is used this way 49 times, on my best interpretation. Examples:

   "Whether we are considering my relations with the things or my relations with the other . . . the question is . . . whether every relation between me and Being, even vision, even speech, is not a carnal relation with the flesh of the world." (VI 83–84)

   "Yes or no: do we have a body—that is, not a permanent object of thought, but a flesh that suffers when it is wounded, hands that touch?" (VI 137)
   - Some associated words: "surface," "density," "massive," "mass," "body," "corporeity," "carnal," "weight," "thickness," "presence," etc.
   - Occurrences in the main text: VI 9, 61, 84, 88 (2×), 114 (2×), 118, 122, 123, 127 (3×), 131, 137, 138 (3×), 144 (3×), 146, 148, 151, 153 (4×). Subtotal: 28 times.
   - Occurrences in the Working Notes: VI 181, 193, 200, 201, 202, 205, 209, 219, 220, 224, 239, 244, 248 (3×), 254, 258, 259 (3×), 274. Sub-total: 21 times.

2. Flesh as *reversibility*. It is used this way 46 times, on my best interpretation. Examples:

   "Once again, the flesh we are speaking of is not matter. It is the coiling over of the visible upon the seeing body, of the tangible upon the touching body, which is attested in particular when the body sees itself, touches itself seeing . . ." (VI 146)

   "But once we have entered into this strange domain, one does not see how there could be any question of *leaving* it. If there is an animation *of* the body; if the vision and the body are tangled up in one another . . . and if finally, in our flesh as in the flesh of things, the actual, empirical, ontic visible, by a sort of folding back, invagination, or padding, exhibits a visibility . . . that is not the proper contribution of a 'thought' but is its condition, a style . . ." (VI 152)

- Some associated words and phrases: "possibility," "latency," "envelop," "cohesion," "coiling over," "folding back," "prototype," "paradox," "constitutive paradox," "style," "archetype," etc.
- Occurrences in the main text: VI 111, 114, 118, 123, 133, 135 (2×), 136, 137, 140, 144, 145, 146 (2×), 147 (2×), 148 (2×), 149, 152 (4×), 153. Subtotal: 24 times.
- Occurrences in the Working Notes: VI 205, 217, 248 (3×), 250 (6×), 255, 259, 261 (2×), 263, 267, 268, 271 (2×), 272, 274. Subtotal: 22 times.

3. Flesh as an *element of being*. It is used this way 8 times.

Example:

"The flesh is not matter, is not mind, is not substance. To designate it, we should need the old term 'element,' in the sense it was used to speak of water, air, earth, and fire, that is, in the sense of a *general thing,* midway between the spatio-temporal individual and the idea, a sort of incarnate principle . . ." (VI 139)

- Some associated words and phrases: "general principle," "exemplar," "concrete emblem of a general manner of Being."
- Occurrences in the main text: VI 139 (4×), 140, 142, 145, 147.

Suggestions and obscure usages:

- Flesh as *mother,* in the Working Notes: VI 267 ("Do a psychoanalysis of Nature: it is the flesh, the mother").
- Flesh as *horizonality,* in the Working Notes: VI 271 ("The flesh of the world = its *Horizonthaftigkeit* (interior and exterior horizon) surrounding the thin pellicle of the strict visible between these two horizons").
- Obscure usages in the main text: VI 111 ("the flesh of time"), 155 ("a sublimation of the flesh").
- Obscure usages in the Working Notes: VI 253, 269, 270 (3×), 273.

Summary of Findings in Other Late Writings

Flesh in "The Philosopher and His Shadow" (late 1958):

- Flesh as *carnality:* PS 167 (2×), 169.

Flesh in the Third Course on nature (1959–1960):

- Flesh as *carnality:* N 218, 223.
- Flesh as *reversibility:* N 209 (4×), 210 (2×), 217 (2×), 218 (2×), 223 (4×).

Flesh in "Eye and Mind" (summer 1960):

- Flesh as *carnality:* EM 125 (3×), 127, 129, 131, 139, 142, 145.
- Flesh as *reversibility:* EM 129, 130.

Flesh in the "Introduction" to *Signs* (February/November 1960):

- Flesh as *carnality:* IS 15 (3×), 16 (2×).
- Flesh as *reversibility:* IS 20.

Notes

Introduction to Merleau-Ponty's Philosophy

1.   Recent important single-author books on Merleau-Ponty in (or translated into) English include: Renaud Barbaras, *The Being of the Phenomenon: Merleau-Ponty's Ontology* (Evanston, 2004); Mauro Carbone, *Thinking of the Sensible: Merleau-Ponty's A-Philosophy* (Evanston, 2004); and Leonard Lawlor, *Thinking Through French Philosophy: The Being of the Question* (Bloomington, 2003).

     Many important essays on Merleau-Ponty are published in the international journal *Chiasmi International: Trilingual Studies Concerning Merleau-Ponty's Thought,* ed. Barbaras, Carbone, and Lawlor; but others appear in edited collections that having been appearing with considerable frequency. Some recent examples are: Carman and Hansen, eds., *The Cambridge Companion to Merleau-Ponty* (Cambridge, 2004); Evans and Lawlor, eds., *Chiasms: Merleau-Ponty's Notion of Flesh* (Albany, 2000); and Hass and Olkowski, eds., *Rereading Merleau-Ponty: Essays Beyond the Continental-Analytic Divide* (Amherst, 2000).

2.   The most extraordinary example of a new text by Merleau-Ponty is *Nature: Course Notes from the Collège de France* (Evanston, 2003). Also of exceptional interest are Merleau-Ponty, *Husserl at the Limits of Phenomenology,* ed. Lawlor and Bergo (Evanston, 2002); *The World of Perception* (New York, 2004); and *The Incarnate Subject: Malebranche, Biran, and Bergson on the Union of Body and Soul,* ed. Bjelland and Burke (Amherst, 2001). This is only a first wave of these new publications: several other texts (including lectures and other texts) have already been published in France.

3.   Merleau-Ponty's name and clear influence is emerging with some frequency in current research in the philosophy of mind, for example: Clark, *Being There: Putting Brain, Body, and World Together Again* (Cambridge, Mass., 1999); Lakoff and Johnson, *Philosophy in the Flesh: The Embodied Mind and its Challenge to Western Thought* (New York, 1999); and Cole, *About Face* (Cambridge, Mass., 1999). This connection is also explored with considerable frequency in the important journal *Phenomenology and the Cognitive Sciences,* ed. Shaun Gallagher. Merleau-Ponty's continuing influence upon philosophers of art can be seen, for example,in Johnson, ed., *The Merleau-Ponty Aesthetics Reader* (Evanston, 1993).

4.   *The Philosophical Lexicon,* ed. Daniel Dennett, can be seen online at: www.blackwellpublishing.com/lexicon/.

5.   It has eluded many commentators, but not *every* commentator by any means. M. C. Dillon's landmark study, *Merleau-Ponty's Ontology* (Evanston, 1997), explores expression in treating Merleau-Ponty's theory of truth and philosophy of language. Henry Pietersma also elucidates the relation of expression to epistemology in *Phenomenological Epistemology* (Oxford, 1999). Recent important

work on the subject of expression has also been done by Leonard Lawlor in "The End of Phenomenology: Expressionism in Merleau-Ponty and Deleuze," in Lawlor, *Thinking Through French Philosophy* (Bloomington, 2003); and Stephen Noble in "Entre le silence des choses et la parole philosophique: Merleau-Ponty, Fink et les paradoxes du langage," in *Chiasmi International* no. 6 (2005), pp. 111–144. Also see Remy C. Kwant's earlier study, *The Phenomenology of Expression* (Pittsburgh, 1967).

6. Heidegger expresses phenomenology as "saying to show" in many places, but an extended discussion of this formulation is found in his "The Nature of Language," in *On the Way to Language* (New York, 1971), pp. 57–108. As Heidegger puts it there: "'to say,' related to the Old Norse 'saga' means to show: to make appear, set free, that is, to offer and extend what we call World" (p. 93).

7. There is no question that much more could be said about Husserl's formative role in the phenomenological movement and his own efforts to escape from subjectivism. Indeed, Merleau-Ponty himself is careful to acknowledge these complexities and tensions in Husserl's thought. Nonetheless, in chap. 6 I will make an argument about a fundamental and irresolvable difference between the thinkers—and it will be the difference between a genuine philosophy of the world and one that is caught in subjective idealism. Even so, the scholarship on the complex relationship between Merleau-Ponty and Husserl has been superb. For a look at the current state of the discussion, see Toadvine and Embree, eds., *Merleau-Ponty's Reading of Husserl* (Dordrecht, 2002). Also see Dillon, *Merleau-Ponty's Ontology* (Evanston, 1997); Galen A. Johnson, "Merleau-Ponty and Husserl: History, Language, and Truth," in *Merleau-Ponty: Critical Essays,* ed. Pietersma (Washington, D.C., 1989), pp. 197–217; and Joseph Margolis, "Phenomenology and Metaphysics: Husserl, Heidegger, and Merleau-Ponty," in *Merleau-Ponty Vivant,* ed. Dillon (Albany, 1991), pp. 153–182. Still very useful is Herbert Spiegelberg's discussion in *The Phenomenological Movement* (The Hague, 1984), esp. pp. 538–585.

8. To see briefly how an equation between phenomenology and subjectivism continues to shape Anglo-American philosophy of mind, we might first consider Thomas Nagel's influential, even iconic paper, "What is it Like to be a Bat?" in Nagel, *Mortal Questions* (Cambridge, 1979), pp. 165–181. As the paper begins, Nagel quickly establishes his foundational distinction between "the subjective character of experience," which is equated with "conscious mental states," and the "objective" properties that "physical theory" will provide, and he equates this distinction with Sartre's bifurcation between "the *pour soi* and the *en soi*" (pp. 165–168). Nagel then immediately starts referring to the subjective side as "the phenomenological features of experience." Once this is in place all the damage has been done: hereafter in this essay, and in the many discussions that take up or challenge this essay, phenomenology is treated as equivalent to the subjective features of experience. As we will see in the prelude, Merleau-Ponty explicitly rejects this whole subject/object framework for discussing phenomenology and experience because it presupposes Descartes's dualistic ontology.

Now, Nagel embraces this dualistic frame to make his argument about the non-reductive character of qualitative experience. It is the frame he uses over and over in his subsequent book, *The View from Nowhere* (Oxford, 1989). But this Cartesian way of thinking about phenomenology can also be found lurking among the most anti-Cartesian thinkers in Anglo-American philosophy of mind. For example, in Dennett's *Consciousness Explained* (Boston, 1991)—an account of mind that will have several areas of close proximity to Merleau-Ponty's views—he depicts and criticizes phenomenology as "first-person," "internal," and "introspective" so that he can install his own alternative model of "heterophenomenology" (in chap. 4). Again, we see the mistaken, although common assumption that phenomenology is equivalent to subjectivism. It is thus, from Merleau-Ponty's perspective, entirely unnecessary to create a new form of phenomenology when the "old" one—the *actual* one practiced by Merleau-Ponty and Heidegger—provides all the resources for intersubjective criticism and confirmation that Dennett seeks.

9. This way of presenting it stresses the direct, ongoing challenge that Merleau-Ponty poses to Descartes's dualistic ontology. I do not want to suggest, however, that Merleau-Ponty's overall treatment of Descartes is one-dimensional or merely polemical. Particularly in his later writings (the *Nature* lecture courses and "Eye and Mind"), Merleau-Ponty is careful to elaborate the innovations of the Cartesian project—however limited it is and problematic in its consequences—as part of a complex historical development that needs to be appreciated in its own terms. Indeed, Merleau-Ponty's overall treatment of Descartes is extremely nuanced, even though I am stressing the central differences of ontology for the purposes of my presentation.

Prelude

1. Descartes, *Philosophical Writings III* (Cambridge, 1991), p. 173.

2. See ibid., pp. 156–157. For an interesting discussion of this plan, see Garber, "Descartes' Physics," in *The Cambridge Companion to Descartes,* ed. Cottingham (Cambridge, 1992), pp. 286–334.

3. The felicitous phrase, "the Cartesian Theater," was coined by Daniel Dennett. His lengthy argument against the Cartesian Theater model unfolds over the course of his *Consciousness Explained* (Boston, 1991), an argument that often brings him very close to Merleau-Ponty's views about intentionality, mind, and self.

4. Merleau-Ponty, *The Visible and the Invisible* (Evanston, 1968), p. 138.

5. For a detailed discussion of these influences see Gaukroger, *Descartes* (Oxford, 1995).

6. For an excellent account of this meeting, Beeckman's views, and Descartes's subsequent apprenticeship in 1618–1619, see ibid., chap. 3.

7. On these widespread cultural transformations, see Crosby, *The Measure of Reality* (Cambridge, 1997).

8. See, for instance, Descartes's criticisms in *Discourse on the Method,* in Descartes, *Philosophical Writings I* (Cambridge, 1985), pt. 1.

9. See Gaukroger, *Descartes* (Oxford, 1995), chap. 4.

10. *Principles of Philosophy,* in Descartes, *Philosophical Writings I* (Cambridge, 1985), p. 186.

11. Descartes, *Philosophical Writings II* (Cambridge, 1985), p. 12.

12. This is Descartes's analogy from the Seventh Reply: "if we have a basket or tub full of apples and want to make sure there are no rotten ones, we should first tip them all out, leaving none at all inside, and then pick up again . . . only those apples in which no flaw can be detected" (ibid., p. 349).

13. Ibid., p. 13.

14. Ibid., p. 15.

15. Ibid., p. 18. There is considerable scholarly debate surrounding this second phase of the *cogito* argument. Bernard Williams, in chap. 4 of his *Descartes* (East Rutherford, N.J., 1978), defends the view (dating back to Hobbes and Gassendi), that Descartes is making here what is referred to as "the real distinction," that is, the metaphysical distinction between mind and body. Other commentators, such as Margaret D. Wilson, have argued that Descartes does not make the real distinction until the Sixth Meditation with his argument by way of clear and distinct ideas. See Wilson, "The Epistemological Argument for Mind-Body Distinctness," in *Descartes,* ed. Cottingham (Oxford, 1998), pp. 186–196. In my view, the truth rests between these views: Descartes does not lay down the "real" distinction in the second phase of the *cogito* argument, but the metaphysical distinction is made when Descartes draws his later conclusion that perception is something the mind does and not the body. Consider: "But as I reach this conclusion I am amazed at how prone to error my mind is. . . . We say that we see the wax itself, if it is there before us, not that we judge it to be there from its colour or shape; and this might lead me to conclude . . . that knowledge of the wax comes from what the eye sees, and not from the scrutiny of the mind alone" (*Philosophical Writings II* [Cambridge, 1985], p. 21). The real distinction between mind and body is being drawn in this passage, and necessarily so for Descartes's reasoning: if perception really just is one's body, then those perceptions cannot be made incorrigible as mental ideas and the wax argument could not be mounted. In sec. 3, below, I will explain this problem fully and lay bare the fallacy that is involved in Descartes's reasoning here.

16. Aristotle, *On the Soul,* in *The Basic Works of Aristotle* (New York, 1941), 424a19–20.

17. Descartes, *Philosophical Writings II* (Cambridge, 1985), p. 20.

18. As Descartes puts it: "I normally say that I see men themselves. . . . [Yet] I *judge* that they are men. And so something which I thought I was seeing with my eyes is in fact grasped solely by the faculty of judgment which is in my mind" (ibid., p. 21).

19. Ibid., p. 24, emphasis added.

20. Descartes, *Philosophical Writings I* (Cambridge, 1985), p. 172.

21. Descartes, *Philosophical Writings II* (Cambridge, 1985), pp. 22–23.

22. Williams, *Descartes* (East Rutherford, N.J., 1978), chap. 4.

23. Descartes, *Philosophical Writings II* (Cambridge, 1985), p. 20.

24. Ibid., p. 18.

25. Ibid., p. 19.

26. See, in particular, Merleau-Ponty, *The Visible and the Invisible* (Evanston, 1968), pp. 44–49. As Merleau-Ponty puts it there: "The reflection finds itself therefore in the strange situation of simultaneously requiring and excluding an inverse movement of constitution. It requires it in that, without this centrifugal movement, it should have to acknowledge itself to be a retrospective construction; it excludes it in that, coming in principle after an experience of the world . . . which it seeks to render explicit, it thereby establishes itself in an order of idealization and of the 'after-the-fact' which is not that wherein the world is formed" (p. 45).

27. Descartes, *Philosophical Writings II* (Cambridge, 1985), p. 50.

28. As Descartes says: "I therefore think that today's meditation [i.e., the Fourth Meditation] . . . has been very profitable. . . . [F]or if, whenever I have to make a judgment, I restrain my will so that it extends to what the intellect clearly and distinctly reveals, and no further, then it is quite impossible for me to go wrong. This is because every clear and distinct perception . . . must necessarily have God for its author" (ibid., p. 43).

29. Ibid., p. 55.

30. The phrase quoted in this sentence is ibid., p. 50. As Descartes puts it in *Principles of Philosophy:* "The matter in the entire universe is thus one and the same, and it is always recognized as matter simply in virtue of its being extended. All the properties which we clearly perceive in it are reducible to divisibility" (*Philosophical Writings I* [Cambridge, 1985], p. 232). My discussion of extension and motion in this paragraph is indebted to Garber, "Descartes' Physics," in *The Cambridge Companion to Descartes,* ed. Cottingham (Cambridge, 1992). Also see Garber, *Descartes' Metaphysical Physics* (Chicago, 1992).

31. Descartes, *Philosophical Writings I* (Cambridge, 1985), p. 233.

32. See Daniel Garber's extended discussion of this problem in "Descartes' Physics," in *The Cambridge Companion to Descartes,* ed. Cottingham (Cambridge, 1992), pp. 292–297.

33. See ibid., pp. 303–310.

34. Descartes, *Philosophical Writings II* (Cambridge, 1985), p. 58.

35. Ibid., p. 60.

36. This claim is only implied in the *Meditations* itself, but is explicitly made in the Sixth Reply (ibid., pp. 294–295).

37. There is no question that Descartes legitimates this central distinction for classical science and philosophy, but it was already suggested by Galileo in *The Assayer* (1623). For Galileo's influence on Descartes in this matter, see Hacker, *Appearance and Reality* (Oxford, 1987), chap. 1.

38. "Onto-theology" is Heidegger's artful term for any metaphysical view that explicitly or implicitly involves theological premises or notions. Clearly Descartes's ontology is an example of "onto-theology," but it isn't the only one: Heidegger argues that most post-Platonic metaphysics—until at least Nietzsche—has been theological in one way or another. See "The Onto-theo-logical Constitution of Metaphysics" in Heidegger, *Identity and Difference* (Chicago, 2002).

39. Locke, *An Essay Concerning Human Understanding* (Oxford, 1975), p. 117.

40. Ibid., p. 48.

41. While Nietzsche's tacit use of the representation theory of perception can been seen in a number of places in *The Gay Science,* a paradigmatic passage is in Nietzsche, *Beyond Good and Evil* (New York, 1966), sec. 192: "Our eye finds it more comfortable to respond to a given stimulus by reproducing once more an image that it has produced many times before. . . . [E]ven in the 'simplest' processes of sensation the affects dominate, such as fear, love, hatred."

42. *The Cambridge Companion to Descartes,* ed. Cottingham (Cambridge, 1992), pp. 2–3.

1. The Sensation Fallacy

1. Wittgenstein, *Philosophical Investigations* (New York, 1953), p. 121.

2. Ibid., p. 31.

3. Merleau-Ponty, *Phenomenology of Perception* (London, 1962), p. 3.

4. Merleau-Ponty's evocative expression, *l'ouverture au monde,* is an artful phrase used throughout *The Visible and the Invisible* (Evanston, 1968). For example: "We will miss that relationship—which we shall here call the openness upon the world (*l'ouverture au monde*)—the moment that the reflective effort tries to capture it" (pp. 35–36; *Le Visible et l'invisible* [Paris, 1964], p. 57).

5. Locke, *An Essay Concerning Human Understanding* (Oxford, 1975), p. 119.

6. We can see Kant's commitment to a sense-data picture of sensation early in the *Critique of Pure Reason* (New York, 1965), where he is defining his basic terms: "while the matter of all appearance is given to us *a posteriori* only [as sensation], its form must lie ready . . . *a priori* in the mind . . . apart from all sensation. Thus, if I take away from the representation of a body that which the understanding thinks in regard to it, substance, force, divisibility, etc., and *likewise what belongs to sensation, impenetrability, hardness, colour,* etc., something still remains over from this empirical intuition, extension and figure" (p. 66, emphasis added).

7. There is no question that Quine and Sellars are both trying to circumvent the fundamentality of sense-data that marks traditional empiricism. Nonetheless, they discuss perception and sensibility in ways that still identify them as atomistic qualities rather than complex relations. For some examples, see Quine, *Word and Object* (Cambridge, Mass., 1960), chap. 1; and "Phenomenalism," in Sellars, *Science, Perception, and Reality* (London, 1963).

8. As Locke puts it: "As simple *Ideas* are observed to exist in several Combinations united together, so the Mind has a power to consider several of them united together, as one *Idea*. . . . *Ideas* thus made up of several simple ones put together, I call *Complex;* such as *Beauty, Gratitude, a Man, an Army, the Universe*" (*An Essay Concerning Human Understanding* [Oxford, 1975], p. 164).

9. In Merleau-Ponty, *Phenomenology of Perception* (London, 1962), intro. and chap. 1.

10. There is a remarkable similarity in this argument (and many others) made by Wittgenstein and Merleau-Ponty. Even so, in chap. 2 I will say some things about

the substantial differences between Wittgenstein's so-called "grammatical investigations" and Merleau-Ponty's commitment to phenomenology.

11. Hume, *A Treatise of Human Nature* (Oxford, 1978), p. 27.

12. This argument is offered by G. E. Moore in "Visual Sense-Data," in *Perceiving, Sensing, and Knowing* (Garden City, N.Y., 1965), pp. 130–137. A more recent case of the "wall" argument is in Jackson, *Perception* (Cambridge, 1977), pp. 20–29.

13. Hubert L. Dreyfus has done a great deal of work on this pre-predicative meaning in embodied perceptual experience and the theory of intentionality that it implies. Dreyfus argues that this non-predicative *Gestalt* intentionality is what marks the essential, irreducible difference between computers and humans, between artificial and embodied intelligence. See Dreyfus, *What Computers Can't Do* (Cambridge, Mass., 1993); and *Mind Over Machine* (New York, 1986). For a condensed look at some of the arguments, see Dreyfus, "The Current Relevance of Merleau-Ponty's Phenomenology of Embodiment," *Electronic Journal of Philosophy* no. 4, Spring 1996: http://phil.indiana.edu/ejap/1996.spring/dreyfus.1996.spring.txt.

14. For a memorable evocation of how we can be "drawn out" by things such as a sculpted work, see Abram, *The Spell of the Sensuous* (New York, 1996), pp. 49–59.

15. In chap. 3 of *Philosophy in the Flesh* (New York, 1999), George Lakoff and Mark Johnson refer to this new paradigm for understanding perception as "interactionism," and argue vigorously on its behalf. This is just one of the places where their work overlaps very closely with Merleau-Ponty. For a partial discussion of this overlap, see Hass, "Rays of the World: Merleau-Ponty and the Problem of Universals," in *Chiasmi International* no. 6 (2005), pp. 225–236.

16. A recent example of someone offering the "argument by illusion," replete with reference to the Müller-Lyer illusion, can be seen in Robinson, *Perception* (London, 1994), chap. 2.

17. See bk. 2 of the "Transcendental Analytic" in Kant, *Critique of Pure Reason* (New York, 1965), esp. pp. 201–208.

18. As Merleau-Ponty puts it: "The two straight lines in Müller-Lyer's optical illusion are neither of equal nor unequal length; it is only in the objective world that this alternative is posed. . . . We must recognize the indeterminate as a positive phenomenon. It is in this atmosphere that quality arises" (*Phenomenology of Perception* [London, 1962], p. 6, trans. modified).

19. In his "Critical Remarks Concerning the General Part of Descartes' Principles," in Leibniz, *Monadology and Other Philosophical Essays* (New York, 1965), pp. 22–24.

20. For an argument to this effect, see Hass, "Merleau-Ponty and Cartesian Skepticism: Exorcising the Demon," in *Rereading Merleau-Ponty,* ed. Hass and Olkowski (Amherst, 2000).

21. The term "physicalism" has at times been used to refer to any view that isn't substance dualism. I am using the term in a narrower way that has come to be common in contemporary discussions: the view that neurophysiological explanation can tell us everything (or everything important) about consciousness or perception. Clearly, there have been many philosophers who are physicalists in the *first*

sense, but not in the second: Merleau-Ponty, for instance, but also Spinoza, Nietz-sche, Wittgenstein, Thomas Nagel, and Colin McGuinn. Well-known physical-ists in the *second* sense include Daniel Dennett, Paul Churchland, and Patricia Churchland. While Merleau-Ponty would share several points of agreement with these thinkers, particularly in their critical arguments, my subsequent arguments work against the reductive thrust of this second type of physicalism.

22. There is an interesting ambiguity in contemporary physicalist work on the mean-ing of "*qualia*." In many cases, the word is used to refer to the empiricist sense of simple, monadic sense-data that are present to consciousness. In other cases, the word refers to experience itself as experienced—its so-called "felt qualities." Merleau-Ponty's phenomenology of the relational complexity of perceptual ex-perience is a series of arguments against the first of these meanings. And it might well be said that his phenomenology is all about revealing the rich, complex char-acter of *qualia* in this second sense. Indeed, what physicalists call "*qualia*" in the second sense is what Merleau-Ponty calls "phenomena." One caution, however, is that the way physicalists talk about *qualia* in this second sense often remains at-omistic and reductive, rather than complex and holistic. Further, they usually talk about *qualia* in this sense as distinct from material processes, and this is to repeat Descartes's dualistic ontology rather than to express an "experiential realism."

23. Dennett, *Consciousness Explained* (Boston, 1991), pp. 370–371.

24. Churchland, *A Neurocomputational Perspective* (Cambridge, Mass., 1989), p. 57.

25. Ibid., p. 31.

26. For Merleau-Ponty's flawed critique of the neurophysiological attempt to define the sensation, see *Phenomenology of Perception* (London, 1962), intro. and chap. 1, esp. pp. 7–10. In later chapters when Merleau-Ponty argues against the empiricist treatment of sensation (for instance, in the chapter on "Association") he is argu-ing, once again, against sense-data and not physicalism. The result is that in *Phe-nomenology of Perception* Merleau-Ponty has a large battery of arguments against the empiricist tradition on sensation, which bleed into the intellectualism of Des-cartes and Kant, but little to say about the physicalist turn to neurophysiology.

27. The variability and flexibility of neuronal action as distinct from a constancy hy-pothesis is widely acknowledged in the field. For an example of such a treatment see Anderson, *Cognitive Psychology and Its Implications* (New York, 1990), chap. 2.

28. The most famous of these cases is Gelb and Goldstein's study of "Schneider," a World War One veteran who received a piece of shrapnel in the brain and who, as a result, experienced a pervasive disassociation between abstract intellectual op-erations and practical actions. We will see more of Schneider in chap. 3, below.

29. In "The Philosopher and His Shadow," in Merleau-Ponty, *Signs* (Evanston, 1964), p. 167.

30. In this regard, my argument meshes with Merleau-Ponty, for he makes clear that his own arguments are not out to reject scientific explanation, but rather to think about its presuppositions and limits. As Merleau-Ponty puts it in an early foot-note in *Phenomenology of Perception* (London, 1962): "Each consciousness is born in the world. . . . In this perspective the 'immediate' data of perception can always

be challenged . . . as complex products of an origin. For the philosopher . . . there is therefore always a problem of origins, and the only method possible is to follow, in its scientific development, the causal explanation in order to make its meaning quite clear, and assign to it its proper place in the body of truth. That is why there will be found no *refutation,* but only an effort to understand the difficulties peculiar to causal thinking" (p. 7).

31. This line of argument connects up with one developed by Merleau-Ponty in the section on science and the perceptual faith in *The Visible and the Invisible* (Evanston, 1968), pp. 14–27. For instance, Merleau-Ponty says: "The sole attitude proper to [an explanatory science] is to take 'objective' thought for what it is, that is, a method that has founded science and is to be employed without restriction, unto the limit of the possible, but which . . . [only] represents a first phase of elimination [of the irrational] rather than a means of total explanation" (pp. 24–25).

32. Pirsig, *Zen and the Art of Motorcycle Maintenance* (New York, 1999), chap. 6.

33. The argument I have been making against physicalism, in terms of the limits of analytic thinking, has some proximity with Colin McGuinn's position as developed in *The Character of Mind* (Oxford, 1997) and *The Mysterious Flame* (New York, 1999). A notable similarity is that we both argue against physicalism by pointing to the limits of certain ways of thinking which are essential to the explanatory project: I focus on analysis; McGuinn focuses on what he calls "combinatorial" thinking. These are not equivalent foci, but closely related. I believe studying both sets of arguments in conjunction clarifies the limits of physicalism even further. However, I entirely reject McGuinn's way of referring to consciousness (or perception) as essentially "mysterious" or to his position as "mysterian," for this way of speaking by itself has little bite against physicalist explanations. More: it ignores the kind of knowledge and life-value that phenomenological understanding offers. I will explore this issue in some detail below.

34. For some details on this research, see "Dysfunctional Network in Brain's Left Hemisphere Linked to Dyslexia": www.medscape.com/govmt/NIMH/1998/07.98.

35. My argument here has several points of overlap with the one Dennett develops in his paper, "Real Patterns," in Dennett, *Brainchildren* (Cambridge, Mass., 1998). Here Dennett argues that beliefs and intentions are no less real than brain processes, but are to be understood as different "levels" of observation and discussion about the same reality. In my view, this "different levels" approach is far better for dealing with perceptual experience than is his effort to "Disqualify Qualia" (Dennett, *Consciousness Explained* [Boston, 1991], chap. 12) because it doesn't throw the baby out with the Cartesian bathwater.

2. The Secret Life of Things

1. From "The Thing and Its Relations," in James, *The Writings of William James* (Chicago, 1977), p. 214.

2. Merleau-Ponty, *Phenomenology of Perception* (London, 1962), p. 58.

3. "[I bring] out the [sense] quality by fixing my eyes on a portion of the visual field: then and only then have I found myself before a certain *quale* which absorbs my

gaze. Now what actually is fixing one's gaze? . . . [I]t is separating the region under scrutiny from the rest of the field, it is interrupting the total life of the spectacle. . . . The sensible quality, far from being co-extensive with perception, is the peculiar product of an attitude of curiosity or observation" (ibid., p. 226).

4.   "For each object, as for each picture in an art gallery, there is an optimum distance from which it requires to be seen, a direction viewed from which it vouchsafes most of itself: at a shorter distance we have merely a perception blurred through excess or deficiency. We therefore tend towards the maximum of visibility, and seek a better focus as with a microscope. This is obtained through a certain balance between the inner and outer horizon [that is, the living body and the world as a surrounding field]" (ibid., p. 302).

5.   "All understanding and objective thought owe their life to the inaugural fact that with this color (or whatever the sensible element in question may be) I have perceived, I have had, a singular existence which suddenly stopped my glance yet promised it an indefinite series of experiences. . . . [T]he sensible order is *being at a distance*—the fulgurating attestation here and now to an inexhaustible richness" (Merleau-Ponty, *Signs* [Evanston, 1964], p. 167).

6.   Perception is "just that act which creates at a stroke, along with the cluster of data, the meaning which unites them—indeed which not only discovers the meaning *which they have* but moreover sees to it *that they have a meaning*" (Merleau-Ponty, *Phenomenology of Perception* [London, 1962], p. 36).

7.   In sense experience "we are given not 'dead' qualities, but active ones. A wooden wheel placed on the ground is not, *for sight,* the same thing as a wheel bearing a load. . . . The light of a candle changes its appearance for a child when, after a burn, it . . . becomes literally repulsive. Vision is already inhabited by a meaning [*sens*] which gives it a function in . . . our existence. Sense experience is that vital communication with the world which makes it present as a familiar setting of our life. . . . It is the intentional tissue that the effort to know will try to take apart" (ibid., pp. 52–53, trans. modified).

8.   My arguments in this section will follow Merleau-Ponty's work on phenomena relating to vision. As Merleau-Ponty argues in the "Sense Experience" chapter of *Phenomenology of Perception,* each sense-modality has its own features loosely comparable to color, shadow, and reflection: for instance, within hearing there is tone, melody, echo, and the like. As a result, Merleau-Ponty's work is not ignorant of the facts of blindness, but explicitly sensitive of those facts and the ways the living experience of blind people is profoundly different than that of sighted people. See, for example, ibid., pp. 222–229.

9.   This second notion can be seen, for instance, in the Fourth Discourse of Descartes's *Optics* where he valorizes engravings as revealing geometric form, and dismisses color as mere ornament (*Philosophical Writings I* [Cambridge, 1985], pp. 164–166). It can also be seen in sec. 14 of the third *Critique,* where Kant infamously argues that aesthetic judgments (of beauty and sublimity) are rooted in the object's *form* rather than the manifold of sensory content: "In painting, sculpture, and in all the formative arts . . . the *delineation* is the essential thing; and here it is not what gratifies in sensation [i.e., color and tone], but what pleases by means of

its form that is fundamental for [judgments of] taste." See Kant, *Critique of Judgment* (New York, 1951), p. 61.

10. "[P]erception goes straight to the thing and by-passes the colour, just as it is able to fasten upon the expression of a gaze without noting the colour of the eyes" (Merleau-Ponty, *Phenomenology of Perception* [London, 1962], p. 305).

11. "I say that my fountain-pen is black, and I see it as black under the sun's rays. But this blackness is less the sensible quality of blackness than a somber power which radiates from the object, even when it is overlaid with reflected light" (ibid., p. 305).

12. As Merleau-Ponty puts it: "Only after centuries of painting did artists perceive that reflection on the eye without which the eye remains dull and sightless as in the paintings of the early masters. The reflection is not seen as such, since it was in fact able to remain unnoticed for so long, and yet it has its function in perception, since its absence deprives objects and faces of all life and expression. The reflection is seen only incidentally. It is not presented to our perception as an objective element, but as an auxiliary or mediating one. It is not seen itself, but causes us to see the rest" (ibid., p. 309).

13. Merleau-Ponty's discussion of perceptual constancy is in *Phenomenology of Perception*, pp. 224–228, 299–317. My understanding of this point has been enhanced by the careful, provocative analysis in Helen Fielding, "White Logic and the Constancy of Color," in *Feminist Interpretations of Merleau-Ponty*, ed. Olkowski and Weiss (University Park, 2006). Part of Fielding's claim is that Merleau-Ponty's work on color constancy helps us understand certain structures of racism, but also fails to appreciate the ways in which those levels are mediated by social forces.

14. Concerns about Merleau-Ponty's tendency to "privilege" vision are fairly widespread in the secondary literature. Particularly influential statements of this problem have been made by Luce Irigaray in her chapter on *The Visible and the Invisible*, in Irigaray, *An Ethics of Sexual Difference* (Ithaca, 1993), pp. 151–184; and by Judith Butler in "Sexual Ideology and Phenomenological Description: A Feminist Critique of Merleau-Ponty's *Phenomenology of Perception*," in *The Thinking Muse*, ed. Allen and Young (Bloomington, 1989), pp. 85–100. There is a lot to be said in support of these (and other) concerns about Merleau-Ponty's overemphasis on vision. At the same time, I believe it is important not to overstate the problem, for in both the early and late writings, Merleau-Ponty's attention to vision is frequently augmented by discussions relating to synaesthetic perception and the overlapping of vision and touch, touch and hearing, hearing and vision. For nuanced discussion of the complexities in this issue, see Holland, "In a Different Ch[i]asm: A Feminist Rereading of Merleau-Ponty on Sexuality," in *Rereading Merleau-Ponty*, ed. Hass and Olkowski (Amherst, 2000).

15. "The sight of sounds or the hearing of colours come about in the same way as the unity of the gaze through the two eyes: in so far as my body is, not a collection of adjacent organs, but a synergic system, all its functions are exercised and linked together in the general action of being in the world, in so far as it is the congealed face of existence" (Merleau-Ponty, *Phenomenology of Perception* [London, 1962], p. 234, trans. modified).

16. "[T]here is a total logic of the picture or the spectacle, a felt coherence of the colours, spatial forms and significance of the object. . . . We now begin to see a deeper meaning in the organization of the field: it is not only colours, but also geometrical forms, all sensory givens and the significance of objects which go to form a system. Our perception in its entirety is animated by a logic which assigns to each object its determinate features in virtue of those of the rest" (ibid., p. 313).

17. Lingis, *Sensation* (Atlantic Highlands, N.J., 1996), chap. 3. As Lingis puts it, in his own inimitable language: "The world in which we perceive . . . extends on *levels*— the level of the light which our gaze adjusts to and sees with as it looks at the il- luminated contours that surface and intensify, the level of sonority our hearing attunes to as it hearkens to sounds and noises that rise out of it, the level of the tangible our posture finds as our limbs move across the contours and textures of tangible surfaces, the level of verticality and depth and of rest that emerges as our position becomes functional in the layout of tasks. The level is found sensorially, by a movement that does not grasp it as an objective but adjusts to it, is sustained by it, moves with it and according to it" (p. 33).

18. Ibid., p. 33, emphasis added.

19. My thanks to Samir Pandya.

20. As seen in the *Nicomachean Ethics,* bks. 1–4. Despite this provocative affinity, Aris- totle's "practical philosophy" does not advocate sensibility as a specific virtue. In fact, as I will suggest at the end of this chapter, the Merleau-Pontian virtue of sen- sibility is violated by the substance metaphysics of Aristotle's "theoretical phi- losophy."

21. There is a quickly expanding body of work on the relation of Merleau-Ponty's phi- losophy to contemporary environmental thought. In particular, see Abram, *The Spell of the Sensuous* (New York, 1996); Mazis, *Earthbodies* (Albany, 2002); and Brown and Toadvine, eds., *Eco-Phenomenology* (Albany, 2003). An earlier, impor- tant essay on the subject is Monika Langer, "Merleau-Ponty and Deep Ecology," in *Ontology and Alterity in Merleau-Ponty,* ed. Johnson and Smith (Evanston, 1990), pp. 115–129. Some of the most recent work in this area was inspired by the re- cent publication of Merleau-Ponty's 1956–1960 lecture notes from the Collège de France, published under the title *Nature: Course Notes from the Collège de France* (Evanston, 2003). For an excellent collection of this scholarship, see *Chiasmi Inter- national* no. 2 (2000).

22. Levinas, *Totality and Infinity* (Pittsburgh, 1969), pp. 37–38.

23. Writers sometimes suggest that Merleau-Ponty's emphasis on this transcendence of things and others is a late development of his thought. On the contrary, there is plenty of evidence that this emphasis runs throughout *Phenomenology of Per- ception.* Consider, for example, the following passage: "My set of experiences is presented as a concordant whole . . . in that they are all collected together . . . in the ipseity of the thing. The ipseity is, of course, never *reached*: each aspect of the thing which falls to our perception is still only an invitation to perceive beyond it. . . . If the thing itself were reached, it would be from that moment arrayed be- fore us and stripped of its mystery. It would cease to exist as a thing at the very moment when we thought to possess it. What makes the 'reality' of thing is there-

fore precisely what snatches it from our grasp. The aseity of thing, its unchallenge-able presence and the perpetual absence into which it withdraws, are two insepa-rable aspects of transcendence" (*Phenomenology of Perception* [London, 1962], p. 233).

3. Singing the Living Body Electric

1. Whitman, *Leaves of Grass* (New York, 1965), p. 82.

2. Nietzsche, *Thus Spoke Zarathustra* (New York, 1954), p. 34.

3. Descartes, *Philosophical Writings II* (Cambridge, 1985), p. 58.

4. Foucault, *Discipline and Punish* (New York, 1979), p. 136.

5. Locke, *An Essay Concerning Human Understanding* (Oxford, 1975), p. 118.

6. Foucault, *Discipline and Punish* (New York, 1979), pt. 3, chap. 1: "Docile Bodies."

7. For example, Charles Taylor says: "If one had to sum up Merleau-Ponty's philo-sophical legacy in a phrase, one might say that he more than any other taught us what it means to understand ourselves as embodied agents. I mean both that he has made the most convincing case for this view, and that he has explored its ramifications to unparalleled distance and depth" (*Merleau-Ponty: Critical Essays,* ed. Pietersma [Washington, D.C., 1989], p. 1).

8. "[F]urthermore the presentation of objects in perspective cannot be understood except through the resistance of my body to all variation of perspective. If objects may never show me more than one of their facets, this is because I am myself in a certain place from which I see them and which I cannot see" (Merleau-Ponty, *Phenomenology of Perception* [London, 1962], p. 92).

9. As Merleau-Ponty puts it: "We have just seen that the two hands are never simul-taneously in the relationship of touched and touching to each other. When I press my two hands together, it is not a matter of two sensations felt together as one per-ceives two objects placed side by side, but of an ambiguous set-up in which both hands can alternate the roles of 'touching' and 'being touched'" (ibid., p. 93). This image of the two hands not coinciding in the touch will become a thematic exem-plar in *The Visible and the Invisible,* and will be explored further in chap. 5, below.

10. As Merleau-Ponty puts this point: "What prevents its ever being an object, ever being 'completely constituted' is that it is that by which there are objects" (*Phe-nomenology of Perception* [London, 1962], p. 92).

11. Descartes, *Philosophical Writings II* (Cambridge, 1985), p. 60.

12. Dewey's famous piece on this subject is "The Reflex Arc Concept in Psychology" (1896), which he developed further in "Conduct and Experience" (1930). Both es-says are collected in *The Essential Dewey, Volume 2: Ethics, Logic, Psychology,* ed. Hickman and Alexander (Bloomington, 1998), pp. 3–10, 67–87.

13. Merleau-Ponty, *The Structure of Behavior* (Pittsburgh, 1983), p. 13. Further discus-sion of this point can be found in *Phenomenology of Perception* (London, 1962), pp. 75–79.

14. "If a given area of skin is several times stimulated with a hair, the first percep-

tions are clearly distinguished and localized each time at the same point. As the stimulus is repeated, the localization becomes less precise, [and the sensation] is no longer a contact, but a feeling of burning. . . . Later still the patient thinks the stimulus is . . . describing a circle. . . . Finally nothing more is felt. It follows that the 'sensible quality' . . . and even the presence or absence of a perception, are not *de facto* effects of the situation outside the organism, but represent the way in which it meets stimulation and is related to it. An excitation is not perceived when it strikes a sensory organ that is not 'attuned' to it" (Merleau-Ponty, *Phenomenology of Perception* [London, 1962], p. 75).

15. Dennett, *Consciousness Explained* (Boston, 1991), p. 333.

16. Adhémar Gelb and Kurt Goldstein's most extended discussion of Schneider is in their edited collection, *Psychologische Analysen hirnpathologerischer Fälle* (Leipzig, 1920), chap. 2. Kurt Goldstein, in particular, published many case studies of his patients with neurological damage toward a more holistic account of neural function. See, for instance, his 1934 work *The Organism: A Holistic Approach to Biology Derived from Pathological Data in Man* (New York, 1995).

17. "The world in its entirety no longer suggests any meaning to [Schneider] and conversely the meanings that occur to him are not embodied any longer in the given world. We shall say, in a word, that the world no longer has any *physiognomy* for him" (Merleau-Ponty, *Phenomenology of Perception* [London, 1962], p. 132).

18. See Varela (with Thompson and Rosch), *The Embodied Mind: Cognitive Science and Human Experience* (Cambridge, Mass., 1992); and Varela, *Ethical Know-How: Action, Wisdom, and Cognition* (Palo Alto, Cal., 1999). See Clark, *Being There: Putting Brain, Body, and World Together Again* (Cambridge, Mass., 1999). For Lakoff and Johnson's work, see Lakoff, *Women, Fire, and Dangerous Things* (Chicago, 1987); Johnson, *The Body in the Mind* (Chicago, 1987); and Lakoff and Johnson, *Philosophy in the Flesh* (New York, 1999).

19. "The fact that the normal subject immediately grasps that the eye is to sight as the ear is to hearing shows that the eye and ear are immediately given to him as a means of access to the *world,* and furthermore that the world is ante-predicatively self-evident. . . . The Kantian subject posits a world, but, in order to be able to assert a truth, the actual subject must in the first place have a world or be in the world, that is, sustain round about it a system of meanings whose reciprocities, relationships and involvements do not require to be made explicit in order to be exploited" (Merleau-Ponty, *Phenomenology of Perception* [London, 1962], p. 129).

20. For further arguments as to why Merleau-Ponty's living body should not be understood as the transcendental subject, see Dillon, *Merleau-Ponty's Ontology* (Evanston, 1997), pp. 146–148.

21. The term "body image" was introduced by Henry Head, in his *Studies in Neurology* (Oxford, 1920). In the psychological literature since then, the term is used in a couple of main ways: (1) as the body's *visual* image of itself, or (2) as the body's *felt* schema, also referred to as "proprioception." Throughout this section, I am using term in the second way.

22. Contemporary support for Merleau-Ponty's view can be gleaned from Jonathan Cole's *Pride and a Daily Marathon* (Cambridge, Mass., 1995). Cole's book is about

Ian Waterman, a man who has literally lost his body image from the neck down due to a rare neurological disease. More severely than Schneider, Waterman doesn't know where the other parts of his body are and cannot coordinate their movements in space. It is evident that the cause of this disruption is not a breakdown in customary associations or mechanistic reflexes, as behaviorism would have it. Nor is it the loss of positing, representing consciousness; on the contrary, Waterman's positing consciousness is fully functional, and he learns to use it to compensate for his lack of proprioception. Waterman's case and Cole's research support Merleau-Ponty's claim that we need a holistic account of the body and neural functioning that does not start from a picture of consciousness as fundamentally representational.

23. Merleau-Ponty's main source for these claims about phantom limb and anosagnosia is François Lhermitte in *L'Image du notre corps* (Paris, 1939). Contemporary cases that bear them out can be found throughout the works of Oliver Saks, for instance, see Saks, *The Man Who Mistook His Wife for a Hat* (New York, 1985), chaps. 1, 3, and 6.

24. Merleau-Ponty's appreciation of Freud is not unlike his appreciation of Husserl, Hegel, and Saussure. That is to say, cautious, critical, and yet profound: he seeks to amplify what he sees as the best aspects of their work. With Freud it is the notion of repression, the unconscious, and eros as rooted in the two-fold dynamic of the living body. For one example: "Whatever the theoretical declarations of Freud may have been, psychoanalytical research is in fact led to an explanation of man [*sic*], not in terms of his sexual substructure, but to a discovery in sexuality of relations and attitudes which had previously been held to reside *in consciousness*. Thus the significance of psychoanalysis is less to make psychology biological than to discover a dialectical process in functions thought of as 'purely biological,' and to reintegrate sexuality into the human being" (*Phenomenology of Perception* [London, 1962], p. 158). For particularly deft treatments of Merleau-Ponty's fertile relationship to psychoanalysis, see James Phillips, "From the Unseen to the Invisible," and Edward S. Casey, "The Unconscious Mind and the Prereflective Body," both in *Merleau-Ponty, Interiority and Exteriority, Psychic Life and the World,* ed. Olkowski and Morley (Albany, 1999), pp. 47–56, 69–88.

25. The imagination is not thematized by Merleau-Ponty, but his texts are richly suggestive about how an embodied theory of the imagination might go. Important work on this topic has been done by James Morley. See, for example, Morley, "The Texture of the Real: Merleau-Ponty, Imagination, and Psychopathology," in *Imagination and Its Pathologies,* ed. Morley and Phillips (Cambridge, Mass., 2003). Also, see David Abram's treatment of imagination in *The Spell of the Sensuous* (New York, 1996), chap. 2. Merleau-Ponty's account of the erotic is most fully developed in the chapter of *Phenomenology of Perception* entitled "The Body in its Sexual Being," though a schematic late treatment can be found in Merleau-Ponty, *Nature: Course Notes from the Collège de France* (Evanston, 2003), pp. 274–284. The chapter in *Phenomenology of Perception* has been the subject of a great deal of scrutiny and criticism. Important work on this subject has been done by Dorothea Olkowski, for example in "Chiasm: The Interval of Sexual Difference Between Irigaray and Merleau-Ponty," in *Rereading Merleau-Ponty,* ed. Hass and Olkowski

(Amherst, 2000), pp. 339–354. Her arguments in relation to Merleau-Ponty's theory of sexuality also run throughout Olkowski, *Gilles Deleuze and the Ruin of Representation* (Berkeley, 1999). Merleau-Ponty's theory of sexuality and erotic life is also central to Alphonso Lingis's book *Libido: The French Existential Theories* (Bloomington, 1985). I will have something to say about problems in this aspect of Merleau-Ponty's account of the living body in sec. 5 of this chapter.

26. In chap. 5, I will explore Merleau-Ponty's later development toward a language of "the flesh." The flesh is one of Merleau-Ponty's most celebrated concepts, but since in the late writings it is so ontologically rich—referring to far more than the living body—it requires extended treatment on its own.

27. Foucault, "Nietzsche, Genealogy, History," in Faubion, ed., *Michel Foucault: Aesthetics, Method, and Epistemology* (New York, 1998), pp. 375–376, emphasis added.

28. Foucault, *The History of Sexuality, Volume 1* (New York, 1980), pp. 42–44, final emphasis added.

29. It is clear that Foucault became unhappy with his analysis of power in *The History of Sexuality, Volume 1* and worked to revise it in ways that both distinguish it from violence and show how resistance is structurally possible. His important late treatment of these questions is in "The Subject and Power," which is attached as an afterword to Dreyfus and Rabinow, *Michael Foucault: Beyond Structuralism and Hermeneutics* (Chicago, 1983), pp. 208–226. For example, Foucault says in this essay: "In itself the exercise of power is not violence. . . . It is . . . always a way of acting upon an acting subject or acting subjects by virtue of their acting or being capable of action. . . . Power is exercised only over free subjects, and only insofar as they are free. By this we mean individual or collective subjects who are faced with a field of possibilities in which several ways of behaving, several reactions, several diverse comportments may be realized" (pp. 220–221).

30. Judith Butler makes the case for changing the terms from "construction" to "materialization" in the introduction to her book on the way cultural norms and practices coerce the formation of living bodies: Butler, *Bodies That Matter: On the Discursive Limits of Sex* (New York, 1993).

31. For his extended treatment of this see Foucault, *Discipline and Punish* (New York, 1979), pt. 3, chaps. 1, 2, and 3.

32. On Merleau-Ponty's contribution to these questions, see Kruks, *The Political Philosophy of Merleau-Ponty* (Atlantic Highlands, N.J., 1981); Whiteside, *Merleau-Ponty and the Foundation for an Existential Politics* (Princeton, 1988); and Bernard P. Dauenhauer, "Democracy and the Task of Political Amelioration," in *Rereading Merleau-Ponty*, ed. Hass and Olkowski (Amherst, 2000), pp. 235–252.

33. This kind of survey is carried out by Olkowski and Weiss in their anthology *Feminist Interpretations of Merleau-Ponty* (University Park, 2006).

34. Young, "Throwing Like a Girl: A Phenomenology of Feminine Body Comportment, Motility, and Spatiality," in *The Thinking Muse*, ed. Allen and Young (Bloomington, 1989), pp. 51–70.

35. Ibid., p. 65.

36. Ibid., p. 66.

37. See her essay "Foucault, Femininity, and the Modernization of Patriarchal Power," in Bartky, *Femininity and Domination: Studies in the Phenomenology of Oppression* (New York, 1990), pp. 63–82.

38. In Butler, "Sexual Ideology and Phenomenological Description: A Feminist Critique of Merleau-Ponty's *Phenomenology of Perception*," in *The Thinking Muse*, ed. Allen and Young (Bloomington, 1989), pp. 85–100.

39. Weiss, *Body Images: Embodiment as Intercorporeality* (New York, 1999).

40. See, in particular, Grosz's book *Volatile Bodies: Toward a Corporeal Feminism* (Bloomington, 1994).

41. The theme of sexual difference runs throughout all of Irigaray's writings, but it receives special emphasis in relation to Merleau-Ponty in Irigaray, *An Ethics of Sexual Difference* (Ithaca, 1993). Merleau-Ponty's thought and its difficulties is also a theme in Irigaray, *To Be Two* (New York, 2001).

42. From the essay, "Sexual Difference," in Irigaray, *An Ethics of Sexual Difference* (Ithaca, 1993), p. 5.

43. Irigaray's explicit critique of Merleau-Ponty in these terms, "The Invisible of the Flesh: A Reading of Merleau-Ponty, *The Visible and the Invisible*, 'The Intertwining—The Chiasm'," is in Irigaray, *An Ethics of Sexual Difference* (Ithaca, 1993), pp. 151–184.

44. Grosz, *Volatile Bodies* (Bloomington, 1994), p. 19.

45. For an account of Merleau-Ponty's promising approach to generality see Hass, "Rays of the World: Merleau-Ponty and the Problem of Universals," in *Chiasmi International* no. 6 (2005), pp. 225–236.

46. The only focused treatment of desire in Merleau-Ponty occurs in the final sketch for his third and last course on nature. See Merleau-Ponty, *Nature: Course Notes from the Collège de France* (Evanston, 2003), pp. 274–284. But since this is literally a "sketch," that is, thought-fragments written by Merleau-Ponty to be fleshed out in class, I believe it is hard to find anything like a "theory" in them. At best, I think we get gestures toward a theory in these late notes.

47. Lingis first makes this argument against Merleau-Ponty in his *Libido: The French Existential Theories* (Bloomington, 1985), but also in *Sensation: Intelligibility in Sensibility* (Atlantic Highlands, N.J., 1996), chap. 4.

48. Olkowski has explored this problem in Merleau-Ponty's thought in many of her essays, for example, "Chiasm: The Interval of Sexual Difference Between Irigaray and Merleau-Ponty," in *Rereading Merleau-Ponty*, ed. Hass and Olkowski (Amherst, 2000), pp. 339–354; but it is also thematic in chap. 3 of Olkowski, *Gilles Deleuze and the Ruin of Representation* (Berkeley, 1999).

4. Elemental Alterity

1. Lingis, *Sensation: Intelligibility in Sensibility* (Atlantic Highlands, N.J., 1996), p. 104.

2. Descartes, *Philosophical Writings II* (Cambridge, 1985), p. 21.

3. Berkeley, *A Treatise Concerning the Principles of Human Knowledge* (Indianapolis, 1982), sec. 148, p. 88.

4. Kant, *Critique of Pure Reason* (New York, 1965), in "The Paralogisms": see p. 332.

5. Scheler's influential work on the epistemological problem of other minds is best seen in Scheler, *The Nature of Sympathy* (Hamden, Conn., 1973), pt. 3. His work on this subject is also developed in his *magnum opus* from the same year (1913): *Formalism in Ethics and Non-Formal Ethics of Value* (Evanston, 1973), chap. 6. For a survey of the contemporary empirical research confirming this, see Gopnik, Meltzoff, and Kuhl, *The Scientist in the Crib: Minds, Brains, and How Children Learn* (New York, 1999).

6. Sartre, *Being and Nothingness* (London, 1958).

7. Ibid., p. 256.

8. Ibid., p. 261.

9. "The Battle Over Existentialism," in Merleau-Ponty, *Sense and Non-Sense* (Evanston, 1964), p. 72. This early critical assessment by Merleau-Ponty is rather gently made, offered while he and Sartre are close friends and co-editors of *Les Temps Modernes*. Later, Merleau-Ponty will make this critique of *Being and Nothingness* in unflinching terms: "Whether we are considering my relations with the things or my relations with the other . . . the question is whether in the last analysis our life takes place between an absolutely individual and absolutely universal nothingness behind us and an absolutely individual and absolutely universal being before us— in which case we have the incomprehensible and impossible task of restoring to Being . . . everything that we are—or whether every relation between me and Being, even vision, even speech, is not a carnal relation, with the flesh of the world" (*The Visible and the Invisible* [Evanston, 1968], pp. 83–84).

10. Wittgenstein, *Philosophical Investigations* (New York, 1953), sec. 309, p. 103e.

11. It is clear that in offering this view Merleau-Ponty is influenced by Husserl's treatments of the problem in the *Cartesian Meditations* and *Ideas II*. The notion of pre-predicative "pairing" or "coupling" is most richly developed by Husserl in the Fifth Cartesian Meditation, the one that wrestles with other minds. The manifest problem in this account, which Merleau-Ponty is aiming to correct, is that Husserl's argument proceeds, à la Descartes, from a transcendental reduction to the thinking ego, the so-called "sphere of ownness." From this egoistic and idealistic position, it is a priori impossible to get to the otherness of the other in the flesh, and it seems that Husserl, as Descartes before him, smuggles the idea of otherness into the *Eigensphäre* and leaves it unexplained. Merleau-Ponty's breakthrough idea was to take Husserl's basic notion and export it into living, organic experience. For extended discussion of the crucial differences between Husserl's and Merleau-Ponty's different ways of rendering this solution, see Dillon, *Merleau-Ponty's Ontology* (Evanston, 1997), chap. 7.

12. Merleau-Ponty uses this language and develops this distinction between "syncretic" and "synthetic" in his 1951 course at the Sorbonne, transcribed as "The Child's Relation With Others," in *The Primacy of Perception and Other Essays*

(Evanston, 1964), pp. 96–155. In this way of speaking, Merleau-Ponty is drawing on Henri Wallon, *Les origines du caractère chez l'enfant* (Paris, 1949).

13. For a survey of the contemporary research see Gopnik, Meltzoff, and Kuhl, *The Scientist in the Crib* (New York, 1999), chap. 2. Also see Stern, *The Interpersonal World of the Infant* (New York, 1985); and Mahler, Pine, and Bergman, eds., *The Psychological Birth of the Human Infant* (New York, 1975), pt. 2.

14. As Merleau-Ponty says: "There is simply no radical distinction in the child between his own hand and that of another. The child's extraordinary facility in recognizing parts of the body in a drawing . . . the promptness and skill with which he identifies parts of his own body in the bodies of animals that scarcely resemble the human body or familiar domestic animals, the plasticity of vision that allows him to recognize homologous structures of the body in different organisms—all this can be explained by the state of neutral indistinction between self and other in which he lives" (*The Primacy of Perception and Other Essays* [Evanston, 1964], pp. 149–150). In this passage, Merleau-Ponty is drawing upon the findings of Wallon, but the contemporary research to support this claim is fully discussed in Myers, *Children and Animals: Social Development and Our Connections to Other Species* (Boulder, 1998).

15. Glen Mazis is particularly good at articulating our multifaceted relations with animals in Mazis, *Earthbodies: Rediscovering Our Planetary Senses* (Albany, 2002).

16. There is a typo in the English text of *The Visible and the Invisible* (Evanston, 1968) that has significant implications for understanding the relationship between Merleau-Ponty and Irigaray. The typo occurs in a place where Merleau-Ponty is discussing the separation relation, or *écart*. The published text says the body and things are welded together and separated as "two laps" (p. 136), when in fact the original has *deux lèvres*—"two lips" (*Le Visible et l'invisible* [Paris, 1964], p. 179). "Lips" is a near-perfect metaphor for the divergent relation Merleau-Ponty envisions between self and other, for between two lips there is flesh and a distinct similarity of contour, but also a constitutive separation that is essential for their intimate contact. In the next chapter I will have much more to say about this separation relation (*écart*) and its centrality in Merleau-Ponty's late writings.

17. As Merleau-Ponty puts it: "I can evolve a solipsist philosophy but, in doing so, I assume the existence of a community of men endowed with speech, and I address myself to it. . . . I must choose between others and myself, it is said. But we choose one *against* the other, and thus assert both" (*Phenomenology of Perception* [London, 1962], p. 360).

18. Derrida first develops this striking claim in his important essay "Force of Law: The 'Mystical Foundation of Authority,'" in Derrida, *Acts of Religion* (New York, 2002), pp. 228–298.

19. See, for instance, his eulogy, "Adieu," in Derrida, *Adieu to Emmanuel Levinas* (Stanford, 1999), pp. 1–13.

20. As Levinas says in *Totality and Infinity* (Pittsburgh, 1969), with Merleau-Ponty clearly in mind: "The [self] and the other do not constitute a simple correlation which would be reversible. The reversibility of a relation where the terms are indifferently read from left to right and from right to left would couple them the *one*

to the *other;* they would complete one another in a system visible from the outside. The intended transcendence would thus be reabsorbed into the unity of the system, destroying the radical alterity of the other" (pp. 35–36).

21. As indicated, much of Levinas's critique of Merleau-Ponty is only implied in his two main works, *Totality and Infinity* (Pittsburgh, 1969), and *Otherwise than Being* (Pittsburgh, 1998). However some criticisms (and appreciations too) are explicitly developed in "Meaning and Sense," in Levinas, *Collected Philosophical Papers* (Dordrecht, 1987), pp. 75–107; and "Two Texts on Merleau-Ponty," in *Ontology and Alterity in Merleau-Ponty,* ed. Johnson and Smith (Evanston, 1990), pp. 53–66.

22. Is such a thing—"elemental alterity"—contradictory? While the categories of *Totality and Infinity* would make it seem impossible, the arguments of this chapter are an attempt to show that this type of account is utterly necessary: an account which respects the irreducible alterity of others, but which remains rooted in the elements of flesh, animality, and nature. I am inspired toward such an account by work already begun by thinkers such as Elizabeth Grosz, Luce Irigaray, and Alphonso Lingis.

23. Levinas, *Totality and Infinity* (Pittsburgh, 1969), p. 43.

24. See Robert Bernasconi, "One-Way Traffic: The Ontology of Decolonization and its Ethics," in *Ontology and Alterity in Merleau-Ponty,* ed. Johnson and Smith (Evanston, 1990), pp. 67–80.

25. This comment touches on a very large issue that goes beyond the limits of the present discussion: the question of what "priority" means in Levinas, as in the "priority of ethics to ontology," and whether he fully earns that claim. In my view, a first difficulty is that his use of "priority" seems to waffle between two senses that are not obviously commensurable: the sense of "prior" as temporally *before,* and the sense of "prior" as a "breach," as interrupting the flow of time. I will show some problems in certain related equivocations below. But secondly, in cases where temporal priority is clearly intended, some of Levinas's claims seem empirically false. Indeed, developmental research does not support the claim that the most basic sense of self, desire, and pleasure is *wholly derivative* upon the shocking experience of alterity, but rather that those senses are rooted in the infant's experience of his/her body in relation to others (playing, contact, and eating). For a synthesis of the medical and scientific research to this effect see Greenspan, *Building Healthy Minds* (Cambridge, 2000), chap. 4. For a look at what happens to the infant's sense of self and sense of other when such physical engagement and reciprocity are missing, see Jay Belsky, Kate Rosenberger, and Keith Crnic, "The Origins of Attachment Security: Classical and Contextual Determinants," in *Attachment Theory,* ed. Goldberg, Muir, and Kerr (Hillsdale, N.J., 1995), pp. 153–184.

26. Levinas, *Totality and Infinity* (Pittsburgh, 1969), p. 50.

27. Ibid., p. 159.

28. See, for example, ibid., pp. 158–159.

29. Ibid., p. 115.

30. Ibid., p. 57, emphases added.

31. Ibid., pp. 155, 91.

32. Ibid., pp. 196–197.

33. Ibid., p. 195.

34. Ibid., p. 97.

35. Ibid., p. 73.

36. As he puts it in Levinas, *Otherwise than Being* (Pittsburgh, 1998): "The Infinite is non-thematizable, gloriously exceeds every capacity and manifests . . . its exorbitance in the approach of the neighbor, obedient to its measure. . . . It is the breaking-point, but also the binding place" (p. 12).

37. Ibid., p. 51.

38. Ibid., pp. 51–52.

39. Ibid., p. 15.

40. Ibid., p. 70.

41. Ibid., p. 49.

42. Ibid., p. 123.

5. Later Developments

1. A working note from September 1959, in Merleau-Ponty, *The Visible and the Invisible* (Evanston, 1968), p. 203.

2. These self-critical reflections can be found in the notes on pp. 168–169, 175–176, 183, and 200 of Merleau-Ponty, *The Visible and the Invisible* (Evanston, 1968). It should be mentioned that the Working Notes collected in that volume are by no means exhaustive: they contain only a select number of Merleau-Ponty's many late notes, those that editor Claude Lefort deemed most pertinent to clarify the meaning of the manuscript (ibid., pp. xxxviii–xxxix).

3. It is quite clear that Merleau-Ponty's late phase of thinking and writing was inspired by certain themes in Husserl's writings on the life-world, but more particularly by Merleau-Ponty's renewed engagement with Heidegger's work. This influence is indicated by the many references to Heidegger in the late writings and Working Notes, but also by the language of Being and *Wesen* that permeates *The Visible and the Invisible*. Part and parcel of this interest, Merleau-Ponty devoted a lecture course at the Collège du France in 1959–1960 to themes in Heidegger's late work; see Merleau-Ponty, *Notes de cours 1959–1961 par Merleau-Ponty* (Paris, 1996).

4. Merleau-Ponty died of a heart attack in May 1961 at the age of 53. The painful shock of his sudden death can be felt in the elegies written by his colleagues. See, for instance, Sartre, *Situations IV* (Greenwich, Conn., 1969); "Merleau-Ponty: In Memoriam," in Lacan, *Merleau-Ponty and Psychology* (Atlantic Highlands, N.J., 1993); Claude Lefort's forward to Merleau-Ponty, *The Visible and the Invisible* (Evanston, 1968), pp. xi–xxxiii; and Stephen Spender's poem, "One More New Botched Beginning," in Spender, *Selected Poems* (London, 1965), pp. 79–80. I am grateful to my good friend, Dr. Alec Marsh, for bringing this poem to my attention.

With regard to the character of the manuscript of *The Visible and the Invisible* (Evanston, 1968), Lefort states that the 150 handwritten, heavily corrected pages comprising pt. 1 were found among Merleau-Ponty's papers along with several conflicting bare outlines for the entire book (pp. xxxiv–xxxvii). As Lefort says, "these few indications do not permit us to imagine what the work would have been in its matter and in its form" (p. xxxvi).

5. Although Merleau-Ponty does not quote him, this is how Augustine puts it in *Confessions* (New York, 1961), bk. 11, sec. 14, p. 264: "What, then, is time? I know enough what it is, provided that nobody asks me; but if I am asked what it is and try to explain, I am baffled."

6. As Merleau-Ponty says later in *The Visible and the Invisible* (Evanston, 1968): "philosophy interrogates the perceptual faith—but neither expects nor receives an answer in the ordinary sense . . . because the existing world exists in the interrogative mode. . . . If we are ourselves in question in the very unfolding of our life . . . it is because we ourselves are one continued question, a perpetual enterprise of taking our bearings on the constellations of the world" (p. 103).

It is reasonably clear that Merleau-Ponty's turn toward this notion and language of "interrogation" is one which was inspired by Heidegger. For already by the late 1930s, Heidegger had argued that "questioning" is the proper mode of philosophy itself. This is true, Heidegger suggests, because any "answer" worth its name is always an invitation to further seeking, always an invitation to explore what is concealed by the revelation. As Heidegger puts it in 1937–1938, such "questioning of the truth of Being is . . . philosophy. Here questioning already counts as knowing, because no matter how essential and decisive an answer might be, the answer cannot be other than the penultimate step. . . . In the domain of genuine seeking, to find does not mean to cease seeking, but is the highest intensity of seeking" (*Basic Questions of Philosophy* [Bloomington, 1994], p. 7).

7. Merleau-Ponty uses this phrase in a passage of "Eye and Mind" that mirrors the opening arguments of *The Visible and the Invisible*. See *The Merleau-Ponty Aesthetics Reader,* ed. Johnson (Evanston, 1993), p. 124.

8. The reader will notice here that Merleau-Ponty is both criticizing and inverting the Hegelian project. For Hegel, we begin with contradictories that a sublime thought (dialectic) must resolve; for Merleau-Ponty we start with experiences of divergent unities that thought tears into contradictories. From Merleau-Ponty's perspective, dialectic only compounds the errors, and we need a new philosophical method (that is, expression) that will offer a way of *knowing* the perceptual faith without deforming it. Again, we will see Merleau-Ponty's "expression" as a way of knowing, in subsequent chapters, and we will see how it works without "representation" or deformation to reveal the experiences we live.

9. See Merleau-Ponty, *Phenomenology of Perception* (London, 1962), pp. 13–14. Just as *écart* is prefigured in this early work, Merleau-Ponty also makes clear in several working notes that the divergence-spread is closely related to the *Gestalt* and the perceptual meaning that opens up there. For instance, he says: "understand perception as differentiation. . . . Understand that the 'to be conscious' = to have a figure on a ground . . . the figure-ground distinction introduces a third term be-

tween the 'subject' and the 'object.' It is *that separation (écart)* first of all that is the perceptual *meaning*" (*The Visible and the Invisible* [Evanston, 1968], p. 197).

10. As he says in *The Visible and the Invisible* (Evanston, 1968), Sartre's philosophy of the negative "begins by opposing being and nothingness absolutely, and it ends by showing that the nothingness is in a way within being. . . . When are we to believe it? At the beginning or the end? . . . there is a difference between Being in the restricted sense with which one begins—which over its whole extension is absolutely exclusive of nothingness . . . and Being in the broad sense which one ends up with—which in a way contains nothingness" (p. 66). After a few pages of elaborating this equivocation, Merleau-Ponty sums it up: "Negativist thought oscillates between these two images without being able to sacrifice one of them nor to unite them. . . . it is the 'ventriloquial' thought that Plato speaks of, that which always affirms or denies in the hypothesis what it denies or affirms in the thesis" (p. 73).

11. As Merleau-Ponty puts this point: "[Can Sartre plausibly say] that there is the In Itself as position, and that the For Itself inexists [*inexiste*] as negation? This formula is evidently abstract: taken literally it would make the experience of vision impossible, for if being is wholly in itself, it is itself only in the night of identity, and my look, which draws it therefrom, destroys it as being; and if the For Itself is pure negation, it is not even For Itself, it is unaware of itself for want of *there being* something in it to be known" (ibid., p. 75; *Le Visible et l'invisible* [Paris, 1964], p. 106).

12. "Hence . . . we know that, since vision is a palpation with the look, it must also be inscribed in the order of being that it discloses to us; he who looks must not be foreign to the world that he looks at. As soon as I see, it is necessary that the vision . . . be doubled with a complementary vision or with another vision: myself seen from without, such as another would see me. . . . [H]e who sees cannot possess the visible unless he is possessed by it, unless he *is of it*" (Merleau-Ponty, *The Visible and the Invisible* [Evanston, 1968], pp. 134–135).

13. While some commentators have thought the word "chiasm" is a neologism, in fact Merleau-Ponty draws the word from the field of anatomy where "chiasm" refers to the juncture where the two separate optic nerves and interior nasal fibers weave together. The term is thus appropriate enough to express his carnal intertwining through difference.

14. For Levinas's version of the solipsism criticism, see *Totality and Infinity* (Pittsburgh, 1969), pp. 35–36. Irigaray's comments to this effect are found in her early essay on Merleau-Ponty, "The Invisible of the Flesh," in Irigaray, *An Ethics of Sexual Difference* (Ithaca, 1993), see pp. 154–157. Lefort's concerns are voiced in "Flesh and Otherness," in *Ontology and Alterity in Merleau-Ponty,* ed. Johnson and Smith (Evanston, 1990), pp. 3–13.

15. Levinas, *Totality and Infinity* (Pittsburgh, 1969), p. 35.

16. "Différance," in Derrida, *Margins of Philosophy* (Chicago, 1982), pp. 1–27.

17. As Derrida puts it: "What is written as *différance,* then, will be the playing movement that 'produces' . . . these differences, these effects of difference. . . . *Différance*

is the non-full, non-simple, structures and differentiating origin of differences" (ibid., p. 11).

18. This phrase is from the interview "Semiology and Grammatology," in Derrida, *Positions* (Chicago, 1981), p. 27.

19. As Derrida puts it: "I try to respect as rigorously as possible the internal, regulated play of philosophemes or epistememes by making them slide—without mistreating them—to the point of their . . . closure. To 'deconstruct' philosophy, thus, would be to think—in the most faithful, interior way—the structured genealogy of philosophy's concepts, but at the same time to determine . . . what this history has been able to dissimulate or forbid, making itself into a history by means of this somewhat motivated repression" (ibid., p. 6).

20. For the record, I believe that Derrida has satisfactorily answered these objections. Early on, Derrida flatly denied that his philosophy is a linguistic or textual reductionism. For example, in "Deconstruction and the Other" (in *Dialogues with Contemporary Continental Thinkers,* ed. Kearney [Manchester, 1984], pp. 105–126), Derrida says: "It is totally false to suggest that deconstruction is a suspension of reference. Deconstruction is always deeply concerned with the 'other' of language. I never cease to be surprised by critics who see my declaration that there is nothing beyond language [as saying] that we are imprisoned in language; it is in fact saying the opposite. The critique of logocentrism is above all else the search for the 'other' and the 'other of language'" (p. 123). This interview has been reprinted in Kearney, ed., *States of Mind: Dialogues with Contemporary Thinkers* (New York, 1995), pp. 156–176.

   As for the concern that deconstruction is an essentially skeptical, nihilistic philosophy, Derrida has vigorously rejected this interpretation (vilification?) in print and in voice more times than I have been able to count. One excellent place to see his answer—his insistence that deconstruction is about systematically affirming what is excluded by this or that discourse—is in Derrida, *Deconstruction in a Nutshell: A Conversation with Jacques Derrida,* ed. with comm. Caputo (New York, 1997). Derrida also addresses this question in detail in an interview at Oxford, available on film as *Jacques Derrida* (Princeton, 1992). On this issue, I would also refer the reader to Rodolphe Gasché's early, but still important work, *The Tain of the Mirror: Derrida and the Philosophy of Reflection* (Cambridge, Mass., 1986).

21. The two later texts by Derrida that centralize visibility and the flesh are *Memoirs of the Blind* (Chicago, 1990); and *On Touching—Jean-Luc Nancy* (Stanford, 2005).

22. May, *Gilles Deleuze* (Cambridge, 2005), see chap. 1.

23. This important argument is developed over the course of *Memoirs of the Blind* (Chicago, 1990), but particularly in the last twenty pages of the text. As Derrida puts it: "Now if tears *come to the eyes,* if they *well up in them,* and if they can also veil sight, perhaps they reveal, in the very course of this experience . . . an essence of the eye. . . . Deep down, deep down inside, the eye would be destined not to see, but to weep. For at the very moment they veil sight, tears would also unveil what is proper to the eye . . . nothing less than *aletheia,* the *truth* of the eyes . . . : to have imploration rather than vision in sight, to address prayer, love, joy, or sadness

rather than a look or gaze. Even before it illuminates, revelation is the moment of 'tears of joy'" (p. 126).

24. Derrida, *On Touching—Jean-Luc Nancy* (Stanford, 2005), p. 211.

25. On the complex question of Merleau-Ponty's late ontology to animal life, particularly in light of the *Nature* lectures, I have been educated by a wonderful unpublished paper by Randall Johnson, "Animal Appeal: Derrida, Merleau-Ponty, and *The Call of the Wild*." This paper is especially interesting in this context because of its explicit references to Derrida's work on animality.

26. So far, I believe the best work in this spirit has been done by Leonard Lawlor. I refer the reader to any of the essays in Lawlor, *Thinking Through French Philosophy* (Bloomington, 2003).

27. Derrida, *On Touching—Jean-Luc Nancy* (Stanford, 2005), p. 215.

28. Deleuze and Guattari, *A Thousand Plateaus* (Minneapolis, 1987), p. 249.

29. I am particularly indebted to the work of Dorothea Olkowski, Fred Evans, and Leonard Lawlor, all of whom have rigorously challenged aspects of Merleau-Ponty's thought through ideas and arguments that are at least partly inspired by Deleuze. For some examples, see Dorothea Olkowski, "A Psychoanalysis of Nature?"; and Fred Evans, "'Chaosmos' and Merleau-Ponty's Philosophy of Nature," both in *Chiasmi International* no. 2 (2000); and "The End of Phenomenology: Expressionism in Deleuze and Merleau-Ponty," in Lawlor, *Thinking Through French Philosophy* (Bloomington 2003), pp. 80–94.

30. Deleuze, *Difference and Repetition* (New York, 1994).

31. As Deleuze puts it, "it matters [little] whether . . . identity be considered analytic or synthetic. In either case, difference remains subordinated to identity, reduced to the negative, incarcerated within similitude and analogy. . . . On what condition is difference traced or projected on to a flat space? Precisely when it has been forced into a previously established identity, when it is placed on the slope of the identical which makes it reflect or desire identity, and necessarily takes it where identity wants it to go—namely, into the negative" (ibid., pp. 50–51).

32. I say Deleuze "seems to agree" because seeing the agreement requires some interpretive work. One of the two places Merleau-Ponty is mentioned in *Difference and Repetition* is when Deleuze mentions that "Merleau-Ponty . . . undoubtedly followed a more thoroughly Heideggerian inspiration in his speaking of 'folds' and 'pleating'" (ibid., p. 64). This reference is followed by a brief, schematic survey of the main theses of Heidegger's philosophy of difference, and one thesis, he says, is Heidegger's view that "Difference cannot . . . be subordinated to the Identical or the Equal but must be thought as . . . in the same" (ibid., p. 65). Thus, he seems to be saying that Heidegger (and Merleau-Ponty by extension) is not performing the subordination of difference to identity.

Nonetheless, the second place Merleau-Ponty is mentioned in *Difference and Repetition* (in a footnote to chap. 3) hints toward a different criticism: that Merleau-Ponty's *Phenomenology of Perception* at times appeals to "common sensibility" in a way that remains tethered to the Cartesian-Kantian "image of thought," with all its commitments to representation, order, and unification among the faculties. This is, I think, a perceptive line of concern, for Merleau-Ponty from time to time lapses into the language of unity and synthesis when discussing the character of perceptual experience. For example, from the pages to which Deleuze refers us, Merleau-Ponty says: "That is why we said with Herder that man *is a sensorium commune*. In this primary layer of sense experience . . . I have the living experience of the unity of the subject and the intersensory unity of the thing" (*Phenomenology of Perception* [London, 1962], pp. 238–239). And Merleau-Ponty does assume the "commonness" of *Gestalt* perception in a way that is analogous to the "subjective assumptions" that Deleuze demonstrates in Kant and Descartes. Yet, I must also say that as Deleuze's "image of thought" emerges in his text, it rather quickly seems remote both from Merleau-Ponty's intention and his text itself. For example, the quote just given occurs in a passage where Merleau-Ponty is working to dramatically complicate the notions of "unity" and "synthesis" that inhere in post-Cartesian philosophy. (Indeed, as observed before, the unit of thought in Merleau-Ponty is not the "sentence" but *the passage*.) Further, as will be shown in chap. 6, below, it gradually emerges that for Merleau-Ponty these "organizations" occur through creative, productive, expressive operations rather than the mapping and modeling of representation. In short, articulating the relationship between Deleuze's and Merleau-Ponty's thought is an extremely complicated task and not a simple or obvious binary, as Foucault alleges in his essay "Theatrum Philosophicum" (in Faubion, ed., *Michel Foucault: Aesthetics, Method, and Epistemology* [New York, 1998]). To be sure, despite their manifest differences and Deleuze's several successful lines of criticism, one of which will soon be developed, I believe these two thinkers remain closely connected in their efforts toward a "philosophy of difference." If Deleuze's thought performs a provocative "radicalization" of Merleau-Ponty's ontology (which I think is true), it might also be that Merleau-Ponty's philosophy provides a perfect path for appreciating both the achievements and limits of Deleuze's thought.

33. Deleuze, *Difference and Repetition* (New York, 1994), p. 28, trans. modified.

34. Ibid., p. 35, emphasis added.

6. Expression and the Origin of Geometry

This chapter is a significantly expanded version of an earlier paper I co-authored with Marjorie Hass, "Merleau-Ponty and the Origin of Geometry," in *Chiasms: Merleau-Ponty's Notion of Flesh*, ed. Evans and Lawlor (Albany, 2000), pp. 177–188.

1. Merleau-Ponty, *The Visible and the Invisible* (Evanston, 1968), p. 149.

2. Heyting, "The Intuitionist Foundations of Mathematics," in *Philosophy of Mathematics: Selected Readings*, ed. Benacerraf and Putnam (Cambridge, 1983), p. 53.

3. See, for example, "Cézanne's Doubt," in *The Merleau-Ponty Aesthetics Reader*, ed. Johnson (Evanston, 1993); and "Metaphysics and the Novel," in Merleau-Ponty, *Sense and Non-Sense* (Evanston, 1964).

4. Halfway through "The Unpublished Text," after having summarized the general arguments from *The Structure of Behavior* and *Phenomenology of Perception*, Merleau-Ponty indicates that his future studies will be concerned with the field of

knowledge a theory of truth. He also says that an important focus will be on the "characteristic operation of the mind" by which it "sublimates rather than suppresses our incarnation" (in Merleau-Ponty, *The Primacy of Perception and Other Essays* [Evanston, 1964], p. 7). This operation is what he elsewhere calls "expression," and we will see its essential characteristics in the pages that follow.

5. Plato, *Meno* (Indianapolis, 1981), p. 13 (80d).

6. As Merleau-Ponty puts this: "At the root of our experiences and all our reflections, [we seem to find], then, a being which immediately recognizes itself, because it is knowledge both of itself and of all things, and which knows its own existence, not by observation . . . nor by inference from any idea of itself, but through direct contact" (*Phenomenology of Perception* [London, 1962], p. 371).

7. This last phrase connotes that there are two different ways to be transcendental about mathematics: one is to see mathematical statements as representations of ideal forms or objects, as in Plato; the other is to see them as representations necessitated by the a priori structures and categories of the transcendental subject, as in Kant. In what follows we will see how Merleau-Ponty's account of mathematics as expression amounts to a rejection of both versions.

8. See also Merleau-Ponty's closely related argument that our categories for "objective" space draw upon the spatiality of living embodiment, in *Phenomenology of Perception* (London, 1962), pp. 98–102. Consider: "It will perhaps be [objected] that the figure-background structure . . . [itself] presuppose[s] the notion of objective space. . . . But what meaning could the word 'against' have for a subject not placed by his body face to face with the world? When I say that an object is *on* a table, I always mentally put myself either in the table or in the object, and I apply to them a category which theoretically fits the relationship of my body to external objects. Stripped of this anthropological association, the word *on* is indistinguishable from the word 'under' or the word 'beside'" (p. 101).

9. Merleau-Ponty, *The Prose of the World* (Evanston, 1973). In the "Algorithm" chapter, the primary example Merleau-Ponty uses for his argument is an algebraic proof that derives from Sn the formula, $n/2 (n + 1)$. (His proof proceeds from a breakthrough insight that the first ten natural numbers are composed of five pairs of numbers whose sum is constant and equal to $10 + 1$.) I should also mention that *The Prose of the World,* as we have it, is an unfinished manuscript that Merleau-Ponty wrote between 1949 and 1952. Claude Lefort argues in his preface to the published volume that Merleau-Ponty's discontinued work on it should not be interpreted as condemnation of the book: written notes indicate that he was still contemplating revisions of the manuscript as late as 1955; and further, in 1959 Merleau-Ponty excised and revised a lengthy portion of chap. 3 for publication (this appears as "Indirect Language and the Voices of Silence" in *Signs* [Evanston, 1964], and is reprinted with a revised translation in *The Merleau-Ponty Aesthetics Reader,* ed. Johnson [Evanston, 1993]). Needless to say, *The Prose of the World* is extremely important for understanding Merleau-Ponty's philosophy of expression.

10. Merleau-Ponty reiterates and further develops this claim in *The Prose of the World* (Evanston, 1973): "When I introduce a new line into a drawing that changes its

signification . . . there is no longer the same object before me. When the chimpanzee, wanting to get something beyond his reach, picks up a branch of a tree to use as a stick . . . his conduct shows that the branch in its new function is no longer a branch for him. . . . The transformation is irreversible, and now it is not the *same* object which is treated each time from two perspectives. It is a branch which becomes a stick . . . the way a shake of a kaleidoscope makes a new pattern appear without my being able to recognize the old one in it" (pp. 119–120).

11. Identifying this widespread concern is not to imply that there haven't been attempts to defend transcendental accounts of mathematics. For instance, a contemporary defense of mathematical Platonism can be found in Maddy, *Realism in Mathematics* (Oxford, 1990).

12. Merleau-Ponty puts the same point this way, in *The Prose of the World* (Evanston, 1973): "Instead of saying that we establish certain *properties* of mathematical *entities,* we would be more exact if we said that we establish the possibility of the principle of enriching and making more precise the relations that served to define our object, of pursuing the construction of coherent mathematical wholes which our definitions merely outlined. To be sure, this possibility is not an empty thing, this coherence is not accidental, this validity is not illusory. But we cannot say the new relations were true *before* they were revealed or that the first set of relations bring the later ones into existence" (p. 122).

13. As Curry says: "According to formalism the central concept in mathematics is that of a formal system. . . . It should be noted that in such a formal system it is immaterial what we take for tokens (and operators)—we make take these as discrete objects, symbols, abstract concepts, variables, or what not. Any such way of understanding a formal system we may call a representation of it" (in his "Remarks on the Definition and Nature of Mathematics," in *Philosophy of Mathematics: Selected Readings,* ed. Benacerraf and Putnam [Cambridge, 1983], p. 203). For an excellent extended discussion of formalism, see Körner, *The Philosophy of Mathematics* (New York, 1968), chaps. 4 and 5.

14. For this foundational view see Brouwer, "Intuitionism and Formalism," in *Philosophy of Mathematics: Selected Readings,* ed. Benacerraf and Putnam (Cambridge, 1983); and the general discussion in Körner, *The Philosophy of Mathematics* (New York, 1968), chap. 6. I describe Dummett's view as idiosyncratic because it attempts to ground the intuitionist program in the view, attributed to Wittgenstein, that the meaning of a mathematical statement is exhaustively determined by its use. For his classic statement of the program, see "The Philosophical Basis of Intuitionistic Logic," in Dummett, *Truth and Other Enigmas* (Cambridge, Mass., 1978), pp. 215–247.

15. It is interesting to note here that Merleau-Ponty's view of the *cogito* (or unified self), as a reflective collection of the disparate actions and processes of our embodied life, is extremely close to Daniel Dennett's view as expressed in *Consciousness Explained* (Boston, 1991), chap. 13: "The Reality of Selves." As Dennett puts it, in a very different idiom: "Our fundamental tactic . . . of self-definition is not spinning webs or building dams, but telling stories . . . about who we are. And just as spiders don't have to think, consciously and deliberately, about how to spin their

webs . . . we (unlike *professional* human storytellers) do not consciously and deliberately figure out what narratives to tell and how to tell them. . . . These strings of narrative issue forth *as if* from a single source" (p. 418). One difference is that Dennett's way of putting it makes the process sound automatic—encoded in the genes—when for Merleau-Ponty, the "narratives" of self-unity and permanence are creative-expressive.

16. Toward the end of "The *Cogito*" chapter, Merleau-Ponty will sometimes talk of the living body and actions that precede the expressive act of framing a unified self as "the tacit *cogito*." Merleau-Ponty later repudiates this way of putting it, for instance, in *The Visible and the Invisible* (Evanston, 1968), p. 175. He does so, I believe, with excellent reason: this "tacit *cogito*" revives the sense of a substantial, thinking self, after he has worked so long in the chapter to undermine that notion; and he discusses it with a language of unity that has been undermined by his own premises. It is a strange fact indeed that this crucial, pivotal chapter of the book winds up in a paradoxical confusion. For an excellent treatment of the problem of the tacit *cogito* and an analysis of its roots, see Dillon, *Merleau-Ponty's Ontology* (Evanston, 1997), chap. 6.

17. Several times in *Phenomenology of Perception* (London, 1962), Merleau-Ponty refers to the movement of expression as the *Fundierung* relation. His most extensive reference to this is: "The relation of reason to fact, or eternity to time . . . of thought to perception is this two-way relationship that phenomenology has called *Fundierung*: the founding term, or originator—time . . . the fact . . . perception— is primary in the sense that the originated[—eternity, reason, thought—]is presented as a determinate or explicit form of the originator . . . and yet the originator is not primary in the empiricist sense and the originated is not simply derived from it, since it is through the originated that the originator is made manifest" (p. 396). What he says here is precisely true of the process of expression, but unless the reader already understands that process, the above passage is rather unhelpful and obscure. A further difficulty with *Fundierung* talk, as we will see in sec. 4, below, is that it falsely suggests a kinship between Merleau-Ponty and Husserl on expression when, in fact, it is a crux of their disagreement.

18. See, for example, Dawkins, *Unweaving the Rainbow* (Boston, 1998).

19. This is the thrust of Derrida's critique of Merleau-Ponty in sec. 8 of his early work, *Edmund Husserl's Origin of Geometry: An Introduction* (Lincoln, 1989). The charge is that, in several essays from the 1950s and in the *Phenomenology of Perception* itself, Merleau-Ponty attributes a worldly, factual, historical fundament to Husserl's thought that simply doesn't hold up to closer examination. In one of his final works Derrida returns to this criticism in great detail—that Merleau-Ponty actively distorts Husserl's thought for his own ends. See Derrida, *On Touching— Jean-Luc Nancy* (Stanford, 2005), esp. chap. 9.

20. In Husserl, *Crisis of the European Sciences and Transcendental Phenomenology* (Evanston, 1970), pp. 353–378.

21. It is clear that Husserl was moved in this direction not only by Heidegger's *Being and Time,* which argues that meaning is fundamentally worldly and historical, but

also by his continued reading of Dilthey, who in fact inspired Heidegger. For excellent discussion of this important turn in Husserl's thought, see Ricoeur, *Husserl: An Analysis of his Phenomenology* (Evanston, 1967), chap. 6. Also see Walter Biemel's "Introduction to the Dilthey-Husserl Correspondence," in *Husserl: Shorter Works*, ed. McCormick and Elliston (Notre Dame, 1981), pp. 198–202.

22. Husserl, *Crisis of the European Sciences and Transcendental Phenomenology* (Evanston, 1970), p. 355.

23. Ibid., p. 354, emphasis added.

24. As Husserl puts it in "The Origin of Geometry": "Our problem now concerns precisely the ideal objects which are thematic in geometry: how does geometrical ideality . . . proceed from its primary intrapersonal origin, where it is a structure within the conscious space of the first inventor's soul, to its ideal objectivity?" (ibid., pp. 357–358).

25. That Husserl's genetic phenomenology remains subtly committed to a Kantian model of transcendental subjectivity is rigorously articulated by Alphonso Lingis in the first chapter of *Deathbound Subjectivity* (Bloomington, 1989), pp. 11–37. As Lingis puts it, Husserl's is "a subjectivity of [a] form that can conceive of absolute self-responsibility. Its own form, its own formative power, is such that it can maintain itself in its identity, can be true to itself. . . . In the form of its presence, it can retain still the *raison d'être* of all its past phases, of the in principle infinite series of moments in which the meaning of its deeds has been constituted" (p. 35). Lingis thus concludes: "The enigmatic original subjection of subjectivity to the idea, the idea-form . . . is the starting point of Kant's practical philosophy" (p. 37).

26. Husserl, *Crisis of the European Sciences and Transcendental Phenomenology* (Evanston, 1970), pp. 374–375.

27. Ibid., p. 375.

28. In this argument we are opening onto a further essential difference between Husserl and Merleau-Ponty that typically goes unnoticed, and which is glossed over by Merleau-Ponty himself. Specifically, that Husserl's "object-horizon" structure is not at all equivalent to Merleau-Ponty's perceptual *Gestalt*. For Husserl, all meaning or sense is formulated *in the mind* against the vicissitudes of the world and history by its using free variation to find the eidetic property of the object. But for Merleau-Ponty the perceptual *Gestalt* is already saturated with meaning; indeed, the mind finds itself already confronted with meaning and sense in the perceptual *Gestalt,* thus requiring creative expression to move thought forward.

29. "Speech and Phenomena: Introduction to the Problem of Signs in Husserl's Phenomenology," in Derrida, *Speech and Phenomena and Other Essays* (Evanston, 1973).

30. Ibid., p. 21, final emphasis added.

31. Ibid., p. 3.

32. The most well-known passage where Derrida seems to sweep Merleau-Ponty along with the critique of Husserl is at the very end of "Speech and Phenomena," when Derrida says: "And contrary to what phenomenology—which is always phenomenology of perception—has tried to make us believe . . ." (ibid., p. 104). In the

world of 1960s French philosophy, it was impossible to read the phrase "phenomenology of perception" without thinking of Merleau-Ponty's book.

33. For an example of Derrida's dilemma, consider the following from his *Edmund Husserl's Origin of Geometry: An Introduction* (Lincoln, 1989): "one has, facing this equivocity [of the depth of development and the past] the choice of two endeavors. One would resemble that of James Joyce: to repeat and take responsibility for all equivocation itself, utilizing a language that could equalize the greatest possible synchrony with the greatest potential for buried, accumulated, and interwoven intentions within each linguistic atom. . . . [T]his writing settles itself *within* the *labyrinthine* field of culture 'bound' by its own equivocations. . . . The other endeavor is Husserl's" (pp. 102–103). Other explicit statements of the dilemma can be seen in the closing pages of "Speech and Phenomena," and in Derrida, *Of Grammatology* (Baltimore, 1998), pp. 49–51.

34. It is noteworthy that expression is centralized in the philosophies of both Deleuze and Merleau-Ponty—arguably the two most important ontologists of mid- to late-twentieth-century French philosophy. To be sure, there are important differences between the thinkers on the range or domain of expressivity. For Merleau-Ponty, expression is—as I have been showing—the "life of the mind"; it is a productive process at work in human cognition which manifests in knowledge, art, language, and thinking. However, for Deleuze, expression is nothing less than the productive, differentiating power of being itself. In short, for Merleau-Ponty, expression is essentially epistemological; for Deleuze it is ontological.

Having drawn this distinction, however, it must be said that both thinkers conceive the nature of expression itself in remarkably similar ways. It is a productive principle which is not creative or emanative in any theological sense, and it always unfolds within and amid natural, historical being—not outside it. In short, Deleuze and Merleau-Ponty are both committed to the ontology of immanence in Deleuze's sense of the phrase, with expression as the excessive power that yields new acquisitions without "grounding" them (as will be seen as my text continues). This is an extraordinary confluence for two thinkers who many scholars have taken to be radically distinct. Further, it is possible and plausible to reconcile their different applications: one might understand Merleau-Ponty's philosophy of expressive *cognition* as a "regional study" of expressive being itself. Once again we see the exceptional fecundity of rigorously pursuing the conversation between Merleau-Ponty and Deleuze.

For Deleuze's theory of expressive being, see Deleuze, *Expressionism in Philosophy: Spinoza* (New York, 1992). For an important discussion of the relationship between Merleau-Ponty and Deleuze on the subject of expression, see the previously mentioned essay by Leonard Lawlor, "The End of Phenomenology: Expressionism in Merleau-Ponty and Deleuze," in Lawlor, *Thinking Through French Philosophy* (Bloomington, 2003), pp. 80–94.

7. Behold "The Speaking Word"

1. Merleau-Ponty, *Phenomenology of Perception* (London, 1962), p. 181.

2. Saussure, *Course in General Linguistics* (New York, 1959), p. 112.

3. For instance, there is Merleau-Ponty's lecture course of 1949–1950 at the Sorbonne, entitled *Consciousness and the Acquisition of Language* (the complete transcribed notes of which are published in English under that title, trans. Hugh Silverman [Evanston, 1973]). There are also two lectures from early during his tenure at the Collège de France, "The Sensible World and the World of Expression," and "Studies in the Literary Use of Language" (the basic outlines of which are published in *In Praise of Philosophy and Other Essays* [Evanston, 1988]). As for written work, there is "On the Phenomenology of Language" from 1951 (published in *Signs* [Evanston, 1964]). *The Prose of the World* (Evanston, 1973) also dates from 1951 and 1952, chap. 3 of which was revised for publication in 1959 as "Indirect Language and the Voices of Silence" (this appears in *Signs,* and is reprinted with a revised translation in *The Merleau-Ponty Aesthetics Reader,* ed. Johnson [Evanston, 1993]).

4. As Plato puts it: "A name, then, it appears, is a vocal imitation of that which is imitated," and that which is imitated is the form (*eidos*) of individual things. And "if anyone could imitate this essential nature of each thing by means of letters and syllables, he would show what each thing really is, would he not?" See Plato, *Cratylus* (Cambridge, Mass., 1926), pp. 135, 137 (423b, 423e).

5. Aristotle, *On Interpretation,* in *The Basic Works of Aristotle* (New York, 1941), p. 40 (16a3–8).

6. For example, Locke says: "The Comfort, and Advantage of Society, not being to be had without Communication of Thoughts, it was necessary, that Man should find out some external sensible Signs, whereby those invisible *Ideas,* which his thoughts are made up of, might be made known to others" (*An Essay Concerning Human Understanding* [Oxford, 1975], p. 405).

7. Ibid., p. 405.

8. See "Ontological Relativity," in Quine, *Ontological Relativity and Other Essays* (New York, 1969).

9. Wittgenstein, *Philosophical Investigations* (New York, 1953), sec. 28, p. 14e.

10. As Merleau-Ponty says, on the intellectualist theory "the word is still bereft of any effectiveness of its own, this time because it is only the external sign of an internal recognition, which could take place without it, and to which it makes no contribution. It is not without meaning, since behind it there is a categorical operation, but this meaning is something which it does not *have,* does not possess, since it is thought which has a meaning, the word remaining an empty container. . . . Thus we refute . . . intellectualism . . . by simply saying *the word has a meaning*" (*Phenomenology of Perception* [London, 1962], p. 176).

11. A similar point is made by Wittgenstein in *Philosophical Investigations* (New York, 1953), when he says: "Augustine describes the learning of human language as if the child came into a strange country and did not understand the language of the country, that is, as if it already had a language, only not this one. Or again: as if the child could already *think,* only not yet speak" (sec. 32, pp. 15–16e). Wittgenstein's point here is that the representation theory is really a depiction of how one who already has a language might learn a second language, and this is very close to Merleau-Ponty's claim that representational language presupposes that we learn and develop language through expression. Despite this, and other interesting con-

vergences between Merleau-Ponty's and Wittgenstein's criticisms of representation theory, Wittgenstein does not have the rich understanding of expressive language that allows Merleau-Ponty to actually resolve some of the traditional problems that this theory encounters.

12. While the translation of *The Prose of the World* (Evanston, 1973) is generally good, the passage in which Merleau-Ponty makes this crucial distinction is ruined by a disastrous mistranslation. In French, Merleau-Ponty refers to the two different sides of language as *le langage parlé et le langage parlant* (*La Prose du monde* [Paris, 1969], p. 17), that is, "the spoken word and the speaking word." However, the translation casts this as "sedimented language and speech." The first problem is that this choice obliterates the meaning and artfulness of Merleau-Ponty's central distinction. That is bad enough. Even worse, this rendering makes it appears as though Merleau-Ponty is repeating Saussure's famous distinction between language (*la langue*) and speech (*la parole*). As I will argue in sec. 3, below, nothing could be further from the truth: Merleau-Ponty's distinction between already acquired language and expressive language has the effect of substantially criticizing and supplanting Saussure's distinction, not sharing in it.

13. This is another place where Wittgenstein's critique of representationalism converges with Merleau-Ponty's. As Wittgenstein puts the point: "But how many kinds of sentences are there? Say assertion, question, and command? There are *countless* kinds. . . . And this multiplicity is not something fixed, given once and for all; but new types of language, new language-games, as we may say, come into existence" (*Philosophical Investigations* [New York, 1953], p. 11e).

14. That the representation theory of language is intimately bound up with a transcendental or supernatural theology is a point also made at length by Heidegger in the important essay, "The Nature of Language," in *On the Way to Language* (New York, 1971); and then later by Derrida in *Of Grammatology* (Baltimore, 1998), pt. 1. Merleau-Ponty's way of putting this point is: "The algorithm [as an exemplar of the representation theory] is an attempt to construct language according to the standard of truth, to redefine it to match the divine mind, and . . . to tear speech out of history. The divine speech, or the language we always presuppose as prior to speech, is [not] to be found in modern languages scattered throughout history and the world. The internal word is the standard of the external word [and it] was created by God at the beginning of the world; it was sent forth by him and received as a prophecy" (*The Prose of the World* [Evanston, 1973], p. 5).

15. Merleau-Ponty says: "Thought is no 'internal' thing, and does not exist independently of the world and of words. What misleads us in this connection, and causes us to believe in a thought which exists for itself prior to expression, is thought already constituted and expressed, which we can silently recall to ourselves, and through which we acquire the illusion of an inner life" (*Phenomenology of Perception* [London, 1962], p. 183).

16. "A thought limited to existing for itself, independently of the constraints of speech . . . would no sooner appear than it would sink into unconsciousness, which means that it would not exist even for itself" (ibid., p. 177).

17. Merleau-Ponty puts the qualification this way: "Although the final effect is not for

me to dwell within Stendhal's lived experience, I am at least brought within the imaginary self and the internal dialogue Stendhal held with it for the fifty years he was coining it in his works" (*The Prose of the World* [Evanston, 1973], p. 12).

18. For Merleau-Ponty's own discussion of this, see ibid., pp. 42–43.

19. That Merleau-Ponty had not read Saussure until the late 1940s—at least not until after he completed *Phenomenology of Perception*—seems confirmed by the fact that Saussure's formative distinctions and concepts are not used in that text, especially not in the chapter on language. Further, Saussure is neither cited nor mentioned at any place in the text or bibliography of *Phenomenology of Perception*. In his foreword to Merleau-Ponty, *Consciousness and the Acquisition of Language* (Evanston, 1973), Hugh Silverman makes this case more fully, and notes that Merleau-Ponty's first use of Saussure's ideas is in a course on language he gave at Lyon in 1947–1948.

20. Saussure, *Course in General Linguistics* (New York, 1959), p. 14.

21. Ibid., p. 15.

22. Ibid., p. 66.

23. As Saussure puts it: "Some people regard language . . . as a naming-process only—a list of words, each corresponding to the thing that it names. . . . This conception is open to criticism at several points. It assumes that ready-made ideas exist before words . . . it doesn't tell us whether a name is vocal or psychological in nature . . . finally it lets us assume that the linking of a name and a thing is a very simple operation—an assumption that is anything but true" (ibid., p. 65).

24. Ibid., p. 66.

25. Ibid., p. 25.

26. Merleau-Ponty's argument is developed on pp. 187–190 of *Phenomenology of Perception* (London, 1962). As he puts it: "The predominance of vowels in one language, or of consonants in another, and constructional and syntactic systems, do not represent so many arbitrary conventions for the expression of one and the same idea, but several ways for the human body to sing the world's praises and in the last resort to live it. . . . Everything is both manufactured and natural in man, as it were, in the sense that there is not a word, not a form of behavior that does not owe something to purely biological being—and which at the same time eludes the simplicity of animal life and causes forms of vital behavior to deviate from their pre-ordained direction" (pp. 187, 189).

27. Saussure, *Course in General Linguistics* (New York, 1959), pp. 116–117.

28. Ibid., p. 116.

29. Ibid., p. 114.

30. Merleau-Ponty, *Signs* (Evanston, 1964), p. 39. Other notable passages where Merleau-Ponty commits himself to the diacritical theory of meaning are *The Prose of the World* (Evanston, 1973), p. 32; and *Consciousness and the Acquisition of Language* (Evanston, 1973), p. 5, and again on p. 80 where he asserts: "The expression of articulated language rests on a different principle from that which renders the imitated word possible. That which makes the word 'sun' signify the sun

is not the resemblance between the word and the thing, nor is it the internal character of either. Rather, it is the relationship between the word 'sun' and the totality of all English words; it is the manner in which it differentiates itself from them. The word only has meaning through the whole *institution* of language."

31. Two places where Merleau-Ponty develops this criticism at some length are *The Prose of the World* (Evanston, 1973), p. 23; and *Consciousness and the Acquisition of Language* (Evanston, 1973), pp. 100–101.

32. Merleau-Ponty, *Consciousness and the Acquisition of Language* (Evanston, 1973), pp. 99–100.

33. Ibid., pp. 99–100.

34. Saussure, *Course in General Linguistics* (New York, 1959), p. 9.

35. Ibid., p. 76.

36. While Deleuze himself employs the language and notions of Saussure's structuralism in his earlier, solo works—for example, *The Logic of Sense*—by the time of *A Thousand Plateaus,* he and Guattari have shaken themselves entirely free of that influence. Indeed, I believe that their "assemblage" or "rhizomatic" theory of language (with which they also use the word "expression") is the first French theory of language to systematically supersede structuralism. Here, then, is one more place where putting their work in conversation with Merleau-Ponty promises new insights and the identification of potential limits in both sets of philosophical projects.

37. Derrida's claim in this regard can be seen in "Deconstruction and the Other," in *Dialogues with Contemporary Continental Thinkers,* ed. Kearney (Manchester, 1984), pp. 111–112. For Lyotard's discussion of this see Lyotard, *The Postmodern Explained* (Minneapolis, 1993), chap. 1.

38. In its deep affinity with embodied experience, Merleau-Ponty's expressive theory of language has distinct resonance with Heidegger's theory of language as the "saying of being." This resonance is clear, even though some of Heidegger's writings appear to suggest a direct conflict between the thinkers. For example, in the essay "Language" in *Poetry, Language, Thought* (New York, 1971), pp. 189–210, Heidegger explicitly rejects the notion that language is expression.

However, a close reading of this essay reveals that the notion of expression Heidegger is criticizing is diametrically opposed to Merleau-Ponty's sense of expression. For Heidegger, in this text, expression means "audible utterance" which, for him, is the "externalization" of a prior internal thought (p. 192). In other words, Heidegger's talk of "expression" is his idiom for the representation theory of language. Thus, the thinkers actually agree in rejecting that theory at the very point they seem to disagree. Indeed, Merleau-Ponty and Heidegger are connected in their view of language as an embodied-cognitive process that can show and reveal elusive features of worldly life. In short, they share a commitment to the phenomenological powers of language.

Nonetheless, there are some important points of disagreement, and they seem to me decisive. For one example, Heidegger often commits himself to a historical-cultural notion that the language of being has undergone degradation and dissipation through western history, and thus a recovery through etymology is appropriate and legitimate. I have no doubt that Merleau-Ponty would reject such a move. For him, as for Deleuze and Guattari, language reveals through genuinely creative articulation amid overwhelming excess rather than by uncovering what has been lost through historical sedimentations. I would say that Heidegger's operation—retrieving what has been lost, uncovering what has been covered over—reveals unhappy vestiges of representational epistemology rather than a clear movement toward a philosophy of expression.

Conclusion

1.   Merleau-Ponty, *The Visible and the Invisible* (Evanston, 1968), pp. 144–145.

2.   "The Origin of the Work of Art," in Heidegger, *Basic Writings* (New York, 1993), p. 177.

3.   From Plato, *Republic* (Indianapolis, 1992), pp. 183–185 (509d–511e). As Plato puts it there: "In any case, you have two kinds of thing, visible and intelligible. . . . It is like a line divided of two unequal sections. Then divide each section—namely, that of the visible and that of the intelligible—in the same ratio as the line. . . . [O]ne subsection of the visible consists of images [shadows and reflections]. . . . In the other subsection of the visible, put the originals of these images, namely, the animals around us, all the plants, and the whole class of manufactured things. . . . In one subsection [of the intelligible] the soul . . . is forced to investigate from hypotheses [to a conclusion, as in geometry and calculation]. . . . Then also understand that, by the other subsection of the intelligible, I mean that which reason itself grasps by the power of dialectic. . . . without making use of anything visible at all, but only of forms themselves, moving from forms to forms, and ending in forms."

4.   Husserl, *Ideas Pertaining to a Pure Phenomenology and to a Phenomenological Philosophy, First Book* (The Hague, 1983), p. 6.

Bibliography

Abram, David. *The Spell of the Sensuous.* New York: Vintage, 1996.

Allen, Jeffner, and Iris Marion Young. *The Thinking Muse: Feminism and Modern French Philosophy.* Bloomington: Indiana University Press, 1989.

Anderson, John R. *Cognitive Psychology and Its Implications.* 3d ed. New York: Freeman, 1990.

Aristotle. *The Basic Works of Aristotle.* Ed. Richard McKeon. Trans. J. A. Smith. New York: Random House, 1941.

Augustine. *Confessions.* Trans. R. S. Pine-Coffin. New York: Penguin, 1961.

Barbaras, Renaud. *The Being of the Phenomenon: Merleau-Ponty's Ontology.* Trans. Ted Toadvine and Leonard Lawlor. Evanston: Northwestern University Press, 2004.

Bartky, Sandra Lee. *Femininity and Domination: Studies in the Phenomenology of Oppression.* New York: Routledge, 1990.

Benacerraf, Paul, and Hilary Putnam (editors). *Philosophy of Mathematics: Selected Readings.* 2d ed. Cambridge: Cambridge University Press, 1983.

Berkeley, George. *A Treatise Concerning the Principles of Human Knowledge.* Indianapolis: Hackett, 1982.

Brown, Charles S., and Ted Toadvine (editors). *Eco-Phenomenology: Back to the Earth Itself.* Albany: State University of New York Press, 2003.

Butler, Judith. *Bodies That Matter: On the Discursive Limits of Sex.* New York: Routledge, 1993.

Carbone, Mauro. *Thinking of the Sensible: Merleau-Ponty's A-Philosophy.* Evanston: Northwestern University Press, 2004.

Carman, Taylor, and Mark B. N. Hansen (editors). *The Cambridge Companion to Merleau-Ponty.* Cambridge: Cambridge University Press, 2004.

Churchland, Paul M. *A Neurocomputational Perspective: The Nature of Mind and the Structure of Science.* Cambridge, Mass.: MIT Press, 1989.

Clark, Andy. *Being There: Putting Brain, Body, and World Together Again.* Cambridge, Mass.: MIT Press, 1999.

Cole, Jonathan. *About Face.* Cambridge, Mass.: MIT Press, 1999.

———. *Pride and a Daily Marathon.* Cambridge, Mass.: MIT Press, 1995.

Cottingham, John (editor). *The Cambridge Companion to Descartes.* Cambridge: Cambridge University Press, 1992.

——— (editor). *Descartes.* Oxford: Oxford University Press, 1998.

Crosby, Alfred W. *The Measure of Reality: Quantification and Western Society.* Cambridge: Cambridge University Press, 1997.

Dawkins, Richard. *Unweaving the Rainbow.* Boston: Houghton Mifflin, 1998.

Deleuze, Gilles. *Difference and Repetition.* Trans. Paul Patton. New York: Columbia University Press, 1994.

———. *Expressionism in Philosophy: Spinoza.* Trans. Martin Joughin. New York: Zone Books, 1992.

———. *The Logic of Sense.* Trans. Mark Lester with Charles Stivale. New York: Columbia University Press, 1990.

Deleuze, Gilles, and Félix Guattari. *A Thousand Plateaus.* Trans. Brian Massumi. Minneapolis: University of Minnesota Press, 1987.

Dennett, Daniel C. *Brainchildren: Essays on Designing Minds.* Cambridge, Mass.: MIT Press, 1998.

———. *Consciousness Explained.* Boston: Little, Brown, 1991.

Derrida, Jacques. *Acts of Religion.* Ed. Gil Anidjar. New York: Routledge, 2002.

———. *Adieu To Emmanuel Levinas.* Trans. Pascale-Anne Brault and Michael Naas. Stanford: Stanford University Press, 1999.

———. *Deconstruction in a Nutshell: A Conversation with Jacques Derrida.* Ed. with comm. John D. Caputo. New York: Fordham University Press, 1997.

———. "Deconstruction and the Other." In *Dialogues with Contemporary Continental Thinkers.* Ed. Richard Kearney. Manchester: Manchester University Press, 1984. This interview is also available in Kearney, ed., *States of Mind* (New York, 1995).

———. *Edmund Husserl's Origin of Geometry: An Introduction.* Trans. John P. Leavey, Jr. Lincoln: University of Nebraska Press, 1989.

———. *Jacques Derrida.* Princeton: Films for the Humanities and Sciences, 1992.

———. *Margins of Philosophy.* Trans. Alan Bass. Chicago: University of Chicago Press, 1982.

———. *Memoirs of the Blind.* Trans. Pascale-Anne Brault and Michael Naas. Chicago: University of Chicago Press, 1990.

———. *Of Grammatology.* Corr. ed. Trans. Gayatri Chakravorty Spivak. Baltimore: Johns Hopkins University Press, 1998.

———. *On Touching—Jean-Luc Nancy.* Trans. Christine Irizarry. Stanford: Stanford University Press, 2005.

———. *Positions.* Trans. Alan Bass. Chicago: University of Chicago Press, 1981.

———. *Speech and Phenomena and Other Essays.* Trans. David B. Allison. Evanston: Northwestern University Press, 1973.

Descartes, René. *The Philosophical Writings of Descartes, Volumes I–II.* Trans. John Cottingham, Robert Stroothoff, and Dugald Murdoch. Cambridge: Cambridge University Press, 1985.

———. *The Philosophical Writings of Descartes, Volume III: The Correspondence.* Trans. John Cottingham, Robert Stroothoff, Dugald Murdoch, and Anthony Kenny. Cambridge: Cambridge University Press, 1991.

Dewey, John. *The Essential Dewey, Volume 2: Ethics, Logic, Psychology.* Ed. Larry A. Hickman and Thomas M. Alexander. Bloomington: Indiana University Press, 1998.

Dillon, M. C. *Merleau-Ponty's Ontology.* 2d rev. ed. Evanston: Northwestern University Press, 1997.

——— (editor). *Merleau-Ponty Vivant.* Albany: State University of New York Press, 1991.

Dreyfus, Hubert L. *What Computers Can't Do.* 3d rev. ed. Cambridge, Mass.: MIT Press, 1993.

———. "The Current Relevance of Merleau-Ponty's Phenomenology of Embodiment." *Electronic Journal of Philosophy* no. 4, Spring 1996: http://phil.indiana.edu/ejap/1996.spring/dreyfus.1996.spring.txt.

Dreyfus, Hubert L., with Stuart Dreyfus. *Mind Over Machine: The Power of Human Intuitive Expertise in the Era of the Computer.* New York: Free Press, 1986.

Dreyfus, Hubert L., and Paul Rabinow. *Michael Foucault: Beyond Structuralism and Hermeneutics.* 2d ed. Chicago: University of Chicago Press, 1983.

Dummett, Michael. *Truth and Other Enigmas.* Cambridge, Mass.: Harvard University Press, 1978.

Evans, Fred. "'Chaosmos' and Merleau-Ponty's Philosophy of Nature." *Chiasmi International* no. 2, 2000.

Evans, Fred, and Leonard Lawlor (editors). *Chiasms: Merleau-Ponty's Notion of Flesh.* Albany: State University of New York Press, 2000.

Faubion, James D. *Michel Foucault: Aesthetics, Method, and Epistemology.* New York: New Press, 1998.

Foucault, Michel. *Discipline and Punish.* Trans. Alan Sheridan. New York: Vintage, 1979.

———. *The History of Sexuality, Volume 1.* Trans. Robert Hurley. New York: Vintage, 1980.

Garber Daniel. *Descartes' Metaphysical Physics.* Chicago: University of Chicago Press, 1992.

Gasché, Rodolphe. *The Tain of the Mirror: Derrida and the Philosophy of Reflection.* Cambridge, Mass.: Harvard University Press, 1986.

Gaukroger, Stephen. *Descartes: An Intellectual Biography.* Oxford: Oxford University Press, 1995.

Gelb, Adhémar, and Kurt Goldstein. *Psychologische Analysen hirnpathologerischer Fälle.* Leipzig: Barth, 1920.

Goldberg, Susan, Roy Muir, and John Kerr (editors). *Attachment Theory.* Hillsdale, N.J.: Analytic Press, 1995.

Goldstein, Kurt. *The Organism: A Holistic Approach to Biology Derived from Pathological Data in Man.* New York: Zone, 1995.

Gopnik, Alison, Andrew N. Meltzoff, and Patricia K. Kuhl. *The Scientist in the Crib: Minds, Brains, and How Children Learn.* New York: William Morrow, 1999.

Greenspan, Stanley. *Building Healthy Minds.* Cambridge: Perseus, 2000.

Grosz, Elizabeth. *Volatile Bodies: Toward a Corporeal Feminism.* Bloomington: Indiana University Press, 1994.

Hacker, P. M. S. *Appearance and Reality.* Oxford: Basil Blackwell, 1987.

Hass, Lawrence. "Rays of the World: Merleau-Ponty and the Problem of Universals." *Chiasmi International* no. 6, 2005.

Hass, Lawrence, and Dorothea Olkowski (editors). *Rereading Merleau-Ponty: Essays Beyond the Continental-Analytic Divide.* Amherst: Humanity, 2000.

Head, Henry. *Studies in Neurology.* Oxford: Oxford University Press, 1920.

Heidegger, Martin. *Basic Questions of Philosophy: Selected "Problems" of "Logic."* Trans. Richard Rojcewicz and André Schuwer. Bloomington: Indiana University Press, 1994.

———. *Basic Writings.* Rev. and exp. ed. Ed. David Farrell Krell. New York: HarperCollins, 1993.

———. *Identity and Difference.* Trans. Joan Stambaugh. Chicago: University of Chicago Press, 2002.

———. *On the Way to Language.* Trans. Peter D. Hertz. New York: Harper and Row, 1971.

———. *Poetry, Language, Thought.* Trans. Albert Hofstadter. New York: Harper and Row, 1971.

Hume, David. *A Treatise of Human Nature.* 2d ed. Ed. L. A. Selby-Bigge. Rev. P. H. Nidditch. Oxford: Clarendon Press, 1978.

Husserl, Edmund. *Crisis of the European Sciences and Transcendental Phenomenology.* Ed. Walter Biemel. Trans. David Carr. Evanston: Northwestern University Press, 1970.

———. *Husserl: Shorter Works.* Ed. Peter McCormick and Frederick Elliston. Notre Dame: University of Notre Dame Press, 1981.

———. *Ideas Pertaining to a Pure Phenomenology and to a Phenomenological Philosophy, First Book.* Trans. F. Kersten. The Hague: Martinus Nijhoff, 1983.

Irigaray, Luce. *An Ethics of Sexual Difference.* Trans. Carolyn Burke and Gillian C. Gill. Ithaca: Cornell University Press, 1993.

———. *To Be Two.* Trans. Monique Rhodes and Marco F. Cocito Monoc. New York: Routledge, 2001.

Jackson, Frank. *Perception: A Representative Theory.* Cambridge: Cambridge University Press, 1977.

James, William. *The Writings of William James.* Ed. John J. McDermott. Chicago: University of Chicago Press, 1977.

Johnson, Galen A. (editor). *The Merleau-Ponty Aesthetics Reader.* Trans. Michael B. Smith. Evanston: Northwestern University Press, 1993.

Johnson, Galen A., and Michael B. Smith (editors). *Ontology and Alterity in Merleau-Ponty.* Evanston: Northwestern University Press, 1990.

Johnson, Mark. *The Body in the Mind.* Chicago: University of Chicago Press, 1987.

Johnson, Randall. "Animal Appeal: Derrida, Merleau-Ponty, and *The Call of the Wild.*" Presented at the 30th Annual International Conference of the Merleau-Ponty Circle, University of Oregon, September 2005.

Kant, Immanuel. *Critique of Judgment.* Trans. J. H. Bernard. New York: Macmillan, 1951.

———. *Critique of Pure Reason.* Trans. Norman Kemp Smith. New York: St. Martin's Press, 1965.

Kearney, Richard. *States of Mind: Dialogues with Contemporary Thinkers.* New York: New York University Press, 1995.

Körner, Stephan. *The Philosophy of Mathematics.* New York: Dover, 1968.

Kruks, Sonia. *The Political Philosophy of Merleau-Ponty.* Atlantic Highlands, N.J.: Humanities Press, 1981.

Kwant, Remy C. *The Phenomenology of Expression.* Pittsburgh: Duquesne University Press, 1967.

Lacan, Jacques. "Merleau-Ponty: In Memoriam." In *Merleau-Ponty and Psychology.* Ed. Keith Hoeller. Trans. Wilfred Ver Eecke and Dirk de Schutter. Atlantic Highlands, N.J.: Humanities Press, 1993.

Lakoff, George. *Women, Fire, and Dangerous Things.* Chicago: University of Chicago Press, 1987.

Lakoff, George, and Mark Johnson. *Philosophy in the Flesh: The Embodied Mind and its Challenge to Western Thought.* New York: Basic, 1999.

Lawlor, Leonard. *Thinking Through French Philosophy: The Being of the Question.* Bloomington: Indiana University Press, 2003.

Leibniz. *Monadology and Other Philosophical Essays.* Trans. Paul Schrecker and Anne Martin Schrecker. New York: Macmillan, 1965.

Levinas, Emmanuel. *Collected Philosophical Papers.* Trans. Alphonso Lingis. Dordrecht: Martinus Nijhoff, 1987.

———. *Otherwise than Being.* Trans. Alphonso Lingis. Pittsburgh: Duquesne University Press, 1998.

————. *Totality and Infinity*. Trans. Alphonso Lingis. Pittsburgh: Duquesne University Press, 1969.

Lhermitte, François. *L'Image du notre corps*. Paris: Editions de la Nouvelle Revue Critique, 1939.

Lingis, Alphonso. *Deathbound Subjectivity*. Bloomington: Indiana University Press, 1989.

————. *Libido: The French Existential Theories*. Bloomington: Indiana University Press, 1985.

————. *Sensation: Intelligibility in Sensibility*. Atlantic Highlands, N.J.: Humanities Press, 1996.

Locke, John. *An Essay Concerning Human Understanding*. Ed. Peter H. Nidditch. Oxford: Oxford University Press, 1975.

Lyotard, Jean François. *The Postmodern Explained*. Trans. Julian Pefanis and Morgan Thomas. Minneapolis: Minnesota University Press, 1993.

Maddy, Penelope. *Realism in Mathematics*. Oxford: Clarendon Press, 1990.

Mahler, Margaret S., Fred Pine, and Anni Bergman (editors). *The Psychological Birth of the Human Infant*. New York: Basic, 1975.

May, Todd. *Gilles Deleuze: An Introduction*. Cambridge: Cambridge University Press, 2005.

Mazis, Glen A. *Earthbodies: Rediscovering our Planetary Senses*. Albany: State University of New York Press, 2002.

McGuinn, Colin. *The Character of Mind*. 2d ed. Oxford: Oxford University Press, 1997.

————. *The Mysterious Flame*. New York: Basic, 1999.

Merleau-Ponty, Maurice. *Consciousness and the Acquisition of Language*. Trans. Hugh Silverman. Evanston: Northwestern University Press, 1973.

————. *Husserl at the Limits of Phenomenology*. Ed. Leonard Lawlor and Bettina Bergo. Trans. John O'Neill and Leonard Lawlor. Evanston: Northwestern University Press, 2002.

————. *In Praise of Philosophy and Other Essays*. Trans. John O'Neill. Evanston: Northwestern University Press, 1988.

————. *L'Oeil et l'esprit*. Ed. Claude Lefort. Paris: Gallimard, 1964.

————. *La Prose du monde*. Ed. Claude Lefort. Paris: Gallimard, 1969.

————. *Le Visible et l'invisible*. Ed. Claude Lefort. Paris: Gallimard, 1964.

————. *Nature: Course Notes from the Collège de France*. Comp. Dominique Séglard. Trans. Robert Vallier. Evanston: Northwestern University Press, 2003.

————. *Notes de cours 1959–1961 par Merleau-Ponty*. Paris: Gallimard, 1996.

————. *Phénoménologie de la perception*. Paris: Gallimard, 1945.

————. *Phenomenology of Perception*. Trans. Colin Smith. Trans. rev. Forrest Williams and David Guerrière. London: Routledge, 1962.

————. *Sense and Non-Sense*. Trans. Hubert L. Dreyfus and Patricia Allen Dreyfus. Evanston: Northwestern University Press, 1964.

————. *Signs*. Trans. Richard C. McCleary. Evanston: Northwestern University Press, 1964.

————. *The Incarnate Subject: Malebranche, Biran, and Bergson on the Union of Body and Soul*. Ed. Andrew G. Bjelland, Jr. and Patrick Burke. Trans. Paul B. Milan. Amherst: Humanity, 2001.

————. *The Primacy of Perception and Other Essays*. Ed. James M. Edie. Evanston: Northwestern University Press, 1964.

————. *The Prose of the World*. Ed. Claude Lefort. Trans. John O'Neill. Evanston: Northwestern University Press, 1973.

———. *The Structure of Behavior.* Trans. Alden L. Fisher. Pittsburgh: Duquesne University Press, 1983.

———. *The Visible and the Invisible.* Ed. Claude Lefort. Trans. Alphonso Lingis. Evanston: Northwestern University Press, 1968.

———. *The World of Perception.* Trans. Oliver Davis. New York: Routledge, 2004.

Moore, G. E. *Perceiving, Sensing, and Knowing.* Ed. Robert J. Swartz. Garden City, N.Y.: Doubleday, 1965.

Morley, James, and James Phillips. *Imagination and Its Pathologies.* Cambridge, Mass.: MIT Press, 2003.

Myers, Gene. *Children and Animals: Social Development and Our Connections to Other Species.* Boulder: Westview Press, 1998.

Nagel, Thomas. *Mortal Questions.* Cambridge: Cambridge University Press, 1979.

———. *The View from Nowhere.* Oxford: Oxford University Press, 1989.

Nietzsche, Friedrich. *Beyond Good and Evil.* Trans. Walter Kaufmann. New York: Vintage, 1966.

———. *Thus Spoke Zarathustra: A Book for None and All.* Trans. Walter Kaufmann. New York: Viking Penguin, 1954.

Noble, Stephen. "Entre le silence des choses et la parole philosophique: Merleau-Ponty, Fink et les paradoxes du langage." *Chiasmi International* no. 6, 2005.

Olkowski, Dorothea. *Gilles Deleuze and the Ruin of Representation.* Berkeley: University of California Press, 1999.

Olkowski, Dorothea, and Gail Weiss. *Feminist Interpretations of Merleau-Ponty.* University Park: Penn State University Press, 2006.

Olkowski, Dorothea, and James Morley (editors). *Merleau-Ponty, Interiority and Exteriority, Psychic Life and the World.* Albany: State University of New York Press, 1999.

Pietersma, Henry (editor). *Merleau-Ponty: Critical Essays.* Washington, D.C.: University Press of America, 1989.

———. *Phenomenological Epistemology.* Oxford: Oxford University Press, 1999.

Pirsig, Robert M. *Zen and the Art of Motorcycle Maintenance.* Exp. ed. New York: Harpercollins, 1999.

Plato. *Cratylus.* Trans. H. N. Fowler. Cambridge, Mass.: Harvard University Press, 1926.

———. *Meno.* Trans. G. M. A. Grube. 2d ed. Indianapolis: Hackett, 1981.

———. *Republic.* Trans. G. M. A. Grube. Rev. C. D. C. Reeve. Indianapolis: Hackett, 1992.

Quine, W. V. O. *Ontological Relativity and Other Essays.* New York: Columbia University Press, 1969.

———. *Word and Object.* Cambridge, Mass.: MIT Press, 1960.

Ricoeur, Paul. *Husserl: An Analysis of his Phenomenology.* Trans. Edward G. Ballard and Lester E. Embree. Evanston: Northwestern University Press, 1967.

Robinson, Howard. *Perception.* London: Routledge, 1994.

Saks, Oliver. *The Man Who Mistook His Wife for a Hat.* New York: Simon and Schuster, 1985.

Sartre, Jean-Paul. *Being and Nothingness.* Trans. Hazel E. Barnes. London: Methuen, 1958.

———. *Situations IV.* Trans. Benita Eisler. Greenwich, Conn.: Fawcett, 1969.

Saussure, Ferdinand de. *Course in General Linguistics.* Ed. Charles Bally, Albert Sechehaye, and Albert Riedlinger. Trans. Wade Baskin. New York: McGraw-Hill, 1959.

Scheler, Max. *Formalism in Ethics and Non-Formal Ethics of Value.* Trans. Manfred S. Frings and Roger L. Funk. Evanston: Northwestern University Press, 1973.

———. *The Nature of Sympathy.* Trans. Peter Heath. Hamden, Conn.: Archon, 1973.

Sellars, Wilfred. *Science, Perception, and Reality.* London: Routledge and Kegan Paul, 1963.

Spender, Stephen. *Selected Poems.* London: Faber and Faber, 1965.

Spiegelberg, Herbert. *The Phenomenological Movement.* 3d rev. exp. ed. The Hague: Martinus Nijhoff, 1984.

Stern, Daniel N. *The Interpersonal World of the Infant.* New York: Basic, 1985.

Toadvine, Ted, and Lester Embree (editors). *Merleau-Ponty's Reading of Husserl.* Dordrecht: Kluwer, 2002.

Varela, Francisco. *Ethical Know-How: Action, Wisdom, and Cognition.* Palo Alto, Calif.: Stanford University Press, 1999.

Varela, Francisco, Evan T. Thompson, and Eleanor Rosch. *The Embodied Mind: Cognitive Science and Human Experience.* Cambridge, Mass.: MIT Press, 1992.

Wallon, Henri. *Les origines du caractère chez l'enfant.* 2d ed. Paris: Presses Universitaires de France, 1949.

Weiss, Gail. *Body Images: Embodiment as Intercorporeality.* New York: Routledge, 1999.

Whitman, Walt. *Leaves of Grass.* New York: Airmont, 1965.

Whiteside, Kerry H. *Merleau-Ponty and the Foundation for an Existential Politics.* Princeton: Princeton University Press, 1988.

Williams, Bernard. *Descartes: The Project of Pure Inquiry.* East Rutherford, N.J.: Penguin, 1978.

Wittgenstein, Ludwig. *Philosophical Investigations.* 3d ed. Trans. G. E. M. Anscombe. New York: Macmillan, 1953.

Index

deconstruction: and alterity, 112; and expression, 168; vs. phenomenology, 5

dehiscence. *See écart*

Deleuze, Gilles: on expression, 141–43, 168; and Merleau-Ponty, 2, 136, 229n32, 235n34

Deleuze, Gilles, and Félix Guattari: and flesh concept, 138, 140–41, 144; on language, 239n36

Dennett, Daniel: on directedness, 81–82; and Merleau-Ponty, 1, 207n8, 232n15; on *qualia*, 41–42

Derrida, Jacques: on alterity, 112; and *écart*, 134–37; and Husserl, 167–68; on language, 172, 192, 228n20; and Merleau-Ponty, 2, 135

Descartes, René: and alterity, 102–103; on the body, 79–80; and Dualism, 15, 79; fallacies in, 100; vs. Merleau-Ponty, 10, 19, 35–36, 100–101, 148–49; and mind/body problem, 74–75; and phenomenology, 8–9; and representation theory, 11–25; on sensation, 21, 26–27; and subjectivism, 7, 8, 19; theology of, 12–13, 20–23; wax argument of, 15–19, 40

desire, problem of, 97–99, 221n46

Dewey, John: on reflex arc, 80

diacritical theory of meaning, 184–89

difference, 130–32, 134, 197–98

Difference and Repetition (Deleuze), 141–43

différance, 112, 134–37, 182

"Différance" (Derrida), 134–36

directedness, 81–82

"divided line" model, 147, 194, 197, 198

doubt, 16, 39–41

dualism: dissolving, 79; vs. *écart*, 111; language of, 15, 22, 28–29, 35–36; ontology of, 40; and physicalists, 43–44

dualistic binaries: external/internal world, 15, 19, 24; mind/body, 4, 22–23, 74–75; subject/object, 105–106, 108, 127, 165–66; visible/invisible, 194

dyslexia, 48–50

écart (irreducible difference): and difference, 130–32, 134, 197–98; vs. *différance*, 134–37; in later transformation of thinking, 123, 125; and others, 111; and reversibility, 132–34; Saussure and, 173; as term, 129–30, 223n16

Edmund Husserl's Origin of Geometry (Derrida), 167–68

"embodied consciousness," 83

embodiment: female, 94–99; in geometry, 152–54; as liberating, 27; living, 74–76, 193; Merleau-Ponty on, 2, 9, 75–99; problems of, 75, 91–99; of self, 73–76, 79, 117–18; two-fold dynamic in, 87–91

emotions, 89

empiricism: body in, 75, 85; and expression, 147; sense-data in, 23–24, 28–32, 51–52

erotic, the, 82, 121, 219n25

ethical, the: Merleau-Ponty and, 71–73; and nature, 118–19, 122; and others, 112–13

Ethiopia, author's experience of, 120–21

excess, 169, 198

exchange, symmetrical, 133–34

experience, perceptual: vs. abstraction, 8–9; and alterity, 101–12; and analysis, 47–48; of color, 63–70; as conceptual, 31; indeterminacy of, 61–63; as intentional, 32–33; and knowledge, 149; and language, 137–39, 179–82; living, 53–54, 57–58, 69–70, 129, 199; Merleau-Ponty on, 2, 9–10, 53–57, 68–70; real, 54–55; "self-others-things" triad in, 55–63; and sensation, 28–52; social aspects of, 40; sublimation of, 155

explanation, 36, 44–51

expression, 2; Deleuze on, 141–43, 168; Heidegger and, 197–98; Husserl on, 9–10, 163–69; and the Invisible, 144–45, 195–96; linguistic, 189–92; and mathematical proof, 147–56; and meaning, 184–86, 199; Merleau-Ponty on, 9–10, 73, 145–48, 160–61, 197–99, 235n34; as term, 3, 160

expressive cognition: and experience, 193; as legacy, 75; as new paradigm, 145, 193–94; vs. representation, 3–4, 162–63

extension (*res extensa*), 20–21

evil demon hypothesis, 14, 17, 20, 22, 108

"Eye and Mind" (Merleau-Ponty), 65–66, 125, 138

faith, perceptual, 126–28

feeling, 48, 51–52

feminist theory, 94–98

field, perceptual, 29–34, 39, 64, 68

figure-ground relation, 29–30, 32, 58, 82, 129

flesh, the: and alterity, 120–23; and being, 139–40; in later transformation of thinking, 123, 125; meanings of, 201–203; Merleau-Ponty on, 2, 91; and reversibility, 137–44

formalism, 157–58

Foucault, Michel: on language, 192; and Merleau-Ponty, 2, 91–94, 136; on man-the-machine, 74–75

freedom, 169

Frege, Gottlob: and language, 174; on mathematical statements, 156

Freud, Sigmund: on repression, 89, 219n24

Fundierung (active transcendence), 162, 171–72, 178, 233n17

May, Todd, 136

meaning: diacritical theory of, 184–89; experiential, 48; and figure-ground, 32; linguistic, 174–76, 184; mathematical, 151–53; and symbiosis, 60–62

Meditations on First Philosophy (Descartes), 13–19

Meno (Socrates), 149

Merleau-Ponty, Maurice: on alterity, 103–22; attention to, 1–2, 147; criticisms of, 2, 4–5, 54–55, 71–72, 91–99, 148–49, 168–69, 183; death of, 125, 225n4; and Deleuze, 2, 136, 141–43, 168, 229n32; and Derrida, 134–37; vs. Descartes, 10, 19, 35–36, 100–101, 207n9; on *écart,* 130–37, 144; on embodiment, 2, 9, 75–99; on expression, 9–10, 146–69, 197–99; on expressive cognition, 3–4, 75, 193–94; ethics of, 71–73; on experience, 53–57; on flesh, 2, 91, 120–23, 137–44; and Foucault, 2, 91–94; and Heidegger, 135, 136, 225n3, 226n6, 239n38; and Husserl, 9, 10, 163–69, 197, 206n7; on intersubjectivity, 2, 6–9, 25, 98–99, 119, 199; and Kant, 84–89; on language, 110–11, 171–92; later transformation of, 56–57, 124–42, 197–99; legacy of, 75–76; and Levinas, 112–22; ontology of, 7–9, 12, 54–57, 124–25, 129, 194–98; on perception, 4, 19, 24–25, 27–28; on "philosophy of reflection," 19; political-cultural lacuna in, 91–99; on Sartre, 129–30; and Saussure, 173, 183–92, 238n19; on "self-others-things" system, 55–56, 100–101, 124, 193, 195; on sensation, 26–28, 30–52; on sexuality, 93–99, 219n25; on visible and invisible, 194–98; and Wittgenstein, 54, 174–76, 236n11

metaphysics: Aristotle's, 73, 194; derived from Descartes, 12–13, 22–24, 35–36; and expression, 147; and perceptual ontology, 27; and representation theory, 3; and sensibility, 63, 70–73; transcendental, 162–63

micro-mechanical movement, 12, 21

mind: and body, 74–75; flexibility of, 197; and matter, 26; and nature, 3; of other, 101–12, 123; philosophy of, 50; and representation, 21–22; understanding of, 193–94

motion, 20–21

Müller-Lyer illusion, 37–38, *37*

Nagel, Thomas, 206n8

natural philosophy, 12–13, 75

nature: and the ethical, as problem, 118–22; and mind, 3; physicalists and, 163

Necker cube, *62*

neurophysiological accounts of perception, 27, 36, 42–44, 51, 212n26

Newton, Isaac: natural philosophy of, 75; and onto-theology, 23; and physical world, 21

Nietzsche, Friedrich, 10; and phenomenology, 8–9; and representation theory, 24, 210n41

"Night Watch, The" (Rembrandt), 65–68, *66, 67*

non-things, 61, 65

object: as abstraction, 23, 73, 194–95; body as, 74, 79–80, 105; color as, 63; perceived, 15–16

objectivity, 26, 38, 50–51, 73, 100–101, 162

Olkowski, Dorothea: on sexual difference, 98

"ontological rehabilitation," 43–44, 72–73

ontology: and alterity, 112–23; and deconstruction, 135–37; dualistic, 40, 207n9; of embodied self, 76–85, 92; grounding reduction in, 197–98; of immanence, 168; perceptual, 4, 25; and phenomenology, 7–9, 53–57, 76, 194–98; subjectivistic, 6–7; of visible and invisible, 194–98

onto-theology, 23, 136, 168, 209n38

opening to the world (*l'ouverture au monde*), 24–25, 28, 51, 72

orgasm, 143

"Origin of Geometry, The" (Husserl), 164–67

other minds, problem of, 101–12, 123

others: animals as, 109; binding oneself to, 120–22; contact with, 33, 127; as machines, 109–10

Otherwise than Being (Levinas), 114–15, 119–22

overlapping, relation of, 131–32, 134, 137

perception: as ambiguous, 61–63; errors of, 17–18, 37–38; extramission theory of, 14–15; living, 50–51; as *Gestalt,* 58–59; as "mine," 126–28; as opening, 24, 28, 33–34, 51; phenomenology of, 53–63; as relational, 39; representation theory of, 10–25; synaesthetic, 68–70; unable to exhaust phenomena, 47–52; of worlds, 23–25, 36

perspective, 47, 50, 61, 77

phantom limb, 86–87

phenomeno-logic, 69–70

phenomenology: and embodiment, 74–91; Husserl and, 6–9, 163–69; and language, 170–79; as method, 5–9; Merleau-Ponty and, 7–9, 53–54, 69–70, 106–108, 124–25, 148–69, 197–99; misunderstandings of, 2, 4–7, 54–55; and ontology, 7–9, 53–57, 76; of perception, 43–44, 50–52; and sexual difference, 95–99; as reductive thought, 197–99

Phenomenology of Perception (Merleau-Ponty): "The *Cogito*" chapter, 148–63, 169; on embodi-

LAWRENCE HASS
is Professor of Philosophy
at Muhlenberg College in
Allentown, Pennsylvania.